Ruth Bader Ginsburg

Ruth Bader Ginsburg

A LIFE IN AMERICAN HISTORY

Nancy Hendricks

Women Making History
Rosanne Welch and Peg A. Lamphier, Series Editors

BLOOMSBURY ACADEMIC
NEW YORK • LONDON • OXFORD • NEW DELHI • SYDNEY

BLOOMSBURY ACADEMIC
Bloomsbury Publishing Inc
1385 Broadway, New York, NY 10018, USA
50 Bedford Square, London, WC1B 3DP, UK
29 Earlsfort Terrace, Dublin 2, Ireland

BLOOMSBURY, BLOOMSBURY ACADEMIC and the Diana logo
are trademarks of Bloomsbury Publishing Plc

First published in the United States of America by ABC-CLIO 2021
Paperback edition published by Bloomsbury Academic 2024

Copyright © Bloomsbury Publishing Inc, 2024

Cover photo: Ruth Bader Ginsburg, 2016. (WDC Photos/Alamy Stock Photo)

All rights reserved. No part of this publication may be reproduced or
transmitted in any form or by any means, electronic or mechanical,
including photocopying, recording, or any information storage or retrieval
system, without prior permission in writing from the publishers.

Bloomsbury Publishing Inc does not have any control over, or responsibility for,
any third-party websites referred to or in this book. All internet addresses given
in this book were correct at the time of going to press. The author and publisher
regret any inconvenience caused if addresses have changed or sites have
ceased to exist, but can accept no responsibility for any such changes.

Library of Congress Cataloging-in-Publication Data
Names: Hendricks, Nancy, author.
Title: Ruth Bader Ginsburg : a life in American history / Nancy Hendricks.
Description: Santa Barbara, California : ABC-CLIO, an Imprint of ABC-CLIO, LLC, [2021] |
Series: Women making history | Includes bibliographical references and index.
Identifiers: LCCN 2020036248 (print) | LCCN 2020036249 (ebook) |
ISBN 9781440874215 (hardcover) | ISBN 9781440874222 (ebook)
Subjects: LCSH: Ginsburg, Ruth Bader. | Women judges—United
States—Biography. | Judges—United States—Biography. | United States.
Supreme Court—Officials and employees—Biography.
Classification: LCC KF8745.G56 H455 2021 (print) |
LCC KF8745.G56 (ebook) | DDC 347.73/2634 [B]—dc23
LC record available at https://lccn.loc.gov/2020036248
LC ebook record available at https://lccn.loc.gov/2020036249

ISBN: HB: 978-1-4408-7421-5
PB: 979-8-2161-9175-9
ePDF: 978-1-4408-7422-2
eBook: 979-8-2161-4117-4

Series: Women Making History

To find out more about our authors and books visit www.bloomsbury.com
and sign up for our newsletters.

To Ruth Bader Ginsburg, Martin D. Ginsburg, and the women on whose shoulders we stand.

"Justice, justice shall you pursue" — Deuteronomy 16:20

Contents

Series Foreword ix

Preface xi

Introduction: Why Ruth Bader Ginsburg Matters xvii

CHAPTER 1
Childhood: The Go-Getter *1*

CHAPTER 2
College: The Brain *19*

CHAPTER 3
Law School: The Young Wife *37*

CHAPTER 4
Academia: The Swedish Connection *55*

CHAPTER 5
ACLU: The Litigator *79*

CHAPTER 6
Federal Court: The Judge's Judge *107*

CHAPTER 7
Supreme Court: The Great Dissenter *127*

CHAPTER 8
Meme Supreme: The Icon *149*

Timeline 163

Appendix A: An Evening with Ruth Bader Ginsburg 171

Appendix B: Pioneering Women Lawyers 177

Primary Source Documents 191

Bibliography 215

Index 223

Series Foreword

We created this series because women today stand on the shoulders of those who came before them. They need to know the true power their foremothers had in shaping the world today and the obstacles those women overcame to achieve all that they have achieved and continue to achieve.

It is true that Gerda Lerner offered the first regular college course in women's history in 1963 and that, since then, women's history has become an academic discipline taught in nearly every American college and university. It is also true that women's history books number in the millions and cover a wealth of topics, time periods, and issues. Nonetheless, open any standard high school or college history textbook and you will find very few mentions of women's achievements or importance, and the few that do exist will be of the "exceptional woman" model, ghettoized to sidebars and footnotes.

With women missing from textbooks, students and citizens are allowed to believe that no woman ever meaningfully contributed to American history and that nothing women have ever done has had more than private, familial importance. In such books we do not learn that it was womens' petitioning efforts that brought the Thirteenth Amendment abolishing slavery to Abraham Lincoln's attention or that Social Security and child labor laws were the brainchild of Frances Perkins, the progressive female secretary of labor who was also the first woman appointed to a presidential cabinet.

Without this knowledge both female and male students are encouraged to think only men—primarily rich, white men—have ever done anything meaningful. This vision impedes our democracy in a nation that has finally become more aware of our beautiful diversity.

The National Bureau of Economic Research said women comprise the majority of college graduates in undergraduate institutions, law schools, and medical schools (56 percent in 2017). Still, women's high college attendance and graduation rates do not translate to equal pay or equal economic, political, or cultural power. There can be little argument that American women have made significant inroads *toward* equality in the last few decades, in spite of the ongoing dearth of women in normative approaches to American history teaching and writing. Hence, this series.

We want readers to know that we took the task of choosing the women to present seriously, adding new names to the list while looking to highlight new information about women we think we know. Many of these women have been written about in the past, but their lives were filtered through male or societal expectations. Here we hope the inclusion of the women's own words in the collection of primary documents we curated will finally allow them to speak for themselves about the issues that most mattered. The timeline will visually place them in history against events that hampered their efforts and alongside the events they created. Sidebars will give more detail on such events as the Triangle Shirtwaist Factory Fire. Finally, the chapter on Why She Matters will cement the reason such a woman deserves a new volume dedicated to her life.

Have we yet achieved parity? We'll let one of our subjects—the Honorable Ruth Bader Ginsburg—remind us that "when I'm sometimes asked when will there be enough [women on the supreme court]? And I say when there are nine, people are shocked. But there'd been nine men [for over 200 years], and nobody's ever raised a question about that."

Preface

Supreme Court Justice Ruth Bader Ginsburg died on September 18, 2020. However, her impact on history will be felt for decades to come. Because of her living legacy, many of the references in this book are in the present tense.

Readers of *Ruth Bader Ginsburg: A Life in American History* will not only find the inspiring story of one woman's triumph against the odds but also how her life journey took place across almost 100 years of American history. As part of the WOMEN MAKING HISTORY series, the book will illustrate the life of Justice Ginsburg through the prism of American history as well as her role in remaking it notably in ways that are taken for granted by many people today.

Ruth Bader Ginsburg, popularly known as RBG, did not exist in a vacuum. She was a part of the historical and cultural tapestry of the United States during the tumultuous years of the post–World War II era. Her life will be illuminated within that context.

The reader will note how she was a product of her family's roots in the Lower East Side of New York City. In a little-known episode as a Supreme Court justice, RBG would have a hand in deciding a case involving Ellis Island, the port of entry for immigrants where her father and soon-to-be-born mother had arrived a century earlier.

Many people whose families were immigrants during the early twentieth century never lost sight of how fortunate they were to live in the United States. They recognized the promise of the American Dream. But many were not blind to its unfulfilled promises and, in the words of African American poet Langston Hughes, the many people whose dreams were so long deferred.

For people of color and the women who were the contemporaries of Justice Ginsburg in the 1950s and 1960s, the dream fell short. Today, it would be relatively inconceivable for job applicants with impeccable references who graduated at the top of their class to be told quite openly that people of their race, religion, or gender need not apply. Yet, that was exactly the nation's culture when the young Ruth Ginsburg sought a job as an attorney. This book will show how that state of affairs changed, thanks in great part to her quiet but determined efforts against the odds.

During the postwar years when Ruth Bader Ginsburg struggled to become an attorney, there were basically three career choices open to educated American women: teacher, secretary, or nurse. And those jobs were only available to them until they married or became pregnant. Ruth Ginsburg was instrumental in expanding the field. When it came to women with children, who had lost their husbands due to death or divorce, her efforts in securing them a place in the workforce was a lifeline. She also fought for the simple concept that two people doing the same work should earn the same salary.

As the millennium turned to the year 2000, women's rights advocate Gloria Steinem married for the first time at age 66 and was criticized for apparently changing her stance regarding whether women needed to be married to be fulfilled. Steinem's response was that *marriage* had changed, stating that if she had wed 30 years before, she would have forfeited many of her civil rights. Ruth Ginsburg was instrumental in making those changes.

RBG did so through painstaking legal work in the face of those who criticized her for quietly litigating rather than loudly protesting, for allowing change to happen incrementally rather than demand that it come all at once. The book will illustrate more than the story of a remarkable life journey; it will focus on the formal legal legacy that transcends the life of one person and changed the lives of millions.

GOALS

Many of those changes had this extraordinary woman at their center. To demonstrate that, this book is arranged in chronological order, the way RBG experienced her life. Dates and current events at the time will be included at appropriate points to clearly illuminate the world in which she lived. It meets the need of filling the gap between voluminous biographies and brief overviews of her life.

The book contributes to the literature on the subject of RBG by including first-hand accounts in her own words. There are also sidebars that add, often with humor, to a better understanding of her life and times.

YOUNG RUTH

Many people today are only familiar with the image of Ginsburg as a person in her 80s. To a young person, a woman of that age, in black robes and big glasses, might well be from another planet, hardly relevant to the lives and challenges of those in their teens. This book will take a long look at the young Ruth Bader as a popular teenager and college student, the age group of many readers.

During those years her course was set: dedication to excelling academically, determination to reach the top, and devotion to the memory of her mother who died on the eve of Ruth's high school graduation. Readers will see what young Ruth inherited emotionally as well as what she left behind, particularly surrounding the events immediately after the death of her beloved mother.

This book will examine the culture of law schools in America when RBG attended Harvard and Columbia in the 1950s. From libraries that banned women to the lack of ladies' restrooms, the few females who were admitted to law school found obstacles every step of the way. Still, women like RBG prevailed.

It will also note the significance of the often-overlooked time RBG spent in Sweden. It gave her not only a greater understanding of the way things were in other parts of the world, but a glimpse of what America might become.

This book will follow Ruth Ginsburg's work as head of the Women's Rights Project at the American Civil Liberties Union (ACLU). That was when the quiet bookish woman who strove to be a "lady" was forced to become a litigator, or a lawyer who argues cases in court. That kind of public exposure and argumentation was never her preferred path. She was physically unnerved during the first day she was forced to stand up in court. In RBG's case, it was not just any courtroom but the highest in the land: the Supreme Court of the United States. We will follow her as she wins almost every case she argued there, changing the course of American life, especially that of American women, hopefully forever.

NUTS AND BOLTS

There were low points, like a dispiriting interview before an all-male panel of Wall Street lawyers, after which a friend said it was the only time she had ever seen RBG dejected. Later, RBG underwent the excruciating process of being appointed to the federal Court of Appeals in Washington, D.C., a route that was almost derailed by political rivalries, world events, and missteps by others. Her work for more than a dozen years as a federal judge is often glossed over as being a "placeholder" until she was named to the Supreme Court but is worth review.

The reader will follow RBG's journey in becoming the 107th justice of the United States Supreme Court, with suggestions for viewing it "backstage," including RBG's private office, through a C-SPAN video tour.

Along with RBG's most famous Supreme Court opinions, the reader will also get a glimpse of cases the justices must decide during an average term on the high court. These are the "nuts and bolts" kind of legal questions often based on complex interpretations of arcane law. They rarely make headlines but mean the world to the petitioners involved, many of whom never thought their case would go all the way to the nation's highest court.

ADDED SPICE

Today, not many people can name the members of the U.S. Supreme Court. But most Americans can certainly name one: Ruth Bader Ginsburg. They may have seen the affectionate parody on television's *Saturday Night Live*, or the documentary *RBG*, or the feature film *On the Basis of Sex*. This book will examine how Justice Ginsburg became popularly known as the "Notorious RBG" when few other Supreme Court justices are known at all.

The *Introduction* will examine exactly why Ruth Bader Ginsburg matters. Her place in America's overall historical context will be explored in terms of how her actions have influenced not only women's history but the lives of all citizens of the United States.

In a narrative as dramatic as any movie, this book will also spotlight the lifelong romance between Ruth and her late husband, of whom she has said publicly that nothing in her life "equals in magnitude my marriage to Martin D. Ginsburg." Marty earned his place in history not only for his personal accomplishments as a leading tax attorney but also by acting as a cheerleader for his wife, spurring her on to greater victories when she lacked confidence in herself.

Sidebars are scattered throughout the book, in which the life of Justice Ginsburg receives added spice, a metaphor that would have pleased Marty, a gourmet cook. For example, during a Supreme Court argument, RBG quoted Sarah Grimké. A sidebar will show who Grimké was and how her words from the 1800s became relevant to a twentieth-century legal argument at the highest level.

To clearly illustrate the chronology, a *Timeline* positions RBG in the panorama of late twentieth-century and early twenty-first-century America. With her popular iconography as a "hip" senior citizen in black robes, it is sometimes hard to remember that she was a pretty and popular college girl at the same time that Elvis Presley was taking the country by storm.

Along with well-known names like Elvis, the reader will also meet unsung heroes like Milicent Tryon, who herself may have altered the course of history.

Appendices will add context to Justice Ginsburg's story. Appendix A includes material not seen elsewhere in which the reader has a front-row seat among 15,000 people at a live appearance by RBG, hearing a firsthand account of her life and observations in her own words. In addition, since RBG has often recognized "the women on whose shoulders we stand," Appendix B illuminate their progress from the earliest days of the American nation.

Through the *Primary Source Documents*, we can see RBG's logic and scholarship through the power of her own words. The written texts of Supreme Court decisions are generally unknown to most people, but many can recite word-for-word RBG's "umbrella" opinion regarding the erosion of civil rights. The section begins with the official wording of the Constitutional amendment whose Equal Protection clause was instrumental in many of her opinions, an amendment that is often referred to but rarely understood.

SOURCES AND USAGE

Along with the sources cited at the end of each chapter, there is a full *Bibliography* of print and electronic media that were used in creating the overall scope of this book. All were useful to the author in ways large and small. Especially helpful were Carmon and Knizhnik's breezy *Notorious RBG*, de Hart's voluminous *Ruth Bader Ginsburg: A Life*, and, of course, Ruth Bader Ginsburg's *My Own Words*.

To flesh out the life of this remarkable individual, the reader is strongly encouraged to view the feature film *On the Basis of Sex*, the documentary *RBG*, and the C-SPAN video *The Supreme Court: Home to America's Highest Court* as noted in the Bibliography.

Regarding usage, like most women, Ruth Bader's name was changed to that of her husband after marriage. The nomenclature in this book will reflect that transition. Some sources have chosen to retain her childhood nickname "Kiki" through her college years. After initial reference to being bestowed with the "Kiki" nickname by her older sister, this book will refrain from using it as she grew up. Her husband Martin D. Ginsburg was generally known as "Marty," a practice that will sometimes be utilized to avoid redundancy.

Above all, the author of this book has endeavored to paint the kind of word pictures that, as a college girl, young Ruth was inspired to do by her professor Vladimir Nabokov. It is sincerely hoped that this book reflects well on them both.

ACKNOWLEDGMENTS

The author wishes to thank Dr. Peg Lamphier and Dr. Rosanne Welch of California State Polytechnic University, Pomona; Dr. Guy Lancaster, editor of the *Encyclopedia of Arkansas History and Culture*, Karen Loop, executive producer of the feature film *On the Basis of Sex*, psychologist Dr. David Welch, and former Hollywood production assistant M. A. Wheeler. And, of course, Ruth Bader Ginsburg and Martin D. Ginsburg for their inspiration as well as the honor of documenting their lives.

Introduction: Why Ruth Bader Ginsburg Matters

On September 18, 2020, tributes to Ruth Bader Ginsburg began pouring in from around the world. She had fought heroically against death, but ultimately her body failed her, succumbing to complications from metastatic cancer of the pancreas. In the days that followed, the world reflected on her legacy. Ruth Bader Ginsburg matters because that legacy continues to impact the lives of countless people. Throughout her life, she fought for their rights as tirelessly as she had fought against death.

Despite her passing, the legacy of the woman known to the world as "RBG" lives on. For that reason, Ruth Bader Ginsburg matters: *present tense*. One event, which took place almost exactly a year before her death, demonstrates why.

On September 3, 2019, Supreme Court Justice Ruth Bader Ginsburg spoke to a sold-out crowd of 15,000 people in Little Rock, Arkansas. News media reported that with an additional 30,000 people on the waiting list for tickets, it was the most anticipated event of the year in a city that is not known for being highly liberal-minded. At the concert arena where RBG spoke, there have been a few near sell-outs like Fleetwood Mac, Bruce Springsteen, George Strait, and the Rolling Stones. But, it seemed, nothing was quite like this.

The crowd lining up all day for Justice Ginsburg's evening program was a cross-section of America: male and female, young and old, black and white, and suits and T-shirts. Some young women wore black robes and frilly jabots; many wore shirts with Justice Ginsburg's image or RBG quotes. The audience included Arkansas's all-Republican congressional delegation. Why were they all there?

They were there because Ruth Bader Ginsburg *matters*.

TIMES A-CHANGIN'

During the 1950s, when RBG was a young woman attending college and law school, the United States was changing. Having emerged victorious from World War II, it was the most prosperous nation in the history of the world. Amid the wealth and optimism of postwar America, anything seemed possible.

A singer named Elvis Presley skyrocketed to fame with a revolutionary new form of music called rock and roll. Rosa McCauley Parks, an African American woman in Montgomery, Alabama, was jailed for not giving up her seat on a city bus to a white man, spurring civil rights protests.

In 1957, *Sputnik*, the first artificial space satellite to orbit the earth, was launched by the Soviet Union, marking the start of America's involvement in what was called the Space Race. America's newly coined astronauts became instant heroes as they prepared to show that the sky was no longer the limit.

In 1959, a boy named Robert Zimmerman graduated from high school, going on to write a song called *The Times They Are A-Changin'* under his stage name, Bob Dylan. That song would become an anthem of the era. Throughout postwar America, change was indeed in the air.

As Dwight Eisenhower's term as U.S. president was coming to an end by the late 1950s, there was talk of a young senator named John F. Kennedy being a candidate for president in the 1960 election. With civil rights, satellites, Elvis, and JFK on people's minds, it was a time when the nation was looking more to its Space Age future than to its recent past, which seemed as far away as the horse-and-buggy era.

IMAGINE

The following imaginary thought experiment might help put things into perspective. It must be noted that it is completely fiction, since no such situation has existed in America to date. Imagine, therefore, America in the Space Age as a blue-eyed person enrolls in law school. That person is one of only nine blue-eyed people in a class of more than 500 students. The school's dean requires each of the nine blue-eyed people to justify taking a spot that would normally go to someone with eyes of a different color. After graduating at the top of the class, it is impossible for a blue-eyed person to find a job because no law firm will hire blue-eyed people. Why? Because they are blue-eyed.

If that seems inconceivable, imagine another scenario in America during the same era. Males are discouraged from working outside the home. If they need an outside job and try looking through the want ads, they find only low-level positions earmarked for males with the qualification that male applicants must be attractive and well-groomed. College-educated males might seek a job in one of the few professions open to men: teacher, nurse, or clerical, although they will be expected to quit when they get married. Any man who tries seeking a job in the legal field finds that no law firm will hire men, even those males who graduated at the top of their class. They are forced to seek lower-level jobs as law clerks but most are often turned down, with the explanation that their presence would make the women in top positions feel uncomfortable. Why? Because they are male.

ROSIE TO LUCY

Such discrimination against men—or blue-eyed people, for that matter—seems inconceivable. And yet, in postwar America, when the nation was firmly poised for its Space Age future, half of the country's population experienced that very thing. All of those slights, and many more, happened to a person named Ruth Bader Ginsburg. Why? Because she was female.

Late in life, she said she was asked what she considered the ideal number of women to serve on the nine-member Supreme Court. She related that people were shocked when she suggested *nine*. Yet for more than 200 years, the Court consisted entirely of nine males. No one raised a question about that.

Growing up in New York City, young Ruth did not live in a backwater. With a supportive, intelligent mother who enjoyed talking with Ruth about current events, the intellectually curious child could hardly have been unaware of the changes that the wartime era of the 1940s had brought to the women of the nation. Images of Rosie the Riveter with the determined message "We Can Do It!" were everywhere, encouraging women to join the workforce and help the nation win the war.

Yet by the time Ruth graduated from high school in 1950, most of the women had lost their wartime jobs and were sent back home. A symbol of women's life in the 1950s can be seen in the top-rated television series *I Love Lucy* that ran from 1951 to 1957. Although series star Lucille Ball herself was a smart businesswoman, her fictional character of Lucy Ricardo depended on husband Ricky to rescue her from the zany situations she got herself into. Though she often tried, the fictional Lucy Ricardo failed at working outside the home, nor could she stay within a budget. For her transgressions, Lucy was spanked like a child by her husband.

After becoming an adult, Ruth Bader Ginsburg's legal skills and her status as a cultural icon proved significant in moving America's female population beyond the *Lucy* model of what was considered to be a woman's place.

As civil rights leader Dr. Martin Luther King Jr. said, "The arc of the moral universe is long, but it bends toward justice." However, in a 2016 interview, former U.S. attorney general Eric Holder, the first African American to hold that position, added that "the arc bends toward justice, but it only bends toward justice because people pull it towards justice. It doesn't happen on its own."

Ruth Bader Ginsburg matters because she has helped bend that arc toward justice for all people.

SUPREME MEME

Unlike many public officials, RBG has served as a positive inspiration for people of all ages, especially the young. In the internet age, her image has become a "meme," that is, images, text, or videos forwarded over the internet. Generally, they reach millions.

When little girls—as well as adults—choose black Supreme Court robes with frilly jabots and large glasses like RBG's as their Halloween costume, it is obvious that something has resonated with a large swathe of the population. Those people believe RBG matters. They want to emulate her.

It is not often that Supreme Court justices become a significant part of the popular culture, defined as the characteristic features of a society in a certain place or time. Forms of popular culture like television programs or movies tend to both reflect and reinforce elements of what members of a society find important.

Popular culture has the power not only to entertain but to inform. It also creates a lasting imprint on a society. Few people had ever heard of Robert LeRoy Parker and Harry Alonzo Longabaugh until a 1969 movie immortalized them as Butch Cassidy and the Sundance Kid. Similarly, not many people remembered Depression-era criminals Clyde Chestnut Barrow and Bonnie Elizabeth Parker until the release of the 1967 feature film *Bonnie and Clyde*. New York City police officer Frank Serpico and California environmental activist Erin Brockovich also became familiar to the mainstream by way of movies about their lives.

Joining the pantheon of popular culture, the documentary *RBG* and the film *On the Basis of Sex* brought the life of Ruth Bader Ginsburg to the masses. Through various media like DVDs and streaming services, those projects will continue to bring her story to life as an inspiration to generations to come.

Television has also portrayed images or references to Ruth Bader Ginsburg as part of our nation's tapestry. On the premier episode of the 2019 courtroom drama *All Rise*, two female judges discuss their inspiration for entering the legal field, with both immediately responding in unison "RBG!" In addition to a recurring character on the comedic *Saturday Night Live*, there have been references to Justice Ginsburg on TV dramas like *Scandal* and *The Good Wife* as well as the Cartoon Network program *Clarence* with a character named Wrath Hover Ginsbot.

RBG also entered the national iconography of music when the diminutive jurist was equated with rap star Notorious B.I.G. Like him, she channeled her ire against injustice into a format meaningful to millions.

Ruth Bader Ginsburg matters because she has inspired others to follow in her footsteps through the medium of popular culture, making her efforts more visible than most Supreme Court justices have ever been.

FACING FEAR, SPEAKING TRUTH

While it is true that Justice Ginsburg may not have sought a role for herself in the world of fame, she has not shrunk from the responsibility of being in the public eye. In our celebrity-driven society, sometimes it takes the status of popular cultural figures to spur progress. Far-reaching change can be driven by a few quiet but well-chosen words by shedding light on archaic practices that people often take for granted with the rationale of "that's the way it's always been."

Justice Ginsburg matters because she has done just that. As in the case of the law student who was inspired to funnel her dismay at the *Shelby County v. Holder* Supreme Court decision into the "Notorious RBG" blog, useful action can replace useless anger.

In her own words, Justice Ginsburg has stated that it is possible to disagree without being disagreeable. In a society that has become increasingly confrontational, the concept of disagreeing in a civil fashion requires strength, intelligence, and tact. It also takes great courage to oppose the entrenched ideology of powerful figures.

As both a jurist and cultural icon, Justice Ginsburg has made a difference in today's world—and that of tomorrow—by what is called speaking truth to power. From the earliest days of her legal career, before she became well known, RBG recognized injustice and courageously challenged it, even when she admitted having personal fears. Those fears were not unfounded. Speaking truth to power often bears consequences.

In an article by Josephine Ensign featured in the online edition of *Psychology Today*, a case is cited about the first female gymnast to speak out against the team doctor who was sexually abusing the young girls in his care. After speaking out, that young woman said she lost her church, her closest friends, and her privacy along with being called an opportunist. Pointing out that the silence of victims is what keeps offenders in power, Ensign stated that fear often causes people to turn away from a problem.

Between 1973 and 1976, attorney Ginsburg repeatedly stepped before the men—and they were *all* men—of the U.S. Supreme Court. She later said she was too nervous to eat lunch before her first Supreme Court appearance for fear of not being able to keep it down. But that was her only concession to fear. Of the six gender discrimination cases she argued before the Supreme Court, she won five. Although fearful, RBG made her case calmly, using well-chosen words to describe legal precedents. She faced her fear with weapons that included wearing her late mother's jewelry as a talisman as well as taking aim at specific discriminatory statutes that were harmful to both men and women.

Ruth Bader Ginsburg matters because she faced her fear, spoke truth to power, and inspired successive generations to do the same.

ACTION FIGURE

Some of RBG's allure to young people may be in the ironic juxtaposition of a tiny octogenarian who faces up to huge entrenched forces. In doing so, RBG has become a powerful cultural symbol for the young. Children's books about the life of Justice Ginsburg are popular items in public libraries.

There are also commercial products featuring her image and/or quotes like address books, birthday cards, coloring books, mugs, tote bags, throw pillows, valentines, blank journals having a cover emblazoned with *"Fight for the Things You Care About—RBG,"* and even an action figure clad in judicial robes.

Ruth Bader Ginsburg matters because her courage, intelligence, and strength have a similar effect on young people in a quest toward human rights for all people, inspiring them to ask, "Why not?"

INTO THE LIGHT

Another direct result of RBG's superstar status on the Supreme Court is using her place in the spotlight to draw increased attention to the workings of the Court itself. Often, celebrities can highlight issues that usually languish in the dark, or in this case, in dusty legal journals.

Some people might be able to name a few of the most far-reaching Supreme Court decisions in our nation's history such as 1954's *Brown v. Board of Education*, which opened the door for civil rights. However, unless they are highly controversial, the vast majority of Supreme Court decisions are not familiar to the average American. It is ironic that so few people are aware of Supreme Court decisions that affect us all. With due respect to the other Supreme Court justices, it is the spotlight on RBG that has come to illuminate many Supreme Court decisions. By raising awareness, issues can often be confronted before it is too late.

However, even after the Court hands down decisions RBG does not support, her dissents clearly delineate the points of law she disputes and how Americans will be affected. Many people were not aware of how the 2013 *Shelby County v. Holder* decision would affect voting rights, such as the eventual closing of more than a thousand polling places in predominantly minority neighborhoods. Her dissent made it perfectly clear.

Ruth Bader Ginsburg matters because she is able to shed light on issues that often languish in the dark until people find it is too late.

UMBRELLA POLICY

Shelby County v. Holder ruled against parts of the 1965 Voting Rights Act that protected minority voters from discrimination. The 5–4 Court decision struck down one of those protections because, in its view, the provision was not based on "current conditions." Minority opponents on the Court like RBG felt that the safeguards were designed by Congress to catch discrimination before it causes harm. The provision was also meant to guard against a return to the kind of discriminatory practices in the past that curtailed the voting rights of citizens like African Americans in the South.

RBG dissented against the decision of the Court's five-man majority. Writing in clear, concise language that was understandable to average people, she declared that throwing out voting rights protections when they work is like throwing away your umbrella in a rainstorm because you are not getting wet. The language of that dissent was a turning point for many people who began to pay more attention to Supreme Court decisions in general and specifically to RBG's written opinions. In one, *Safford United School District v. Redding*, the question was whether the strip search of an eighth-grade girl was unconstitutional. Ginsburg's advocacy is said to have motivated the eventual decision in favor of the student. In simple language, RBG was able to make her point by noting that the other justices, who were at the time all males, had never been a 13-year-old girl. Ruth Bader Ginsburg matters because her efforts have compelled people to pay attention to Court decisions, and in simple language, her arguments convince them why they should.

FAMILIAR PHRASE

RBG's impact can also be found in cases apart from those she adjudicates, and yet her influence comes through loud and clear. In February 2019, a federal district judge in Houston, Texas, declared that the current male-only draft registration system violated the Equal Protection Clause requiring that the genders be treated equally. The Houston judge's decision was in response to opposition against women registering for the military draft along with men. The draft itself ended in 1973, although it could theoretically be reinstated at any time of national emergency. The judge in Houston ruled that the opposition to females relied on assumptions and stereotypes about women regarding their ability to fulfill roles in the armed forces, including combat.

If his phraseology sounded familiar to observers, it may have suggested that the Houston judge was aware of Justice Ginsburg's 1996 opinion declaring that the exclusion of women from the state-supported Virginia Military Institute was unconstitutional. One passage of the precedent that the Houston judge cited contained Justice Ginsburg's words, stating that justifications for excluding one gender or the other should not rely on generalizations about the different talents, capacities, or preferences of males and females.

While T-shirts and tote bags with Justice Ginsburg's image may be amusing, citing an RBG precedent toward gender equality almost a quarter century after the fact may be an accolade that is most meaningful to her.

Ruth Bader Ginsburg matters because, amid her popular acclaim, it is the law that matters—legal precedent that is still being created—and it is based on law that Ruth Ginsburg made.

WHAT'S IN A WORD?

Anyone who is familiar with Aretha Franklin's version of the song *Respect* knows there is power in that word. The Supreme Court's decision on *Bush v. Gore*, regarding the outcome of the year 2000 presidential election between George W. Bush and Al Gore, brought the word and the concept of respect into the limelight in a way that individual words in legal opinions usually do not.

In that decision, the closely contested race in Florida became the determining factor of the election, warranting a recount of thousands of votes due to alleged voting irregularities. Many political observers felt the Supreme Court's decision to end the recount effectively gave Bush the victory.

Justice Ginsburg wrote a dissent disagreeing with the Supreme Court's majority decision. She stated it was a threat to the democratic process by not permitting a recount allowing all valid votes to be counted as required by the Constitution. In issuing her opinion, she wrote "I dissent" instead of adding the word "respectfully" to the phrase. That single omission of one word registered with the public more strongly than a thousand-page decree.

Ruth Bader Ginsburg matters because her words are watched so carefully that even one small omission makes a big difference.

HEROES

It is important for people of both genders and all age groups to have strong role models as heroes. That is especially true of young people trying to determine a path to follow as they find their place in the world.

In the past, many young people named their parents as personal heroes. Others chose athletes such as Althea Gibson, Billie Jean King, Mickey Mantle, or Jackie Robinson. In the 1960s, many chose notables like Cesar Chavez, Helen Keller, John Kennedy, Robert Kennedy, and Martin Luther King Jr. Others over the years have included Neil Armstrong, Nelson Mandela, Rosa Parks, Eleanor Roosevelt, Harriet Tubman, and Mother Theresa along with religious figures like the Dalai Lama and the Pope.

Conversations with professionals who work with youth today can be revealing. In response to a question regarding who the role models are for today's young people, the answer was consistent: "Superheroes."

These fictional characters appear in comic books and comic book–based movies that are enormously popular with young people. Those who are most highly esteemed by today's youth as role models include Batman, Black Panther, Captain America, The Flash, Green Lantern, The Hulk, Iron Man, Spider-Man, and Superman.

Occupying the last place among superheroes alphabetically, as well as being the only female, is Wonder Woman. In her skimpy tight-fitting costume that looks like a strapless swimsuit, bulletproof bracelets (which some say resemble shackles), and knee-high red boots, some say Wonder Woman represents the male fantasy version of a female. Young girls might ponder how to emulate Wonder Woman as a role model on a day-to-day basis in schools where the dress code frowns on strapless swimsuits.

Ruth Bader Ginsburg matters because she has become a heroic role model to emulate, a real-life human being who faced adversities courageously. She overcame them through her personal strength and values without involving fantasy comic book superpowers.

THE BOOK OF RUTH

Like Justice Ginsburg, girls might be able to find inspiration closer to home. RBG has said repeatedly that her mother Celia was the smartest person she ever knew, along with being the bravest and strongest. The tragedy of young Ruth's early life was that after her mother was stricken with cancer, Celia spent many of her daughter's formative years being too sick to get out of bed. But with young Ruth doing her homework at Celia's bedside, the child was able to absorb her mother's support and wisdom.

Celia always stressed the importance of getting a good education, a value that RBG has repeatedly emphasized in interviews. Young Ruth also learned from her mother that education meant independence. It was fine to hope for a "Prince Charming" to come along, but it was vital for a woman to have a way to support herself if he didn't turn out to be a knight in shining armor, if he died, divorced her, or simply never came riding into her life at all.

After Celia's death the day before Ruth's high school graduation, another strong female figure came into her life. It was a somewhat unexpected individual, one whose status is usually relegated to being fodder for comedians, to be portrayed as a monster: Ruth's mother-in-law.

Evelyn Ginsburg was the mother of Ruth's husband, Martin. Along with raising a son who turned out to be a strong male who valued smart women, Evelyn showed the young RBG great kindness, even purchasing a suit for Ruth's first job interview.

There is a parallel in the story of Ruth Bader Ginsburg and her mother-in-law that echoes the biblical Book of Ruth. In the Bible, the character of Ruth is a symbol of loyalty and devotion. After being widowed, the biblical Ruth stays with her mother-in-law, stating the famous phrase, "Wherever you go, I will go; wherever you lodge, I will lodge; your people shall be my people, . . . [where] you die, I will die" (Ruth 1:16–17).

RBG's journey through life spotlights not just one but two strong real-life female role models: both her mother and her mother-in-law. By passing along her mother's wisdom, she illuminated the value of education and independence for a woman. By publicly praising her mother-in-law, she showed how a true "Prince Charming" can be raised from childhood into becoming a true life partner. Carmon and Knizhnik (2015) quote RBG as saying that Marty Ginsburg always made her feel like she was better than she thought herself (99). A strong man helped enable her to become a strong woman.

Ruth Bader Ginsburg matters because she has passed along the lessons of how women can become advocates and role models for girls as well as having the power, as mothers, to shape strong, decent men.

WOMEN'S RIGHTS ARE HUMAN RIGHTS

In an early landmark decision, RBG argued a tax law case over a deduction for caregiver expenses that was denied because the taxpayer was a man, not a woman, who was caring for his aged mother. Following RBG's victory, it was the first time a provision of the Internal Revenue Code was declared unconstitutional. In another case, RBG won a decision on behalf of a male plaintiff who was denied survivor benefits after his wife died because such payments were reserved for widows but not for widowers.

Slowly but surely, RBG was not only establishing legal precedent but also steadily bringing judges along to see the injustice of both men and women not being treated equally as human beings, as well as the effect of that injustice on children. She has said publicly that she litigated cases that were not "women's rights" per se, but the constitutional principle of equal citizenship regardless of race or gender.

Although the failure of the Equal Rights Amendment in 1979 was disappointing to many, RBG recognized that new laws might not be needed: the answer was already in the Constitution with the words "We the People" and in the Equal Protection Clause.

Ruth Bader Ginsburg matters because she recognized the power of making small changes, chipping away at injustice when others criticized her for not storming the battlements, and finding answers that are already in the nation's founding document, the Constitution.

SHAKESPEAREAN PRECEDENT

In the Elizabethan Age, a time not noted for its overwhelming tolerance, William Shakespeare spotlighted the human condition by emphasizing our common humanity. Perhaps that is why his plays have not only survived but remain relevant to each generation for the past 500 years.

In Shakespeare's England, religious intolerance spawned mass murder and destruction. Yet in his play, *The Merchant of Venice*, the character of Shylock takes on religious differences, asking if a person of a different faith is not also "fed with the same food, hurt with the same weapons, subject to the same diseases, healed by the same means, warmed and cooled by the same winter and summer. . . . If you prick us, do we not bleed? If you tickle us, do we not laugh? If you poison us, do we not die?" In short, people are people—aren't they? It was a remarkable concept for Shakespeare's time.

In the same play, one of the most notable speeches is delivered in the courtroom by Portia, a woman who is forced to disguise herself as a male since a female attorney was unthinkable: "The quality of mercy is not strained. It droppeth as the gentle rain from heaven upon the place beneath." To modern ears, the speech would sound more like: "No one shows mercy because they have to. It should just happen, the way a soft rain falls on the ground." In other words, because it is the right thing to do.

Like Shylock, in her legal career, Ruth Bader Ginsburg has asked simply that all people be treated the same as fellow human beings. Like Portia, she spoke softly, asking for relief from discrimination because it is simply the right thing to do.

Slowly, some justices started to come around to that way of thinking. As Stern and Wermiel (2010) state, Justice William Brennan, who served on the U.S. Supreme Court from 1956 to 1990, not only refused to hire female clerks (386), but "if a woman ever got nominated to the Court, Brennan predicted, he might have to resign" (388). Yet his private feelings were not always reflected in legal judgments. In his opinion on the gender bias case of *Frontiero v. Richardson* (1973), Brennan wrote, "Our nation has had a long and unfortunate history of sex discrimination, rationalized by an attitude of 'romantic paternalism' which, in practical effect, put women not on a pedestal, but in a cage" (392).

When the first female justice, Sandra Day O'Connor, joined Brennan on the Supreme Court bench, he did not resign. He served with her for nine more years, eventually retiring from the Supreme Court in 1990. After becoming a Supreme Court justice herself, Ruth Bader Ginsburg wrote a landmark gender discrimination decision of her own in *United States v. Virginia* in 1996, providing a signed copy of her bench announcement for Brennan with the inscription, "See how the light you shed has spread!" Stern and Wermiel (2010) say that despite his earlier biased acts and statements, she personally handed the document to Brennan, saying, "Without you this would not have been possible" (408).

RBG has shown respect to other people by recognizing that their contributions have been valued. She moves slowly, in steady increments, bringing opponents along, understanding that reacting in anger and holding grudges are unproductive.

Ruth Bader Ginsburg matters because, as in the case of Justice Brennan, she acknowledges that with increased understanding, people have the capacity to change.

AGREEING TO DISAGREE

RBG has shown the strength of character to be agreeable even when others disagree. Her long friendship with fellow jurist Antonin Scalia is a major example.

Ruth Ginsburg is not known for being easily amused. This was a woman whose children started a scrapbook called *Mommy Laughed* about the times when RBG found something funny. The book was not a thick one.

But viewers of the documentary *RBG* can see her laughing uproariously over a wisecrack from Scalia, whose political outlook was almost diametrically opposed to hers. While they disagreed many times over points of law, Scalia's wit and intelligence could make her laugh. It was something that may have been a welcome relief from her lifelong sober-minded, all-consuming approach to work. She believes in fostering the ability of "agreeing to disagree," not only by respecting other people but also enjoying their company.

Ruth Bader Ginsburg matters because in an increasingly contentious age, she has shown the value of making friends rather than enemies, that making peace is more productive than waging war, and possibly that laughter is the greatest gift of all.

RESPECT AND REASON

In the 1970s when RBG began her work with the Women's Rights Project at the ACLU, it is said that there were the thousands of state and federal laws on the books that codified discrimination against women such as the *Reed v. Reed* case. That was the 1971 decision that RBG coauthored with ACLU legal director Mel Wulf and was the first major case to address discrimination based on gender. They were able to overturn an Idaho statute from 1864 that automatically mandated a father to be preferred over a mother in administering the estate of a deceased child. That Civil War–era law had remained on the books even after Americans landed on the moon.

From that time, RBG worked slowly and strategically to address the kind of legally sanctioned discrimination across the country that existed just like the Idaho law. Her work focused on convincing lawmakers that women are people too, deserving of the rights and responsibilities of equal citizenship. She has said publicly that her efforts in litigation were not about "women's rights" per se but the constitutional principle that men and women share equal citizenship stature.

But as she methodically did so throughout her career as a litigator, earning success after success, there were those who criticized her for not being more strident, for utilizing male plaintiffs, for not moving fast enough, and for working with people who were considered adversaries.

As evidenced in her Congressional hearings for the Supreme Court nomination, RBG has worked to make allies rather than adversaries. The way she did that was not to protest, not to tell them they were wrong-headed, not to question their intelligence or morality, and not to raise her voice. On the federal court bench as well as on the Supreme Court, she has treated colleagues with respect, trying to reason with them. She often focused on the particular passions of those individuals to bring them around.

Before the Congressional hearings for her Supreme Court nomination, she met with potential opponents. By all accounts, she charmed them. Even strongly right-wing senators later claimed to have told her that while they disagreed with her stance on some issues, they liked RBG herself and would therefore support her nomination. That personal appeal helped her to be confirmed in the Senate by a vote of 96–3.

In Carmon and Knizhnik (2015), there is a noteworthy photograph of a female demonstrator in the 1970s with a sign reading, "Enough is enough! You ignorant men!" (19). It is not known how many male hearts and minds were swayed after reading that. What is known, however, is that such confrontational methods were never part of RBG's style. She proved that demonstrations may be less effective than demonstrating how the law can be used as an instrument of change.

Ruth Bader Ginsburg matters not only because she changed the lives of American women but *how* she did it: by bringing adversaries around to her point of view logically, by making the case for equal citizenship status for both men and women as it already existed in the Constitution, and by making friends out of enemies.

UNBROKEN

In situations that would quite justifiably have broken many people, causing them to bow under the pressure of incredible loss and overwhelming odds, RBG persevered. In a quiet, graceful way, she was ultimately able to overcome.

Ruth Bader Ginsburg matters because at those times when it would have been easier to give up in the face of overwhelming odds, she dug down to find hidden strengths. Through all of the obstacles in her life, she persevered. Ruth Bader Ginsburg matters because she remained unbroken.

LEMONS

Most people have heard the expression, "When life hands you a lemon, make lemonade." Throughout her life, RBG has been pelted with lemons. As a young girl, her mother Celia instilled in Ruth the belief that although she was a female, Ruth was just as valued as a son, even though that was hardly the conventional wisdom at the time. However, Celia, the person who supported Ruth the most, was stricken with cancer when Ruth was in high school. Literally the day before a major achievement—Ruth's graduation from high school with top academic awards—Celia died.

At the graduation ceremony where Ruth was scheduled to speak as a testament to earning top grades, she was not in attendance due to her mother's death. At home, Ruth was not even allowed to attend the religious mourning ritual for her mother because she was not a male.

In college, where males scorned a woman who was seen as a "brain," Ruth studied in remote bathrooms where the boys could not see her. When she married Martin Ginsburg, a man who actually did value her intelligence, he was struck with cancer while they were at Harvard Law School, one of the toughest institutions in the world. Ruth organized a support system for Marty among their friends, continued taking her own rigorous courses, went to his classes to take notes, visited him in the hospital, hurried home to care for their small child, served on the prestigious but time-consuming *Harvard Law Review*, transcribed notes for his senior paper, *and* maintained her position as a top student. She averaged two hours of sleep a night.

After her husband miraculously recovered and they both attained law degrees, RBG was unable to find a job as an attorney despite graduating at the top of her class. Employers were quite open about not hiring her because she was a woman.

Finding work was not the only ordeal she would face as an adult. She was diagnosed with colon cancer at age 66, undergoing surgery, chemotherapy, and radiation. Despite it all, Justice Ginsburg didn't miss a day at the Supreme Court. At age 76, she had surgery for pancreatic cancer, one of the deadliest malignancies. Again, she did not miss a day in court. At age 77, when many loving couples find comfort in each other during their senior years, her beloved husband, Marty, died. At age 79 and again at age 80, RBG injured her ribs after falling, something that often brings about devastating health complications in the elderly. At age 81, RBG had heart stent implant surgery; she carried on her work from the hospital. At age 85, she was hospitalized after falling in her office and breaking three ribs. Doctors then discovered a cancerous abnormality in her lungs that led to more surgery. In August 2019, at age 87, RBG underwent a three-week radiation treatment for a cancerous tumor.

Through it all, she persevered, sharing the details of her health as well as her recovery to empower other older people and cancer survivors. She is not unaware of the reasons people look to her health as a harbinger of her remaining time on the high court bench. Periodically rumors surface that she is dead or dying. RBG treats it with humor. On August 31, 2019, soon after the three-week radiation treatment, she appeared at the National Book Festival sponsored by the Library of Congress in Washington, D.C. There, she stated, "First, this audience can see I am alive."

Ruth Bader Ginsburg matters because she has used those challenges to help others find their own power of resilience. She has demonstrated that obstacles do not have to be permanent and that people can keep overcoming them—at any time of life.

SKY'S THE LIMIT

In the decades since the 1950s when RBG was one of only nine women in a class of more than 500 at Harvard Law School, female enrollment in law school across the board has increased. However, sources in the legal profession note that while there may be more women who are lawyers, there are not more women partners at law firms. Nor do women make up a substantial number of general counsels for Fortune 500 companies, law school deans, or state or federal judges.

Although women make up slightly over half of America's population, the three women on the Supreme Court at this writing comprise only a third of the nation's highest bench. That is of course a major step-up in the Court's long history during which, until 1981, there were no women at all. But compared to the 110 male justices who served in the Supreme Court since its inception in 1787, the number of women who have served there constitute less than a half a hundredth of a percent. So perhaps there is still work to be done, a mantle to be assumed by those following in RBG's footsteps.

Therefore it is fitting to return to the paradigm of Ruth Bader Ginsburg as the Notorious RBG and to Biggie Smalls, the Notorious B.I.G. In Smalls' rap song *Sky's The Limit*, he tells a rag-to-riches story based on his own life, citing the power of holding on to a dream.

All her life Ruth Bader Ginsburg held on to the dream and kept pressing on. She attained her place as a star in the sky by reaching the lofty heights of the Supreme Court, the very top of our nation's government. She then continued to press on for human rights for all people.

It is not known what happened to the long-ago Harvard guard who barred RBG from entering the law library because she was female, or would even show her the smallest "quality of mercy" by having the much-needed article brought out to her.

But what *is* known is that RBG prevailed, RBG inspires, and RBG matters.

SOURCES

Carmon, Irin, and Shana Knizhnik. *Notorious RBG: The Life and Times of Ruth Bader Ginsburg.* New York: Dey Street Books, 2015.

Ensign, Josephine. "The Consequences of Speaking Truth to Power." *PsychologyToday.com*, February 2, 2018. https://www.psychologytoday.com/us/blog/catching-homelessness/201802/the-consequences-speaking-truth-power.

Stern, Seth, and Stephen Wermiel. *Justice Brennan: Liberal Champion.* Lawrence: University Press of Kansas, 2010.

1

Childhood: The Go-Getter

On January 1, 1892, teenager Annie Moore from Ireland's County Cork was the first immigrant processed at Ellis Island, within sight of the Statue of Liberty. In the harbor between New York and New Jersey, the federal property was the gateway to the Promised Land of America. It is the place where the journey of Ruth Bader Ginsburg, the 107th justice of the United States Supreme Court, really begins.

According to Cannato (2009), Annie Moore had no idea she made history by becoming the first immigrant to arrive at Ellis Island. To mark the occasion, she was given a ten-dollar gold piece by the facility's commissioner. After asking if it was hers to keep, "she then thanked him, saying it was the largest amount of money she had ever seen" (58).

Annie Moore had journeyed from Ireland across the Atlantic in steerage for almost two weeks. She carried very little with her other than the American Dream. It was a dream that coursed through the lifeblood of Ruth Bader Ginsburg's family, and it is a theme that can be followed, like a golden thread, through RBG's legal career: freedom and equality.

The American Dream, known around the world, was said to offer freedom for U.S. citizens along with an equal opportunity for success through their own hard work and determination. With American public education readily available, it extended the hope of upward mobility for their children regardless of social class.

The American Dream is what Ireland's Annie Moore had in common with more than 12 million immigrants who walked in her footsteps, passing through Ellis Island between 1892 and 1954, when the immigration center closed. It was the dream that beckoned Ruth Bader's father, Nathan.

Today, more than 100 million Americans can trace their ancestry to people who arrived at Ellis Island.

Ruth Bader Ginsburg's origin story, coming from a family of immigrants, formed the foundation of her life. It is impossible to understand the person she became and the laws she influenced without knowledge of where she came from.

THE DREAM BECKONS

In 1909, the young Nathan Bader, age 13, arrived on American shores via Ellis Island. He had been born in 1896, just four years after the opening of Ellis Island. Nathan was part of a Jewish family who had lived in the Russian Empire near today's city of Odessa in Ukraine.

Like the rest of Eastern Europe, Odessa was not a welcoming place for the region's Jewish population. In 1821, 1859, 1871, 1881, and 1905, it was the site of massive pogroms, which were sudden vicious attacks by gangs of mounted soldiers that left thousands of Jewish people dead, injured, and/or homeless. Today, the vicious pogroms might be called ethnic cleansing, genocide, or simply state-sanctioned mass murder.

The Jewish people usually kept to themselves in small villages away from the rest of the population. However, the repeated outbreaks of deadly violence against them left no illusion that there was much of a future for them in Eastern Europe.

Nathan Bader's father Samuel had arrived at Ellis Island in 1905, after surviving that year's massive pogrom. As in many immigrant stories, Samuel worked at whatever jobs he could find to earn passage for the rest of the family. Because of his efforts, within four years, the rest of the family was able to join him.

In 1909, Yiddish-speaking Nathan arrived with his mother, Ida Milstein Bader, and brothers, including Benjamin and Philip. At that time, those names had of course been Americanized, with Nathan having started life as "Nesen." His name did not matter for school records because he had no formal education apart from learning the English language in night school upon arriving in America. After witnessing the terrifying devastation of the 1905 pogrom as a nine-year-old, Nathan Bader was no doubt happy just to be alive.

THE LOWER EAST SIDE

Like tens of thousands of other Jewish immigrants, Nathan Bader's family settled in the Lower East Side area of New York City. The neighborhood is in the southeastern part of Manhattan Island, located roughly between Canal Street, Houston Street, the Bowery, and the East River.

Crowded tenements offered less expensive housing than other areas of the city for most new arrivals, and poor Jewish immigrants would not have been welcomed elsewhere in the city.

As more immigrants arrived, the neighborhood of the Lower East Side became a place where friends and family from the "old country" had already settled. There, people spoke a familiar language, and many often helped new arrivals make the transition to a vastly different life from what they had known in the tiny, isolated villages of Eastern Europe.

In the immigrants' attempt to escape destitution and enter the mainstream of American life, the Lower East Side has become known as the place where many now-famous Americans began their climb out of poverty. They include popular performers who became legendary, such as Irving Berlin, George Gershwin, and the Marx Brothers.

Like those individuals, Nathan Bader joined what grew to almost a million fellow Jewish residents, mostly from Eastern Europe. There, the Bader family surname was not uncommon. "Bader" is said to be a derivative of the medieval occupation of barbers, who often also acted as surgeons during the Middle Ages. Some people by that name grew to prominence in America, including professional golfer Beth Bader, actor Diedrich Bader, sculptor Gretta Bader, U.S. Ambassador Jeffrey Bader, and Major League Baseball players Art Bader and Lore Bader. RBG's cousin Richard Bader, who was her best friend as a child, went on to serve as executive director of the American Shakespeare Theatre in Stratford, Connecticut.

FEW CAREER CHOICES

However, when 13-year-old Nathan Bader arrived in the United States, such occupations could scarcely have crossed his mind, even in his wildest dreams. In the old country, Jewish people could not own land and were usually barred from most livelihoods except money lending and peddling, although often even those were forbidden; the career choices for Jewish people were narrow, to say the least.

But even with those restrictions, some young men in the old country were able to learn trades like tailoring. They brought those skills with them to the United States, forming the basis for the modern garment industry. By 1910, almost 50 percent of the clothing factories in America were located in New York City. Within the garment industry, Jewish employees made up about three-quarters of the tailors, hat makers, and furriers.

To earn a living, new arrivals were often consigned to noisily hawking their wares on the congested streets of the Lower East Side. They found a place among what was estimated to be about 2,500 peddlers and pushcart vendors.

Immigrants lived in overcrowded tenements amid conditions that most people today would find atrocious, with very little sunlight or fresh air. There was generally no indoor plumbing except for one often-malfunctioning toilet to serve an entire building. Frequently, three generations lived in a cramped one-bedroom apartment.

However, despite extreme overcrowding, horrible sanitation, and lack of air and sunlight, it was not all gloom and doom on the Lower East Side. In his book *The Rest of Us*, Stephen Birmingham (1985) says that living conditions for the Jewish immigrants in New York were not that much better than what they had been in the old country. But—and this is an important distinction—"they were not that much worse either" (22).

EDUCATION: PRICELESS

What mattered to the people jammed into the Lower East Side was that they were in America, no longer living in terror of police descending upon them at night, of a son taken away by the army never to be seen again, or what Birmingham calls "being forced to stand by helplessly as one's mother or sister was raped and disemboweled by drunken cossack soldiers" (23).

Not to be in constant fear for one's life was an important distinction indeed. Even living in a slum was still *living*. It was better than perpetual terror of being killed simply for being who they happened to be. Nevertheless, after finding a safe harbor in the United States, the denizens of the Lower East Side were highly motivated to make it out of the tenements and build something better for themselves and their families.

They had an essential weapon on their side. The Jewish religion placed a high value on education. In fact, Jewish people had an obligation to their religion to be literate in Hebrew. It was their duty to regularly read the scriptures written in that language and to educate their children to do the same.

While Nathan Bader had no formal education beyond night school English classes in America, boys like himself had been required by their religion to learn to read Hebrew. As was the case with enslaved African American people in America's antebellum South, it had been illegal for Jewish people to learn reading and writing in the countries where they had lived. Classes in Hebrew were held secretly in a shed or other hidden spot with one child standing lookout, alert to approaching soldiers who would have taken them into custody.

However, in the United States, not only was public education available—even compulsory—but it was also accessible even to impoverished immigrants who had recently arrived. In colonial days, education in America had been obtainable primarily only by the wealthy via tutors and private academies. But ultimately there came a trend toward public education. By the end of the 1800s, public schools outnumbered private ones in the United States.

Newly arrived immigrants like those who jammed into the Lower East Side recognized the priceless value of public education for their children.

The language spoken among many Jewish immigrants was Yiddish, which was based on elements of German and Hebrew. But even if languages other than English were spoken in many homes like Nathan's, schoolchildren could learn to speak the unaccented American vernacular like any native. That in itself would help enable them climb the ladder out of the slums and into the middle class—the American Dream.

Even if Jewish children had to fight tough Irish, Italian, and Polish gangs in the streets to get their American education, they tenaciously faced them day after day to go to school.

TOUGH LOVE

One woman was particularly important to the slum-dwellers of the Lower East Side. Julia Richman was the first female district superintendent of schools in New York City. As the daughter of Jewish immigrants herself, she treated the denizens of the Lower East Side with what today might be called "tough love." Richman was determined to turn immigrant children into Americans if they were to have any hope of success in their new homeland. If students spoke any language other than English in school, her policy was to rinse out their mouths with soap.

Richman's strategy also emphasized vocational education so immigrant children could grow up to be gainfully employed. In America, many Jewish boys started out with pushcarts, graduating to a horse and wagon, then learned a trade, and finally opened shops of their own.

With a personality described as warm and likeable, Nathan Bader became part of a popular vocation among his countrymen, the garment business. He was fortunate in being able to join his father's firm, Samuel Bader and Sons, specializing in inexpensive furs. Nathan was eventually able to start his own small fur business with his brother and later to find work in a men's clothing store.

Approaching his 30th birthday in the mid-1920s, he felt financially secure enough to marry. Nathan Bader was ready for a good life with a good wife.

THE GOOD WIFE

Celia Amster could also be called a product of Eastern Europe, but only technically. In 1902, her parents, Joseph Amster (sometimes spelled

"Auster") and Rose Dick Amster, arrived in New York from their home near Cracow in today's Poland. Four months after their arrival, Celia was born, with her birth date appropriately listed as July 4, 1902.

She was the fourth of seven children and was the first of her family to be born in the United States. From an early age, Celia was described as being smart and ambitious, perhaps catching some of the spirit of the New World even before she was born.

With a love of reading, she did well in both academic and vocational classes at Julia Richman High School, named after the aforementioned educator. With top grades, Celia graduated from high school at age 15. Her father recognized her intelligence, asking her assistance in figuring the bills for his furniture business. But apart from that recognition, having good grades in school did not help Celia much at home, nor did they help her future prospects. After graduating from high school, she was expected to utilize her commercial coursework, not the classes from the academic side, to find a job.

The point was for her to work in order to help pay for her eldest brother's college education. That brother, Solomon Amster, was the one on whom the family pinned their hopes, and everyone did their part in contributing toward his college expenses. Solomon, or "Chuck" as he began to call himself, was accepted at Cornell University in Upstate New York, which admitted a limited number of Jewish people. He was slated to graduate in 1918; eventually, he would play a significant role in the lives of future family members like the child who became Justice Ruth Bader Ginsburg.

At age 15, after graduation from high school in 1917, Celia Amster went to work as a bookkeeper for a furrier in New York City's Garment District, a few densely packed blocks in midtown Manhattan. Part of Celia's salary went toward paying for her brother Solomon's college education. But at least it was a respectable job that was a step-up for Celia compared to her older sister who went to work in a sweatshop.

WHEN NATHAN MET CELIA

Amid the bustle of New York's Garment District in the 1920s, furrier Nathan Bader crossed paths with garment industry bookkeeper Celia Amster. Although Nathan was somewhat shy, he had a warm nature that apparently attracted the amiable, intelligent Celia. They were married, and their first child, Marilyn Elsa, was born in 1927.

Nathan believed in the conventional wisdom of the time, which dictated that a working wife was a stigma for all the world to see. It supposedly showed that a man was unable to support his family and thus was less of a man. Therefore, Celia left her job.

It was more than just a male prerogative or whim on Nathan's part. All across the United States, but especially for immigrants who were scrambling out of the Lower East Side, it was considered a status symbol for a man to have a wife who did not need to work. For them, it was part of the American Dream. It was also a belief that lasted well into the 1960s. According to Carmon and Knizhnik (2015), the mother of an elementary school friend of RBG's daughter Jane was told to be extra nice to Jane because "[her] mommy works" (101). At the time, RBG was a professor of law at Rutgers University.

Celia Bader was at least able to put some of her education, experience, and intelligence to work from their home. As she had done with her father, Celia helped Nathan keep his business afloat by performing bookkeeping and clerical duties.

Celia's business sense was to become crucial after the Stock Market Crash in 1929. The high-flying, prosperous Roaring '20s plummeted into the soul-crushing poverty of the Great Depression in the 1930s. With most people opting to spend what little money they had during the Depression on food and housing, not many people could afford to buy furs.

ALL IN THE FAMILY

In the 1920s and 1930s, the blended Amster and Bader families found ways to economize even as they fought their way up toward the American Dream. Nathan's brother Benjamin Bader married Celia's sister Bernice Amster. The two couples decided to share the downstairs portion of a house in the Flatbush section of Brooklyn until they could afford to live in separate family homes.

Nathan and Celia Bader were eventually able to move to a modest house at 1584 East 9th Street in Brooklyn. The attached two-family home that had been built in 1920 was—and is—a neat, attractive house in a nice neighborhood, where many other Jewish families made their home. A new addition joined Nathan and Celia Bader when their baby, Marilyn Elsa, was born on July 5, 1927.

Even when the Depression struck after the Crash of 1929, there was cause for joy when another baby arrived. On March 15, 1933, Joan Ruth Bader was born at Brooklyn's Beth Moses Hospital.

The new arrival was so energetic that her five-year-old sister Marilyn nicknamed her "Kiki." Felix (2018) says it was pronounced "Kicky" because she was a "Kicky Baby" (9). It was a nickname that would follow Ruth through college and was one of the few legacies she received from Marilyn, who died of meningitis on June 6, 1934, when Ruth was about 14 months old.

Meningitis is an inflammation involving the brain and spinal cord. Its level of contagion depends on the type of infection, whether bacterial or viral. The illness can often spread when infected people cough or sneeze on others. Nathan and Celia took great pains to keep Ruth, their surviving child, safe.

Marilyn was buried at Mount Carmel Cemetery in the nearby borough of Queens, New York. Her family often went there to visit the narrow gravestone that marked her resting place. It was said that Marilyn's death cast a shadow over the Bader household, a dark cloud that would be tragically echoed later in the family's future.

JOAN BECOMES RUTH

When it came time for Joan Ruth Bader to enroll at the 1,000-student P.S. (Public School) 238 in Brooklyn, her mother noticed that there were many other girls there named Joan. With around 30 children per class, to avoid confusion, the practical-minded Celia advocated calling her daughter by her middle name of "Ruth," setting the lifelong precedent.

As Ruth entered grade school in 1937, the Depression was still very much a part of American life. However, there were some positive signs for recovery under what came to be known as the New Deal of President Franklin Delano Roosevelt. Known popularly as "FDR," he had been inaugurated around the time of Ruth's birth in 1933. FDR was reelected in 1936, going on to be elected again in 1940 and 1944. Later in life, many children of Ruth's generation said that they did not know anyone else could be president.

Ruth did well in school, eventually being admitted to Arista, the elite honor society at P.S. 238. The one area in which young Ruth did not immediately excel was penmanship. Like her mother, Celia, Ruth was left-handed. The conventional wisdom of the era was to "convert" children into using the right hand, by force if necessary. This draconian measure was later found to have unfortunate effects on those for whom the left was the dominant hand (it was said that such a forced conversion contributed to the lifelong stutter of England's King George VI). After Ruth gave her right hand a try and ended up with an uncharacteristic "D" in penmanship, she reverted back to using her left hand and stayed that way for life.

Young Ruth was also not enthralled with reading materials like the Dick and Jane books that were used in the classroom. She noticed that the character of "Dick" was the one who was always doing active things like rescuing their cat from a tree while "Jane" sat on the sidelines in her tidy pinafore, cheering him on. Ruth later said she would rather have been the one climbing the tree.

> ## A New Deal
>
> When Joan Ruth Bader was born in Brooklyn during March 1933, few could have foreseen the impact she would have on the laws of our nation, benefitting millions of Americans, both male and female. That same month, events in Washington, D.C., would also impact the lives of most Americans in ways that are taken for granted today. Democrat Franklin Delano Roosevelt (1882–1945) was inaugurated as U.S. president on March 4, 1933. Some of the programs he implemented, which he called "a new deal for the American people," continue to provide safeguards for the citizens of our nation to this day. These include Social Security to assist senior citizens and the disabled, the Federal Deposit Insurance Corporation to protect people's savings from bank failures, and the Securities and Exchange Commission to help avoid financial disasters like the Great Depression. The Roosevelt years also included the glimmering of hope toward a new deal for women. The day Roosevelt was inaugurated, he appointed Frances Perkins (1880–1965) as Secretary of Labor, the first woman ever to serve on the presidential Cabinet in America's history. At the same time, Roosevelt supporter Hattie Caraway (1878–1950) of Arkansas was sworn in as the first woman elected to a full term in the U.S. Senate. She would go on to be reelected in 1938 and was one of the lawmakers in 1944 who introduced the G.I. Bill, providing educational benefits for veterans and called by many the most significant piece of legislation in U.S. history. Few could have foreseen that a baby named Joan Ruth Bader, born the same month that Roosevelt took office, would bring about her own kind of new deal for the American people.

Fortunately for young Ruth, she would have the opportunity to climb trees herself as well as ride horses and enjoy water sports. It would even provide a significant turning point in Ruth's career as an adult, one she could scarcely have foreseen. From age four to her "retirement" as a counselor when she was 18, Ruth's summers centered around a treasured destination: camp.

CHE-NA-WAH

The death of her older sister Marilyn left Ruth to grow up as an only child. However, having a large extended family with relatives living nearby, especially her cousin Richard Bader with whom she was particularly close, did a lot to alleviate loneliness during most of the year. But it was summertime that provided Ruth with an entirely new set of friends and opportunities.

Each summer from 1937 to 1951, young Ruth attended Camp Che-Na-Wah (pronounced SheNAHwa) amid the fresh mountain air of the Adirondacks in Upstate New York. The campers had the impression that the girls' camp had been named for a "Native American princess."

The camp had been founded in the 1920s by Celia's elder brother Solomon "Chuck" Amster, a teacher, whom she had helped put through college. Having attended Cornell University in Upstate New York, Chuck became fond of the rustic upstate region that can sometimes feel light years away from New York City.

In 1922, Chuck purchased a property near Minerva, New York, on Balfour Lake, which had a natural beach. He and his wife Cornelia opened a summer camp, where girls could enjoy nature, sports, and arts activities while forming close friendships. According to the camp's current website, a large majority of the campers return year after year. Some, like Ruth Bader, eventually became camp counselors as teenagers.

The Amsters also operated the nearby boys' counterpart, Camp Baco. One of the boys Ruth met at camp, Mel Wulf, later became the national legal director for the American Civil Liberties Union (ACLU). Wulf would play an important role in Ruth's future professional life as well as in gender equality for the nation.

LOVE AND LOVINGKINDNESS

In 1946, at age 13, Ruth graduated from Hebrew school, carrying home a prize for being top student. She was able to utilize her spiritual education by serving as camp rabbi for religious services at Camp Che-Na-Wah, an opportunity that was rare for girls.

A different kind of education and spiritual growth for young Ruth came courtesy of Celia. Having grown up in Yiddish-speaking households in Manhattan's Lower East Side, Celia and her husband, Nathan, had been able to move out and move up in the world. But she wanted Ruth to recognize her roots in order to better appreciate where they had come from. Celia took her daughter to visit the Lower East Side, which still retained much of its dirt, noise, and bustling crowds.

Being a first-generation American on her father's side (and only second on her mother's), Ruth was not far removed from her Eastern European antecedents. Her grounding in where she came from would form the foundation of her later career as well as her belief in the law as a means to capture the spirit of the American Dream.

By the time Ruth visited the area as a child, the New York Housing Authority had removed the worst of the slums in the Lower East Side, but it was still a place that was crowded and noisy. Kanefield (2016) says that while young Ruth did not fall in love with what has become today's mythology of the Lower East Side, she did find something else to cherish there (6).

The legendary delicatessen on the Lower East Side called Russ & Daughters was not far from Celia's childhood home in the tenements. The shop claims to be the first in the United States to add "& Daughters" to its name, after founder Joel Russ's three full-time partners. According to Zax (2018), RBG said that even before she heard the word "feminist," it made her happy to see a business based on "the founder's then-untraditional decision to name the restaurant after himself and his daughters" (n.p.). In addition, the food was fabulous. Russ & Daughters deli is still in business, and it is said that Justice Ginsburg often orders a shipment of delicacies from the store for parties at her home in Washington, D.C.

In addition to keeping in touch with the family's roots in the Lower East Side, Ruth's mother also stressed the importance of compassion and acts of loving-kindness. Each year, young Ruth celebrated her birthday at a Jewish orphanage in Brooklyn, where the children residing there would share the cake and ice cream that Celia had brought.

Along with summers at camp, birthday visits to the orphanage, and treks to the Lower East Side, there were other significant memories that were formed in Ruth's childhood.

WORDS AND MUSIC

According to Felix (2018), before Ruth could read, she spent happy moments curled up in her mother's lap while Celia read aloud from books like A. A. Milne's poems about Winnie-the-Pooh as well as Robert Louis Stevenson's *Child's Garden of Verses.*

After Ruth could read on her own, her love of books grew. Each week Celia would go to her hairdresser, which was close to the Kings Highway Branch of the Brooklyn Public Library. While having her hair done, Celia allowed her daughter to peruse the books at the library. Ruth could use the time to select books that she would check out and take home for the week. At the time, that particular library was located above a Chinese restaurant, and in later life, Justice Ginsburg said she grew to associate the aroma of Chinese food with the pleasures of reading. The books young Ruth enjoyed included Greek mythology, biographies of strong, successful women like Amelia Earhart, and according to Felix, "losing herself in Nancy Drew mysteries and the New England lives of Alcott's *Little Women*" (10).

Along with books, Celia also introduced her daughter to the world of art and music, reserving seats at the Saturday children's concerts presented by the Brooklyn Academy of Music. Justice Ginsburg later said when she saw the opera *La Giaconda* at age 11, she loved it so much that she wanted to become an operatic diva. Then a music teacher pointed out that she could not sing very well. According to Kanefield (2016), the teacher allegedly called Ruth "a sparrow, not a robin," instructing her to simply mouth the words when the other children sang (6).

LANDMARKS OF FREEDOM

P.S. 238 ran from kindergarten through 8th grade, and Ruth did well throughout the foundational years of her public school days. Celia went over Ruth's homework, and the girl's good grades reflected it. However, one time Ruth brought home a report card that was less than perfect, perhaps the "D" in penmanship. Celia's disappointed reaction struck such a significant chord in the child that the subpar performance was not repeated.

During the 1930s, many parents, especially those in Jewish homes, tried not to mention the trouble in Europe that was occurring at the time, sparing their children from certain harsh realities. In 1939, World War II began in Europe, with America entering the conflict in 1941. Ruth was in elementary school throughout the war years.

In 1946, when she was in the 8th grade, Ruth Bader served as editor of the school newspaper at P.S. 238. Possibly in response to the global war that had ended the year before, and as a kind of precursor to her later career, Kanefield says that 13-year-old Ruth wrote an article titled "Landmarks of Constitutional Freedom" (4).

In her editorial, she spotlighted important milestones in the formation of American law, including the Ten Commandments of the Bible; the Magna Carta, which was signed by Britain's King John in the year 1215; the English Bill of Rights approved by King William of Orange in 1689; and America's own Declaration of Independence, signed in 1776 to herald the birth of the new nation. Ruth was not content simply to focus on the freedoms enjoyed by contemporary Americans that were based on documents from centuries before. She also took a world view, choosing to include the United Nations Charter, which had been signed the year before, in 1945, with a goal of engendering peace and tolerance for all of the world's people.

WOMEN OF VALOR

Another facet of Celia's influence may also have forged a lifelong theme in her daughter: the Jewish tradition of the "Woman of Valor." First cited in the Bible's Book of Ruth (3:11), many translations of the Old Testament cite Boaz calling the biblical Ruth a "woman of valor."

The word "valor" may be defined as courage, decency, integrity, and strength. It includes compassion for the less fortunate and those who cannot speak for themselves. In Proverbs 31:10–31, the passage generally translated as "A Woman of Valor" is often attributed to King Solomon. It states that for such a woman, "her price is far above rubies."

Celia seems to follow the Biblical tradition of strong women. In many cases, women of her background had to be. Often newly arrived immigrant males found themselves adrift in the strange new world of America, where absolutely everything was different—an assault on their take-charge manhood. Many found refuge in spending the bulk of their time studying the scriptures, which was familiar to them and which was traditionally felt to be a noble calling for men. However, someone had to put food on the table, and the task often fell to the woman of the house.

There is no evidence that the warm, friendly Nathan Bader failed his family. But it is noted by numerous sources that after the devastating loss of their eldest daughter Marilyn, Celia encouraged young Ruth to console her sensitive father in his grief while Celia apparently dealt with her own sadness by herself.

People whom Celia considered to be Women of Valor from her era included Emma Lazarus, whose poem "The New Colossus" is engraved on the Statue of Liberty, and Eleanor Roosevelt, who used her position as First Lady to speak for people who had no voice.

GO-GETTER

Ruth was an elementary school child during the years when America was engaged in World War II, from 1941 to 1945. With the war beginning when she was eight years old, she lived through a time not only of hardship and rationing, but also a sense of the country pulling together for victory. She wrote letters to a cousin who was drafted and sent to fight in the Pacific theater of war.

Adults often tried to keep the harsh realities of Nazi Germany from their children, but for Jewish people, it was impossible to ignore the millions of fellow Jews who were being exterminated by the Nazis. For many Jewish Americans, the feeling was of tremendous gratitude to be in the United States coupled with an overwhelming sense of tragedy. Few families in Brooklyn were untouched by events in Europe.

During World War II, Ruth and her mother could hardly have helped noticing that American women took on a variety of roles they had never played before, both on the home front and in combat zones. Recruitment posters for women were everywhere, including the iconic image of "Rosie the Riveter," a female factory worker performing what had always been

> **BETTER THAN HARVARD**
>
> During the time that Ruth Bader attended James Madison High School in the late 1940s, it was described as an ordinary middle- and lower-middle-class public school like many others in the New York City School System. It served a large number of students whose parents and/or grandparents were newly arrived immigrants, many of whom did not speak English. Yet during that era, Brooklyn's James Madison High School also managed to produce movie director/screenwriter Garson Kanin, actor Martin Landau, historian Robert Dallek, singer/songwriter Carole King, television's "Judge Judy" Sheindlin, and presidential candidate Bernie Sanders, as well as a U.S. Supreme Court Justice, six Nobel laureates, and three U.S. senators. One of them, Senate Minority Leader Charles Schumer, has been quoted as saying he received a better education at James Madison High School than he had at Harvard. Most sources today credit the school's dedicated faculty at the time as well as commitment by the parents of its students, like Ruth Bader's mother, Celia, who came from immigrant backgrounds and valued the privilege of a public school education, having little schooling themselves. One teacher from James Madison arranged for a freshman who did especially well in a civics class to administer the oath of citizenship to a group of immigrants at the Brooklyn courthouse. One can only imagine how the boy's parents, possibly recent arrivals themselves, must have felt.

considered a man's job. Women of the 1940s were building airplanes and ships. They drove trucks and produced munitions. They served as nurses on the front lines and as Women Airforce Service Pilots repositioning combat aircraft. All of that would change after the war when Ruth entered high school. Women were sent back into the home.

In 1946, at age 13, Ruth Bader graduated from P.S. 238, first in her class. For grades 9 through 12, she attended the five-story red brick James Madison High School. Founded in 1925, it was on Brooklyn's Bedford Avenue, near her home.

Outwardly, Ruth Bader's high school years seemed like happy ones. Along with scoring top grades academically, Ruth was a cellist in the school orchestra and served as a baton twirler. Perhaps most notably in the hierarchy of the high school world, she was also a member of Go-Getters pep club, acting as the group's treasurer and cheering for the athletic exploits of Madison High's Golden Knights.

THE SMELL OF DEATH

At just over five feet tall, Ruth was described as petite and slender with bobbed auburn hair. Classmates considered her popular but reserved. She tended not to speak unless she had something substantial to say, which she did in a slow deliberate way.

But the popular, upbeat Ruth, scurrying down the halls in her black satin Go-Getters pep club jacket, had a dark secret. Just before Ruth's 14th birthday, her mother, Celia, had been diagnosed with cervical cancer. Throughout Ruth's high school years, Celia was in and out of the hospital for repeated surgeries. Ruth later said she lived with the "smell of death" in the house. Still, she never let on to classmates, keeping her mother's condition to herself. When Celia became bedridden, Ruth did her homework at her mother's bedside, allowing the two of them to spend time together and enabling Celia to take pride in Ruth's academic achievement.

As with many newly arrived immigrant families, education was extremely important to Celia. In her book *My Own Words* (2016), Ruth said, "My mother was very strong about my doing well in school and living up to my potential" (5). It had not been that long ago when Celia was unable to live up to her own potential, leaving school behind to get a job that would help send her brother to college.

Celia had more motherly advice for her daughter. In *My Own Words*, Justice Ginsburg recalls, "Two things were important to her and she repeated them endlessly. One was to 'be a lady' and that meant conduct yourself civilly and don't let emotions like anger or envy get in your way. And the other was to be independent" (5).

Celia's directive to be independent was, as Justice Ginsburg pointed out later in life, "an unusual message for mothers of the time to be giving their daughters" (5). It was an era when women were absolutely dependent on men to support them and their children. Regardless of how loving a man was and how good a provider, husbands and fathers could be taken by death, illness, injury, or other disasters like business calamities at any time. Celia wanted her daughter to have more options than she did.

Ruth followed Celia's advice to always be a lady by rising above petty, destructive emotions, to remain calm, and to be modest. This tranquil exterior masked young Ruth's inner strength. Before her high school graduation in 1950, she would need that strength in the face of a particularly tragic turn of events.

GRADUATION DAY

At James Madison High School, many students, even females, aimed for college. As graduation approached, Ruth Bader set her sights on Cornell University in Ithaca, New York, which Celia's brother Solomon had attended with Celia's financial assistance. In addition to accepting some students who were Jewish, the school accepted some who were female. The word was that it was a good place for a woman to find a man, with a ratio of four males for each female admitted. However, Celia always stressed that she wanted Ruth to have some sort of career so that she could support herself even if "Prince Charming" came along.

At the time, career paths for women were limited, even for college-educated women whose three basic choices were to be a teacher, nurse, or secretary. With schoolteachers held in high esteem by Celia's generation, she thought Ruth would be best suited to being a high school history teacher.

It would have seemed that the path for Ruth to meet that career goal was secure when the acceptance letter from Cornell arrived. Some might feel that since Celia had been unable to attain a college education at Cornell herself, there was a certain poetic symmetry for her daughter to attend. And it had happened in one generation.

High school graduation is an event that is an important milestone in the life of any young person. As Graduation Day at James Madison High School approached, Ruth won scholarships, including the Madison English Scholarship and the New York State Scholarship. She graduated near the top of her class. As such, she was scheduled to speak at the Round Table Forum of Honor as part of the graduation ceremony. However, she never got the chance.

Celia's doctors had recommended an aggressive treatment of radiation that made her horribly ill but did nothing to relieve her suffering. On Sunday, June 25, 1950, Celia Bader died at age 47. The next day, Monday, she was buried. On Tuesday, June 27, James Madison High School held its graduation ceremony. Ruth Bader did not attend, remaining at home with her distraught father. Teachers brought Ruth's academic awards and medals to her house.

NO GIRLS ALLOWED

The burial of Celia Amster Bader took place at Mount Carmel Cemetery, where Ruth's elder sister Marilyn had also been laid to rest. Celia was buried beneath a double headstone that she would later share with her husband, Nathan. Her inscription reads, "Beloved Wife | Dear Mother."

Not attending graduation would ostensibly at least allow Ruth the opportunity to mourn her mother, who had arguably been the most important person in her life. However, the incident that followed would affect Ruth for the remainder of her life to come.

Having had strong spiritual training and being confirmed at the top of her religious class, Ruth had even served as camp rabbi, leading worship services at Camp Che-Na-Wah. Therefore, Ruth was quite familiar with the traditional Jewish mourner's ceremony. In that rite, a ten-member group over the age of 13 sit together for several days, usually at the home of the deceased, reciting prayers in memory of the departed. Along with mourning the death of the loved one, the ritual also focuses on life, honor, and promise.

However, only males were allowed to do so. Because Ruth was a girl, she was not permitted to be part of the group gathered to honor her mother. At one point, the mourners did not have the required ten men and had to go searching for an additional male to sit with them.

Respecting Celia's instruction to "be a lady," Ruth Bader remained outwardly calm. However, the injustice of that slight outraged her to the point that it caused a breach in her spiritual life. Although she remained proud of her Jewish heritage, she no longer practiced ritual observance. From then on, she was not known to be affiliated with any house of worship.

FROM THE GRAVE

After her mother died, Ruth was in for another surprise, this time of a more pleasant nature. It was as if her mother was reaching out to her from the grave. Ruth discovered Celia had been saving for her daughter's college education. Having been a product of the Great Depression when banks were known to fail, Celia spread her money across five separate bank accounts. In all, Celia had saved $8,000. That was a substantial amount in 1950, worth almost $85,000 in 2018. It is not known if Nathan Bader had saved any money for his daughter's education.

Because of the scholarships Ruth had earned, she returned the $8,000 to her father, although it meant working part-time jobs in college for her to cover expenses beyond tuition. This proved to be a wise and compassionate gesture by Ruth, because after Celia passed away, Nathan's business soon declined. When Ruth was away at camp the summer after Celia's death, relatives found a small apartment for Nathan on Long Island, near the town of Rockville Centre.

Celia Bader may have died, but her influence on her daughter lived on. Along with advice to always be a lady and to get a good education so she could be independent, Celia had also taught Ruth the Jewish value of "tikkun olam," or healing the world. Growing up in the 1940s, an alert, intelligent young person like Ruth was aware of the global devastation brought on by World War II. She saw the slaughter of millions of Jewish people like herself in Europe. A young girl named Anne Frank, soon to become known around the world for the diary she kept during the war years, was around Ruth's age. She died at the hands of the Nazis the year before Ruth entered high school.

As an idealistic young person, Ruth also saw injustices at home in America, the shining light of the world, the country she was proud and grateful to call home. Ruth's years at Celia's side and her regular study of the Bible instilled a phrase from Deuteronomy 16:20. It was the biblical imperative: "Justice, justice shall you pursue."

Neither Celia nor her daughter could have foreseen that someday those words would hang in Ruth's office at the highest pinnacle of American government, as a justice of the United States Supreme Court. In any case, Ruth first had to attend college, a time that would have a monumental impact on the rest of her life.

SOURCES

Birmingham, Stephen. *The Rest of Us*. New York: Berkley Books, 1985.
Camp Che-Na-Wah for Girls. http://www.campbaco.com/camp-che-na-wah-for-girls.
Cannato, Vincent J. *American Passage: The History of Ellis Island*. New York: Harper, 2009.
Carmon, Irin, and Shana Knizhnik. *Notorious RBG: The Life and Times of Ruth Bader Ginsburg*. New York: Dey Street Books, 2015.
Felix, Antonia, with Foreword by Mimi Leder. *The Unstoppable Ruth Bader Ginsburg: American Icon*. New York: Sterling, 2018.
Ginsburg, Ruth Bader. *My Own Words*. New York: Simon & Schuster, 2016.
Kanefield, Teri. *Free to Be Ruth Bader Ginsburg: The Story of Women and Law*. San Francisco, CA: Armon Books, 2016.
Zax, Talya. "Ruth Bader Ginsburg Has an Opinion on Everything, from Feminism to Fish," *Forward*, January 24, 2018. https://forward.com/culture/film-tv/392804/rbg-documentaries-to-know-jewish-american-sturgeon-queens.

2

College: The Brain

In the autumn of 1950, the 17-year-old Ruth Bader arrived at Cornell University in Ithaca, New York. Cornell University had been founded in 1865 when it was authorized by New York as the state's land grant institution. State Senator Ezra Cornell, a founder of the Western Union Telegraph company, offered his farm in Ithaca as a site along with a substantial initial endowment.

In 1870, college officials at Cornell received a letter from a prominent citizen of Cortland, New York, supporting the admission of a local girl, Jennie Spencer. The letter testified to what it called her irreproachable character. Spencer had passed a qualifying exam for admission and won a state scholarship. Because part of its financial support came from public funds, "the leaders of Cornell could not deny Spencer entrance" (Solomon 1986, 52). She was admitted to Cornell in the Fall of 1870 as the university's first female student, making Cornell the first coeducational institution among the eight schools of the Ivy League.

But Barbara Solomon also points out that there were no efforts made at Cornell to accommodate what its president called "flippant and worthless 'boarding school misses'" (52). Cornell was about 40 miles from Spencer's hometown of Cortland, a formidable distance by horse and buggy if she tried to live at home. Some sources say it would have taken her about eight hours to make the trip one way. Cornell did not have lodgings for women on campus. Nor did it even have a dining facility where a female student could eat.

Jennie Spencer was able to find a room with a sympathetic local family, but the daily trek to and from campus was daunting, especially in the cold upstate New York winter. The logistics, isolation, and expense of transportation, lodging, and dining requirements proved insurmountable. Although reluctant to do so, Spencer was eventually forced to leave Cornell in 1871. However, her departure was not in vain, as a benefactor who had been moved by Spencer's experience later came forward to fund a women's residence hall on campus.

Some of Cornell's influential faculty members and trustees remained opposed to the admission of women. Opponents stridently pronounced that "young men would lose a proper sense of dignity of their own pursuits" adding that admitting women was "at variance with the ordinances of God" (Conable 1977, 67).

One woman was ultimately able to surmount such opposition. Conable says that Emma Sheffield Eastman, "a transfer student from Vassar College, became in 1873 the first woman to graduate from Cornell University" (67).

ONE OF SEVEN

In terms of religion, Cornell did not bar Jewish students, as many schools did. However, the numbers remained small, especially for Jewish women. In 1950, when Ruth Bader entered Cornell, which had an enrollment of about 7,000 students that year, she was among only seven Jewish women in the freshman class. All seven were housed near each other on one floor of the same residence hall. Some might interpret it as giving them the opportunity to get to know each other in informal surroundings; others might see it as segregation. In later life, Justice Ginsburg diplomatically ventured the thought that, at the very least, it might not have been pure coincidence.

It was also not a coincidence that Ruth's sorority invitations were limited. Sororities and fraternities were segregated by religious restrictions. She later recalled feeling snubbed when two non-Jewish friends she met during a summer waitressing job not only failed to invite her to join their sorority but also avoided her on campus.

Ruth eventually joined the Alpha Epsilon Phi (AEPhi) sorority, which had been founded in 1909 by a group of Jewish women at Barnard College in New York City. The stated goal of the organization was to foster lifelong friendship and sisterhood, academics, social involvement, and community service while providing a "home away from home" for those who joined. Although membership was open to all college women regardless of religion, AEPhi was considered a Jewish sorority.

BRAVE NEW WORLD

When Ruth Bader arrived at Cornell as an entering freshman in 1950, it was an exciting time to be an American. Much of Europe was still in shambles after the devastation of World War II. But apart from the Japanese attack on Pearl Harbor, which was in the U.S. territory of Hawaii, the American mainland had been blessed by coming through the war unscathed.

Not only that, American industries, which had rolled out bustling assembly lines of battleships, fighter planes, tanks, jeeps, munitions, and other implements of war in the 1940s, quickly retooled after the war ended in 1945. By 1950, America entered what many consider the most phenomenal period of prosperity of any nation in the history of the world, offering a dazzling array of consumer goods that average citizens could easily afford to buy. Even if they could not, there were generous credit plans allowing them to bring the goods home simply by paying what was advertised as "a dollar down and a dollar a week."

Giant gas-guzzling cars with decorative fins and shiny chrome trimmings appeared on suburban driveways. A new invention called television found a prominent place in America's living rooms. In the early 1950s, even eating habits in the United States were changing with the advent of TV dinners and drive-in "fast food" restaurants. To many Americans, it appeared to be a brave new world—and a comfortable, prosperous one at that.

BIGGER BOMBS

However, during Ruth's college years, 1950–1954, not everything in the lives of Americans was as shiny as the chrome on their cars. In 1950, the United States entered the Korean War, just five years after the end of World War II. The ensuing conflict meant several years of young Americans facing combat in Korea.

After the Korean War ended in 1953, the hostility between the United States and the Soviet Union was manifested in what was called the Cold War. This ideological battle against Communist Russia and its ally, the People's Republic of China or "Red China," would last for decades.

If the Cold War turned "hot," the stakes would be high. The concept of warfare changed radically in the 1950s with the rise of nuclear weapons, or what came to be known simply as "The Bomb."

In the blink of an eye, America's atomic bombs had annihilated the Japanese cities of Hiroshima and Nagasaki in 1945, at the end of World War II. In 1952, the first hydrogen bomb, or H-bomb, was exploded by the United States on an atoll in the Pacific Ocean. The H-bomb proved that it packed far more destructive power than the deadly atomic bombs that preceded it.

At first, the Bomb ushered in a period that made Americans feel more secure. As the 1950s began, the United States was the only nation in the world to have a nuclear arsenal, which was thought to be a deterrent against aggressive acts by other countries. But in 1953, the Russians successfully tested their own version of the hydrogen bomb. Before long, nuclear tests throughout the 1950s by both nations were spewing radiation into the Earth's atmosphere.

The arms race seemed to signal what could end in a terrifying confrontation between Russia and the United States. Some felt nuclear warfare would trigger the end of the world. Amid the nation's abundance, many Americans lived with a constant sense of anxiety. Some built underground fallout shelters for their family in case the worst happened.

FAR FROM BROOKLYN

To launch her college career in August 1950, Ruth Bader's father, Nathan, drove her upstate to Cornell in Ithaca, New York, about a half-day's drive from Brooklyn but a world apart. It was a poignant moment in their lives. Both Ruth and her father were still mourning Celia, who had died just two months before. Now, as a college student, Ruth was going to the same school Uncle Solomon had attended, when Celia helped finance his education but was unable to attend herself.

Not only was Ruth a female, but she was also the product of immigrants. She symbolized the remarkable transformation that had taken place for many people in the United States in just one generation.

For much of America's history, higher education was a boys' club—no girls allowed. However, in 1837, Ohio's pioneering Oberlin College admitted four women, becoming the first "coeducational" American college. Others slowly followed suit.

Although some college scholarships were available, such as those that Ruth earned for receiving top grades, for much of the early twentieth century, higher education remained primarily the domain of the well-to-do. By mid-century, just in time for Ruth Bader to go to college, that would change dramatically.

G.I. JOE BECOMES JOE COLLEGE

When Ruth Bader stepped on campus in 1950, it was an especially exciting time to be going to college. There were students from all over the country, with all kinds of backgrounds. Many were older or at least more mature than the typical "Joe College" of the past. That was because they were military veterans of World War II.

A great part of the vibrancy on college campuses across the nation was due to the advent of the Servicemen's Readjustment Act of 1944, popularly known as the G.I. Bill of Rights, or simply the G.I. Bill. It had been passed by the U.S. Congress to provide a wide range of benefits for returning World War II veterans, who were commonly referred to as G.I.s, based on the term "Government Issue."

Benefits from the G.I. Bill were available to all veterans who had been on active duty during the war years and had not been dishonorably discharged. Some advantages included low-cost mortgages, low-interest loans to start a business, and one year of unemployment compensation to tide them over until they could find a job in the civilian world.

But the most notable benefit of the G.I. Bill was the payment of tuition and expenses for recipients to attend high school, college, or vocational school.

By 1956, about ten years after the end of World War II, more than two million veterans were able to attend college, something that had been well out of reach to many before the war. Historians call the G.I. Bill one of America's most significant success stories, greatly contributing to the nation's postwar economic boom. It also injected new life into higher education in America.

That was the time when Ruth Bader began her college education at Cornell.

FOUR EVENTFUL YEARS

She would spend the years 1950–1954 on a leafy, pleasant college campus that was in some ways representative of America's burgeoning suburban landscape. Starting with the founding of New York's Levittown, the country's widespread suburbanization was just one of the transformations that took place in postwar America.

Some people today consider the 1950s to be a time when nothing much happened. Their concept of the decade is that of an unexciting, complacent era captured in black-and-white images. To many, the 1950s seem to be best personified by America's low-key president, Dwight Eisenhower, who was elected in 1952, reelected in 1956, and served until he left office in 1961.

However, a closer look reveals that momentous events happened in the 1950s, from the baby boom to the H-bomb, from beatniks to *Sputnik*. It was a decade that saw conflicts from civil rights in Little Rock to civil war in Vietnam. Its cultural touchstones ran from *The Catcher in the Rye* to

"Rock Around the Clock." It was book-ended by two Graces: Grace Kelly, the American-born princess of Monaco, and Grace Metalious, author of the scandalous novel about steamy passions in small town America, *Peyton Place*.

The decade of the 1950s began with debates over whether America really needed an interstate highway system, but by the decade's end, the country was transformed into a nation that set its sights on the moon with the announcement of America's first astronauts in 1959.

The roots of the social and technological revolution that exploded in the 1960s and 1970s can be found in the 1950s. Someone as intelligent and aware as Ruth Bader had to have been a keen observer.

In just the four years of her college education, change was happening fast. During 1950, the year she entered Cornell as a freshman, Senator Joseph McCarthy first gained national attention for his anti-Communism campaign with his "Enemies from Within" speech. TV's comedic *Your Show of Shows* with Sid Caesar debuted, helping to solidify the dominance of television in American living rooms. Both Doris Day and Marilyn Monroe emerged as national icons in 1950, each personifying one of two types of American womanhood, the "girl next door" and the "sex symbol," respectively.

The year 1951 alone saw monumental events during its 12-month span. Ethel and Julius Rosenberg were convicted of espionage and sentenced to death for allegedly passing atomic secrets to the Soviets, sparking furious debates, especially on college campuses. That year, radio disc jockey Alan Freed played rhythm-and-blues music that he started calling "rock and roll," which would become a musical revolution. *The Catcher in the Rye*, Salinger's groundbreaking novel about disaffected youth, was published in 1951 and went on to become a classic. Hit comedy *I Love Lucy* made its television debut that year, often reaping laughs about a woman who wanted to work outside the home but always ended up humiliated for her efforts, sometimes even being spanked by her husband like a child.

The beginning of 1952 saw England's new queen, Elizabeth II, ascending the throne upon the death of her father. It was exciting for many girls to see a woman on the British throne, the first female ruler of that nation in her own right since Queen Victoria died in 1901.

The nightmares of parents across America were alleviated in 1953 with the successful test of a vaccine to combat the crippling disease of polio, developed by Dr. Jonas Salk. In 1954, arguably the most newsworthy event set the stage for the kind of media frenzy that is commonplace today: the wedding of film star Marilyn Monroe and baseball star Joe DiMaggio.

Also that same year, there were mixed responses across the nation to the landmark *Brown v. Board of Education* decision on May 17, 1954, when the U.S. Supreme Court declared that the racial concept of "separate but

> **COURTROOM DOLLS**
>
> The month of June in 1954 was a busy one for Ruth Bader: she graduated from college and married the love of her life. But even at that hectic, life-changing time, as a socially aware young woman who earned a degree in government, she might have noted an event that was life-changing for others: the African American citizens of the United States, and by extension, the entire country. On May 17, 1954, in its landmark *Brown v. Board of Education* decision, the U.S. Supreme Court declared that the racial concept of "separate but equal" in public schools was unconstitutional. The work of an unlikely woman played a role in that decision; Dr. Mamie Phipps Clark (1917–1983) from Hot Springs, Arkansas, was an African American woman who attended segregated schools in the Jim Crow South. She fought her way to RBG's future alma mater, New York's Columbia University, where Clark was the only female black student pursuing a doctoral degree in psychology. Part of Clark's work was the "Doll Experiment" which involved children being given two identical dolls, one white with yellow hair and the other brown with black hair. Even among African American children, there was a clear preference for the white doll, with the preference even stronger among children attending segregated schools. Based in great part on Clark's research, in the landmark *Brown v. Board of Education* ruling, the Supreme Court declared that the concept of "separate but equal" in education was unconstitutional because it resulted in African American children feeling inferior. RBG's later work in human rights often referenced the *Brown* decision, which rested in large part on the work of a generally unsung woman, Mamie Phipps Clark.

equal" in public schools was unconstitutional. In her future career, Ruth Bader Ginsburg would utilize concepts of the *Brown* decision in a quest toward human rights for all Americans regardless of race or gender.

But that work was a long time coming. In the early years of the 1950s, for college girl Ruth Bader, the first task was to build a foundation for her future by getting a good education.

OBSCURE LIBRARIES, ISOLATED BATHROOMS

Because the number of women admitted to Cornell was limited, the ones who gained admittance were generally outstanding young women who had graduated at the top of their high school class. Some were there with the serious intent to study, but many were thrilled to see that, as had been rumored, there were indeed four men for every woman at Cornell.

American society of the postwar era dictated that whatever kind of diploma they earned, it was the goal of college-educated women, like all other females, to land their so-called MRS degree, pronounced "M-R-S." It was essential to marry a man and be "Mrs." Somebody. The aim was to get married, have children, and stay at home, to be solely someone's wife and someone's mother. Author Brett Harvey (1993) states that throughout the 1950s, even at the elite all-female Radcliffe College in Massachusetts, the school president—a male—informed incoming women students that their education would make them "splendid wives and mothers, and their reward might be to marry Harvard men" (47).

At Cornell, as at most colleges in the 1950s, female students were subject to a variety of rules, from curfews to clothing. According to Conable (1977), "For many years, proper dress and decorum were required . . . and often, instructive booklets on campus manners were distributed to women as they entered the university" (23). Conable adds that the administration rarely intervened in a similar manner for men.

Ruth Bader was always well groomed and easily conformed to the standards of dress. She was considered pretty and popular. However, working part-time jobs to help with expenses limited her social life. Even if she had not been obliged to work, Ruth's study habits, honed by her mother, Celia, would probably have taken precedence over social life. The general consensus was that most males on campus considered Ruth Bader "a brain," which was not intended as a compliment.

Part of her study routine consisted of taking extensive notes on index cards and then memorizing them. At Cornell, female students were

---

GILBERT AND SULLIVAN AND GINSBURG

Future Supreme Court Justice Ginsburg could not have known how her appreciation of Gilbert and Sullivan operettas as a student would later serve her at the highest pinnacle of American law. Gilbert and Sullivan's *Iolanthe* is a satiric portrayal of the legal profession that is not a flattering one. Late in life, U.S. Supreme Court Justice Ginsburg recalled Chief Justice William Rehnquist, who also loved Gilbert and Sullivan, appearing in a new judicial robe with four gold stripes that some said made him look like a master sergeant. Ginsburg knew what he was doing. She had immediately grasped the *Iolanthe* reference which the stripes echoed. Justice Ginsburg also guest hosted a radio program called "On Opera and the Law" in which RBG selected "A Paradox" from Gilbert and Sullivan's *The Pirates of Penzance* to illustrate the concept of strict versus sensible construction in jurisprudence. Not only did RBG appreciate opera, but she became the subject of one when in 2013, the new opera *Scalia/Ginsburg* was launched, inspired by the unlikely friendship of Supreme Court justices Ruth Bader Ginsburg and Antonin Scalia. Much like the work of Gilbert and Sullivan, it has played regularly to appreciative audiences since that time.

required to live in dormitories, whereas males were permitted to live off campus in the housing of their choice. Finding it hard to study in a noisy dormitory, Ruth sought out obscure libraries and even isolated bathrooms around campus, where she could have some privacy, peace, and quiet. Those were also places where she could do schoolwork unobserved by the boys on campus, who were said to look down on the "brains," girls who were smart and studious.

When her studies were done, however, Ruth joined in the fun. She played bridge with friends in the dorm and especially enjoyed attending performances like the operettas of Gilbert and Sullivan.

MAJOR DEVELOPMENTS

Despite her enjoyment of the works of Gilbert and Sullivan, schoolwork took precedence over everything. In addition to the influx of mature, interesting students on college campuses in the early 1950s courtesy of the G.I. Bill, wartime upheavals around the globe often led remarkable émigrés to join American college faculties.

At Cornell, Ruth Bader studied literature with one faculty member who became world famous. Her professor was Russian-born novelist Vladimir Nabokov. As she later wrote in the *New York Times* (2016), Nabokov changed the way she read as well as how she wrote. Nabokov illustrated that choosing "the right word, and the right word order, could make an enormous difference in conveying an image or an idea" (Section SR, Page 4). As a Supreme Court justice whose clarity in legal writings is renowned, Ruth Bader Ginsburg credited Nabokov as a major influence on her development as a writer. In 1955, the year after Ruth graduated from college, came the publication of Nabokov's bombshell novel *Lolita*, which he had been writing for several years. The controversial subject concerns a middle-aged literature professor who is obsessed with an adolescent girl. *Lolita* went on to become both famous and infamous around the world.

Although Ruth was an avid reader, she did not choose to major in literature. Her late mother, Celia, had guided Ruth to become a history teacher. For people of Nathan and Celia's generation, becoming an educator was one of the loftiest goals, a distinction that made the family proud. To honor the wishes of her beloved late mother, Ruth no doubt had that in mind as she took basic academic coursework during the first part of her college years.

During her second year, Ruth did some student teaching at the local high school in Ithaca. She soon determined that becoming a public school teacher was not the path she wished to follow, despite her parents' wishes.

Rationalizing that Celia also valued achievement, Ruth speculated that another field would offer better job opportunities after graduation. She then chose to major in government, which some schools today call political science. It would turn out to be an important choice.

INSPIRING TEACHERS

In her government studies, Ruth crossed paths with other exciting teachers who stimulated her already well-developed mind as Nabokov had done. Some no doubt set her on the course that would define her life's work.

One of Ruth's instructors was Clinton Rossiter, a prize-winning political scientist who wrote almost two dozen books about the nation's government, including *The American Presidency*, published in 1956. It is often cited by historians as one of the most popular books ever published on the office of America's chief executive.

The Italian-born Mario Einaudi was a noted scholar of political theory and comparative government whose father was president of the postwar Republic of Italy from 1948 to 1955.

Milton Konvitz was an authority on labor law as well as on human rights. Along with having Ruth Bader as a student, he drew hundreds of others to his class called "American Ideals." Konvitz is said to have coined the term "civil liberties."

One of the most influential of Ruth's teachers at Cornell was Robert Cushman, who taught constitutional law. His landmark anthology, *Leading Constitutional Decisions*, was published regularly between 1925 and 1982, becoming a standard casebook in the field of constitutional law.

Ruth Bader studied constitutional law with Cushman, who had a passionate commitment to constitutional law and civil liberties. He was said to be impressed by Ruth's logic and reason, advising her to make her writings spare, clear, and without unnecessary embellishments, traits that could be found in her legal opinions throughout her career.

Cushman offered Ruth Bader a job as his research assistant. One of his first projects was assigning her to work on a library exhibit about book burning through the ages, which must have appealed to a young person like herself with a love of the printed page.

At the same time when Ruth was in college, working on that book-burning exhibit, books and their authors were having difficulties in America, being targeted under the banner of what came to be called McCarthyism.

RED SCARE, BLACK LIST

The Red Scare, which was a government investigation of alleged communist sympathizers in the United States, was spearheaded in the U.S.

Congress by the Senate Internal Security Committee and the House Un-American Activities Committee (HUAC). Leading the charge was the face of the investigation, Republican Senator Joseph McCarthy from Wisconsin. Reflecting his highly publicized influence, the term "McCarthyism" became a household word, referring to the search for alleged communists and often unfounded accusations that cost people their livelihoods.

America was locked in the Cold War with the Soviets during the 1950s, and McCarthy claimed to be uncovering communist threats but was usually unable to prove his allegations. Some observers noted that much of his investigation tended to center around celebrities whose famous names generated headlines and television coverage.

Many of the accused were blacklisted and prevented from working at their jobs, although most claimed their innocence. Witnesses were pressured to "name names" of other people who they thought might have communist leanings. Those who did not wish to be informers were cited for contempt and often jailed. The constant turmoil was unsettling to many people, fearing the thought of being called before McCarthy's committee and being tarnished despite what they felt was their innocence.

The major part of the McCarthy hearings took place between 1950 and 1954. With Ruth starting at Cornell in 1950 and graduating in 1954, the era of McCarthyism exactly spanned the years when she was in college.

HITTING CLOSE TO HOME

Working as a research assistant for her instructor Robert Cushman who oversaw Cornell's Civil Liberties program, Ruth was tasked with following Red Scare activities. One area of her assignment was to track entertainment industry blacklists, primarily the publication *Red Channels*, a pamphlet that listed people who, it was suggested, should be barred from working due to their supposed communist sympathies.

Among those listed in *Red Channels* and recommended for blacklisting were author Dashiell Hammett (*The Maltese Falcon, The Thin Man*), playwright Arthur Miller (*The Crucible, Death of a Salesman*), poet Langston Hughes ("What happens to a dream deferred? Does it dry up like a raisin in the sun?"), singer/songwriter Pete Seeger ("If I Had a Hammer," "Turn, Turn, Turn," "Where Have All the Flowers Gone?"), and actor/director Orson Welles (*Citizen Kane, The Magnificent Ambersons*, radio adaptation of *The War of the Worlds*).

As assigned, Ruth Bader tracked the growing number of celebrities and others who were targeted. One name from the high-level academic world hit close to home. Cornell professor Marcus Singer was indicted by HUAC in 1953 for not naming names of people in a study group he joined while he was at Harvard. The group's meetings had taken place during wartime when Russia was an ally of the United States. Singer maintained that he was not a member of the Communist Party. He invoked his Fifth Amendment right to silence rather than betray what he called his honor and conscience by becoming an informer when told to "name names" of others in the group. Students at Cornell collected money for his trial, and many lamented what they felt was the apparent demise under McCarthyism of constitutional rights like freedom of speech and freedom of assembly. Marcus Singer was convicted of contempt of Congress, after which Cornell barred him from teaching but did allow him to stay on as a researcher. Singer was eventually acquitted, moving to another university.

In later life, Justice Ginsburg said that it was at this time when she saw how lawyers defended the people's rights to think, to speak, and to write freely as guaranteed by the Constitution. In the documentary *RBG* (2018), she says she then got the idea "that you could do something that would make your society a little better." That motivation was part of her decision to pursue a study of law.

#MeToo

Her experience at Cornell shaped other aspects of her legal career. In interviews such as one at the 2018 Sundance Film Festival, Justice Ginsburg recalled a #MeToo moment of her own when she was at Cornell, years before there was a #MeToo label.

The current #MeToo movement is an effort to expose and eliminate sexual harassment and sexual assault. The movement spread virally in 2017 as a hashtag on social media to demonstrate the widespread prevalence of sexual malfeasance and sexual predators, especially in the workplace. The phrase became prevalent as more women, including high-profile celebrities, shared their stories, as in "It happened to me too."

Justice Ginsburg said in interviews that when she was at Cornell, she was in a chemistry class and did not feel confident with the laboratory work. Seeking help before a big test, she went to the teaching assistant for the class who offered to give her what he said was a practice exam before the actual test. When she looked at the actual exam paper on the day of the test, she found that it was the so-called practice exam. She says she knew exactly what he wanted in return, what was expected as a payoff. Instead of being shy, she refused to be intimidated. She went to his office, confronted him, and said, "'How dare you? How dare you do this?" Justice Ginsburg stated, "That was the end of that," adding that on the actual exam, she deliberately made two mistakes.

In later life, she cited the prevalent belief at the time that if a woman complained about such behavior by a male superior, she stood a good chance of being accused of making it up, thus facing severe consequences. There was, as Justice Ginsburg put it at Sundance and in the *RBG* documentary, a dominant "boys will be boys" attitude toward sexual harassment and predatory behavior at the time.

As history would prove, the same college girl who was expected to give something in return for a chemistry exam would be instrumental in making those laws.

However, during her college years, Ruth Bader was also to discover that there were males who exhibited something beyond the traditional "boys will be boys" mindset. There was a supremely confident young man on campus who was light years ahead of his time. Luckily, they would connect.

WHEN MARTY MET KIKI

To many of her friends, the 17-year-old Ruth was still known by her childhood nickname Kiki. During her freshman year at Cornell, she concentrated primarily on her studies, although she was still sociable when she had the time and inclination.

One day, a friend of Ruth's who lived in the same area of the dorm proposed an idea. As a freshman, Ruth was sporadically dating a boy she had known at Camp Che-Na-Wah who was at the time a law student at Columbia University in New York City. But the distance between Ithaca and Manhattan was daunting. Even verbal communication was difficult in the days when the primary means of connecting between dates was writing letters or making contact by expensive long-distance telephone calls. Ruth's dormitory friend suggested that meeting a suitable young man right on the Cornell campus with whom to socialize might be a good idea.

Ruth's friend was dating a boy who was a roommate of an 18-year-old sophomore named Martin David "Marty" Ginsburg. Marty was extremely outgoing, serving as social chairman of his fraternity, and was widely known as the "life of the party." Like Ruth, he had been born in Brooklyn, but Marty's well-to-do family moved to the upscale community of Rockville Centre on Long Island, New York, where he grew up. Coincidentally, it was the town where Ruth's father, Nathan Bader, then lived.

The Ginsburg family descended from Russian immigrants. By the time Marty was growing up, his parents were affluent enough to hold season tickets to New York's Metropolitan Opera. The family also loved golf. However, even though their home was adjacent to the Rockville Centre Golf Course and Country Club, that establishment banned Jewish people.

The Ginsburgs then became founding members of the Cold Spring Country Club, where Marty's mother, Evelyn Bayer Ginsburg, played golf almost every day, often joined by her son. Marty's father, Morris Ginsburg, was vice president of the Federated Department Store chain that currently owns Target. Morris had started as a stockroom boy with an eighth-grade education, working his way up. Both parents doted on Martin, their only son.

There are those who say that Ruth's mother-in-law must have been an exceptional woman to have raised such an exceptional son. Evelyn lived long enough to see her son's wife appointed to the U.S. Supreme Court. During the ceremony marking the appointment of Ruth Bader Ginsburg, along with her own mother, Celia, Ruth credited Evelyn with being the most supportive parent a person could have.

AWFULLY CUTE, AWFULLY SMART

Like Ruth, when they first met, Marty was also involved with another person. He had a girlfriend at Smith, an elite women's liberal arts college in Northampton, Massachusetts, which was also quite a distance from Ithaca.

Ruth's matchmaking friend understood the difficulties of long-distance romances. More importantly, she also knew that Marty owned a roomy gray Chevrolet automobile. It seemed highly beneficial that the four of them could double date, going places in Marty's gray Chevy.

Ruth agreed to a "blind date" arrangement in order to meet sophomore Martin Ginsburg, who was one year ahead of her in school. However, in later years, the truth emerged that their first date was really only blind on her side. According to writer Liz McNeil (2018), their encounter was set up after Marty had already had the chance to observe the pretty, petite Ruth from afar and decided that she was "awfully cute" (65). He was soon to discover that she was also awfully smart.

On her part, Ruth's first consideration was not Marty's looks, although the tall, handsome young man cut quite a dashing figure. As quoted by Felix (2018), RBG said, "Marty was an extraordinary person. Of all the boys I dated, he was the only one who really cared that I had a brain. And he was always—well, making me feel that I was better than I thought I was" (16).

Even with her razor-sharp mind, Justice Ginsburg would later be somewhat hazy on the exact nature of their first meeting, speculating that it might have been a fraternity party. But the couple liked each other enough to become friends, double-dating with their respective matchmakers in Marty's car.

MEETING OF THE MINDS

During the first year of their acquaintance, Ruth and Marty were good friends, able to tell each other what was on their minds. Their personalities meshed, although they were quite different: he was outgoing, and she was more reserved.

According to Ruth, they shared an intense intellectual and emotional connection. In the literature class with Vladimir Nabokov that they took together, Ruth was impressed with Marty's intelligence when he was the only one to answer the great writer's question about classic author Charles Dickens correctly.

The admiration was mutual, and the friendship blossomed into love. In circular but unassailable logic, the ultra-confident Marty believed that if he loved her, she must be someone special.

They decided to marry after graduation and dreamed of a future together. For most women of the 1950s, even college graduates, their assigned place after marriage was considered to be in the home, raising children and keeping house. In an unusual departure for men and women of that era, the young couple agreed that Ruth would work outside the home after marriage. Moreover, it was not even as a teacher, secretary, or nurse, the acceptable jobs for women of the era. Even more remarkably, they decided to go into the same field.

MAJORING IN GOLF

When he started college, Marty had originally been a chemistry major, with some thought to becoming a doctor. But his true passion was golf. He was a member of the Cornell golf team and played a few rounds on the links between classes. His career path took an unexpected turn when he discovered that the required chemistry labs, which were necessary for a premed degree, were held in the afternoon. Thus, they interfered with his time on the golf course. He dropped the chemistry labs and looked at other majors that would leave his afternoons free for golf.

The couple knew they both wanted to pursue graduate degrees after leaving Cornell and eventually to work in the same field. Although Ruth had also given some thought to becoming a doctor like Marty, medical school was no longer a part of the plan.

In any case, Marty had his heart set on going to Harvard for graduate school. He considered a career in finance, but Harvard's business school did not accept women, even exceptional students like Ruth. Studying law then became a real possibility, since Harvard Law School began accepting women in 1950, the same year Ruth entered college at Cornell. Her interest in government and her observation of how lawyers helped people during the McCarthy hearings made law school a suitable choice.

When Ruth talked to her father, Nathan Bader, about her plan to study law, he was worried. He understood—quite correctly—that there were not many female attorneys who were able to find work in the legal profession.

With his own financial status continually in a precarious state, he feared Ruth would not be able to support herself. Fortunately, Nathan's own version of a "knight in shining armor" eased his mind. After learning that Ruth and Martin Ginsburg were to be married, Nathan had no doubts that Marty would be a good provider even if Ruth was unable to make it in the law.

Nathan Bader lived until 1968, joining his wife Celia at Mount Carmel Cemetery in Queens, New York, 18 years after her death. By the time he died at age 71, he was able to take pride in seeing his daughter Ruth become a college professor at the prestigious Rutgers University Law School, as well as being the mother of his two grandchildren. He knew that she had found a good husband in Marty Ginsburg. Although life for the sweet-natured Nathan might not have turned out as he had hoped when he arrived in America as a 13-year-old immigrant unable to speak English, at least he knew that his daughter Ruth had chosen well.

A LITTLE DEAF

The engagement party for Martin Ginsburg and Ruth Bader was held at New York City's Plaza Hotel on December 27, 1953. Marty had received his bachelor's degree from Cornell earlier in 1953. The couple decided to wait until after Ruth's graduation in June 1954 to marry.

Marty's family was very fond of Ruth, who, they felt, motivated their son and gave him direction. They extended their affection for her into kindness toward her father, who, with the Ginsburgs' quiet intervention, was offered a job at a men's clothing store.

On June 14, 1954, Ruth Bader graduated at the top of her class at Cornell. She earned a bachelor's degree in government and was awarded recognitions, including Phi Beta Kappa, Phi Kappa Phi, and College of Arts and Sciences Class Marshal. Along with high honors in government, she graduated with distinction in all subjects.

Her wedding ceremony with Marty took place on June 23, 1954. To save on costs (traditionally paid by the bride's family), Mr. Martin Ginsburg and Miss Ruth Bader were married in a small ceremony with 18 people present at the home of Marty's parents on Long Island. As a wedding gift that solidified her place in the family, Morris and Evelyn Ginsburg gave a set of golf clubs to their new daughter-in law, who played golf with Marty on weekends.

The new bride's name was now styled Ruth Bader Ginsburg. She would come to be known by her initials as "RBG."

There was one important moment on their wedding day that took place when Marty's mother took Ruth aside, saying she was going to share some advice that would serve the new bride well. In interviews, RBG has stated Evelyn told her that in every good marriage, it sometimes pays to be "a little deaf." Evelyn then placed a set of wax ear plugs in Ruth's hand. Later in life, RBG said she recalled that advice regularly, understanding that sometimes people say unkind or thoughtless things and it was best not to snap back in anger. This was reminiscent of advice Ruth had received from her own mother, Celia—that anger was simply a waste of her time. In 1954, Ruth Bader Ginsburg had no time to waste; she had more important things to do.

First, the newlyweds departed on an ocean liner for their honeymoon in Europe. Characteristically, Ruth took her notes from her college art history classes so they could visit important sites.

PARTNERSHIP

They were an unusual couple, not only for the 1950s, when they wed, but for decades to follow. It was a true partnership of two loving, intelligent people; Marty and Ruth were each other's first love, devoted to each other until the end.

It was also a partnership in which both partners did whatever needed to be done. In their marriage, cooking, cleaning, and childcare were not automatically considered the "second shift" for a female; in other words, the household jobs that women had to do after getting home from outside work.

In the next century, when their nephew wrote the screenplay for the movie *On the Basis of Sex*, he was questioned about the film's portrayal of Marty as "Mr. Wonderful" (the title of a popular song in the 1950s). Their nephew, who had the opportunity to observe the couple up close, confirmed that Marty really was ahead of his time, even ahead of *our* time.

The couple retained their devotion to each other throughout their lives. Along with their love for each other, part of the equation was their own individual self-assurance. Their nephew said Marty was such a confident man that he felt he deserved to have the most beautiful, brilliant wife, and he wanted to celebrate her.

For her part, RBG has said publicly that while she appreciates all the luck she had in her life, "nothing equals in magnitude my marriage to Martin D. Ginsburg. I do not have words adequate to describe my supersmart, exuberant, ever-loving spouse." She also said that without him, she would not have gained a seat on the U.S. Supreme Court.

All of that was far in the future. But throughout the years, the devotion that was born on that first date in college during the early 1950s never diminished. Their union ended only after Marty was taken from Ruth when he died of cancer in 2010.

But fortunately, before she lost Marty to death, the couple had a long, happy, exciting life together that would take them to the very top of their respective professions. They would become parents to successful children and were much loved by the relatives in their extended family. First, however, they had an obligation to a more symbolic relative, "Uncle Sam."

SOURCES

Conable, Charlotte Williams. *Women at Cornell: The Myth of Equal Education.* Ithaca, NY: Cornell University Press, 1977.

Felix, Antonia, with Foreword by Mimi Leder. *The Unstoppable Ruth Bader Ginsburg: American Icon.* New York: Sterling, 2018.

Ginsburg, Ruth. "Ruth Bader Ginsburg's Advice for Living," Opinion, *The New York Times*, October 1, 2016, Section SR, p. 4. https://www.nytimes.com/2016/10/02/opinion/sunday/ruth-bader-ginsburgs-advice-for-living.html.

Harvey, Brett. *The Fifties: A Women's Oral History.* New York: HarperCollins, 1993.

McNeil, Liz. "Ruth Bader Ginsburg: Her Great Love Story," *People*, December 31, 2018, pp. 65–67.

"Ruth Bader Ginsburg at Sundance on #MeToo and Sexual Harassment," YouTube, January 25, 2018. https://www.youtube.com/watch?v=zoCLz3QDT_g.

Solomon, Barbara Miller. *In the Company of Educated Women: A History of Women and Higher Education in Education in America.* New Haven, CT: Yale University Press, 1986.

3

Law School: The Young Wife

By the time Ruth completed her undergraduate work at Cornell in time for Commencement in 1954, two significant events had happened both in the United States and on the other side of the world. In America, the era of McCarthyism was winding down as Senator Joseph McCarthy was widely discredited for what were being called smear campaigns that were based on unfounded and politically biased allegations. However, the repercussions of the anti-communist investigations in Congress that he spearheaded were still being felt by those who had lost their livelihood to being blacklisted and/or endured jail time on charges of contempt for not "naming names."

On the far side of the globe, the Korean Armistice Agreement, which had been signed on July 27, 1953, ended the fighting in that conflict. Before that happened, with the Korean War being hotly contested during his college years, Martin Ginsburg had decided that if he was going to be drafted and sent to fight, it would be as an officer. At Cornell, he enrolled in the Army Reserve Officers' Training Corps (ROTC), a nationwide program on college campuses to prepare commissioned officers for America's armed forces. In the army, commissioned officers are those holding the rank of lieutenant and above.

Both Ruth and Martin Ginsburg had been accepted at the notoriously selective Harvard Law School where Marty began his first year while Ruth completed her undergraduate work at Cornell. Sometimes on visits to Marty in Cambridge, Massachusetts, where Harvard was located, Ruth would sit in on his law classes. But it soon became obvious that law school for the newlyweds would have to be deferred for two years when Uncle Sam came calling.

Martin Ginsburg was drafted into the army. Although his first assignment was not overseas, his assignment was almost as foreign an environment as Korea might have been to a pair of New Yorkers: Fort Sill, Oklahoma.

LAWLESS

When Ruth and Marty arrived at Fort Sill in 1954, there was still a certain sense of lawlessness about the region. As one of the last territories to attain statehood, Oklahoma had joined the Union as recently as 1907, less than 50 years before the Ginsburgs arrived. By comparison, their home state of New York had been one of the 13 original colonies, becoming a state in 1788.

At the time the Ginsburgs arrived, Oklahoma had a higher percentage of Native Americans than any other U.S. state, about one in 12 residents. It was not by accident. In 1830, Congress passed the Indian Removal Act. The U.S. Army began the forced migration of Native Americans living in the East, moving them westward at gunpoint. Another act was passed in 1834, creating what became known as Indian Territory, containing much of modern-day Oklahoma. That was the inhospitable destination for those who survived the infamous "Trail of Tears."

The expansion of the railroads after the Civil War brought more white settlers into Indian Territory, with the accompanying loss of more Native American lands. Whites claimed yet more land on the reservations after the discovery of oil in Indian Territory.

When the Ginsburgs arrived, the state still carried the aura of the Wild West.

ARTILLERY AND AMENITIES

Despite the area's reputation for lawlessness, Fort Sill, like many Army bases, was a world unto itself. Therefore, it was at once a strange new kind of environment for Lt. and Mrs. Ginsburg from New York, but at the same time, among fellow college graduates from all over the country, it could also be also oddly familiar.

In later life, both Ruth and Marty agreed that the two years of military service was a blessing in disguise, freeing them to get to know each other far from the pressures of law school and the outside world. Their home was in the post's Artillery Village—small single-family housing units for married officers. There they met other college graduates who became their friends, many of whom had taken ROTC at Ivy League schools as Marty had done.

Within the boundaries of Fort Sill, there were many amenities. At the base library, they were able to borrow recordings of the operas they had grown to love. As Marty's family had been season ticket holders for New York's Metropolitan Opera, it was especially enjoyable for the young couple when the "Met" went on tour and they could drive to Dallas for performances.

In addition, they could swim at the officers' club and play golf at no cost. Marty's passion for golf may have derailed his pre-med courses at Cornell but definitely became an asset in his military service. Growing up in the pleasant suburban atmosphere of Long Island and attending school in the leafy upstate New York town of Ithaca, there had not been many opportunities for him to come across military weaponry. When Marty arrived at Fort Sill, his training officer asked how familiar he was with artillery. Lt. Ginsburg confessed he had never seen a piece of field artillery other than the one that, at that moment, was sitting on a truck outside the officer's window. The piece of equipment he was pointing to turned out not to be a weapon at all, but a mechanical fence-post digger.

However, Marty's skill at judging angles and distances, sharply honed from his years of playing golf, gave him a distinct advantage. RBG later said publicly that Marty could appraise the distance between a piece of artillery and its intended goal by estimating that the target was a "five-iron away," referring to a middle-distance type of golf club. His ability to judge distances and adjust for the needed firepower advanced him to the position of gunnery instructor at the base for the rest of his duty assignment rather than going overseas.

BUREAUCRATIC INACTION IN ACTION

Ruth was less successful landing a position. Money for the newlyweds tended to run short and she wanted to contribute. An early attempt in a clerical position at a law office ran aground due to her poor typing skills. She took a government civil service exam, qualifying as a clerk. She was eventually hired as a claims adjuster at the Social Security office in Lawton.

It was there that she had a first-hand encounter with the power of bureaucracy to impact people through the kind of intractable regulations she would later repudiate in court. Ruth regularly saw the weathered faces of Native Americans coming to the office to try registering for Social Security, only to be turned away for not having required documentation like a birth certificate. Rules are rules, they were told. No one stopped to consider that Native Americans who reached the age of 65 in the year 1955 had been born in 1890. That was well before Oklahoma became a state, and the Native Americans had been part of a culture in which, unlike white society, Indian children were not issued birth certificates. The compassionate Ruth made her own quiet determination that if they looked 65 and could provide a hunting or fishing license, they qualified.

Along with compassion, Ruth also had a sense of honesty. She was to discover that sometimes honesty was not the best policy when dealing with an intransigent bureaucracy. In January 1955, about six months after their wedding, Ruth and Marty discovered they were going to become parents the following summer. At the Social Security office where she worked, Ruth shared the happy news that she was three months pregnant only to be told that her pregnancy disqualified her from flying to a training session in Maryland that would have qualified her for a more advanced position.

Ruth was dropped in pay grade, position, and responsibility. Another Army wife in the same office kept quiet about her own pregnancy as long as possible and went to the training, advancing accordingly. However, like Ruth, that woman would ultimately lose her job with Social Security as well. The rule in their federal office, as well as most workplaces of the era, was that a woman was expected to leave her job when she gave birth, even though, in this case, Fort Sill had a fine daycare center. With an extra mouth to feed, women lost their jobs at a time when the family needed more income, not less.

WHAT'S COOKING?

Ruth, who was known for her studiousness, apparently did not spend a great deal of time studying cookbooks. She chose seven dishes from a book called *60-Minute Chef*, one for each day of the week, in which none took longer than an hour to prepare. It has become the stuff of legend that one day she served an unidentifiable dish to Marty, who cautiously asked what it was. She replied that it was tuna fish casserole. As diplomatically as possible, he pronounced it inedible. Then he took action.

Ruth's cousin Richard Bader, who had been her best friend growing up in Brooklyn, now proved to be a good friend to Marty too. As a wedding gift, Bader had given the couple the *Escoffier Cookbook: A Guide to the Fine Art of Cookery*. Marty, as a former chemistry major, worked his way through the book, stating that cooking was just like chemistry: the right formulation combined with the proper amount of heat would transfigure individual components into a new entity. He found that he enjoyed the

> **CHEF SUPREME**
>
> Auguste Escoffier (1846–1935) was the most renowned French chef of the late nineteenth and early twentieth century. He became known as the "King of Chefs and Chef of Kings." Escoffier's name (pronounced Ess-KOFF-ee-ay) was—and remains—synonymous with fine cuisine throughout the world. His cookbooks are still used as standards. Escoffier served as executive chef for the very highest tier of luxury establishments such as Monte Carlo's Grand Hotel, owned by César Ritz, and the Savoy Hotel in London. Escoffier's name and reputation attracted the top level of society to dine in his establishments, including members of the British Royal Family. He is usually recognized as the finest master chef of the twentieth century. He was an inspiration for America's beloved "French chef" Julia Child, who wrote that Escoffier had only the highest standards for the quality and perfection of his food. He not only created such dishes as Peach Melba and Cherries Jubilee, but also revolutionized the way we eat, inventing such concepts as ordering "a la carte." As a celebrity chef, he used his influence to make it acceptable for women to dine in public. Escoffier created the template of the chef as an artist, and today would have been a leader among celebrity chefs like Mario Batali, Bobby Flay, Emeril Lagasse, Wolfgang Puck, and Gordon Ramsay. Among his friends, Martin Ginsburg was also renowned for his culinary skill, having learned them from Escoffier's cookbook. After Marty's death, the U.S. Supreme Court Historical Society published *Chef Supreme* in his memory. It is a cookbook of Marty's favorite recipes that is also full of fond memories about a man who was cherished not only for his good humor but also for his great cooking—a skill he said he taught himself in "self-defense."

relaxing, rewarding pastime. Taking up cooking in what he called "self-defense," Martin Ginsburg went on to become an excellent amateur chef. In later life, he was often quoted as saying, "I did the cooking and she did the thinking."

BABY MAKES THREE

Ruth's pregnancy advanced, although she became concerned when a local physician in Lawton said he detected what could prove to be complications. During a trip back to New York to visit the family, Ruth's mother-in-law, Evelyn, arranged an appointment for her with a noted obstetrician who was able to set her mind at ease. Ruth went back to Fort Sill, but in June 1955, she returned to the home of her in-laws in Rockville Centre. There, she awaited the birth of the baby who was due in about another month. On July 21, 1955, a month after Ruth and Marty's first wedding anniversary, their daughter Jane Carol Ginsburg was born at nearby Freeport Hospital. Marty was able to fly home for the occasion.

When Martin Ginsburg returned to Fort Sill, Ruth stayed with his parents for about a month before returning to her home on the Army base with the baby. Marty was a good husband and father, getting up for feedings at 2:00 a.m. At those times, he played classical recordings to give the baby a head start on music appreciation.

When Marty's military service concluded in the summer of 1956, the threesome moved back to the East Coast to begin the next phase of their lives. It looked bright, although not without challenges.

Both Ruth and Martin Ginsburg had been accepted at Harvard Law School in Cambridge, Massachusetts, near Boston, and were now readmitted. Having been founded in 1817 and often abbreviated as Harvard Law, it is the oldest continuously operating law school in the United States and is considered one of the most prestigious in the world, with rigorous admission policies. For example, in the 2017–2018 admissions cycle, the acceptance rate at Harvard Law was just 12.8 percent of those who applied. For a woman in the 1950s, the challenge would have been considerable. For both Ruth and Martin Ginsburg, a husband and wife team, to have been accepted would be considered by many to be a remarkable achievement.

LEGENDARY

The only cloud on the horizon was a conundrum that worried Ruth. While at Fort Sill, caring for baby Jane had not been difficult. There was an officers' nursery for children's daycare during those times when neither she nor Marty could be at home. However, after they left Fort Sill, even the usually confident Ruth was concerned about whether she could handle both the demands of the notoriously rigorous Harvard Law School and the needs of a toddler.

Once again her close relationship with her in-laws served her well. Martin's father, Morris, offered a piece of advice, reassuring Ruth that if she chose not to go to law school in order to stay home with her small child, it was the best reason in the world—no one would think any less of her if she chose to do that. However, he added that if going to law school was something Ruth really wanted, he was sure that she would find a way. As time would prove, she not only excelled in law school but also in caring for her daughter and husband under the most demanding circumstances.

She therefore made the decision to attend Harvard Law. She entered in 1956 as one of only 9 women in a class of 552 students.

Harvard Law has traditionally been—and remains—a place of legendary proportions. Surviving its rigors is often a badge of courage and tenacity as well as brilliance.

It has even attracted Hollywood. Movies with the Harvard Law School in their storyline include *The Paper Chase, Legally Blond, The Firm, Love Story,* and the controversial comedy *Soul Man.*

In 2018, there came another: *On the Basis of Sex,* a hit feature film about Ruth Bader Ginsburg's own experiences at Harvard Law. But that would come more than a half century later. In 1956, the woman who would become known as RBG had to work at finding her foothold as a female student in a place that did not even accept women until 1950.

WOMEN IN THE "LEARNED PROFESSION"

In order to admit women to Harvard Law School in 1950, the institution had to change its traditional male-only policy, which had been in place since its founding in 1817. By way of comparison, the Harvard Graduate School of Education admitted women in 1920. Harvard Medical School accepted its first female students in 1945.

In New Haven, Connecticut, rival Yale Law School accidentally admitted its first female student (who had applied using only her initials) in 1885, but after that, Yale specified in its catalog that its courses were only open to men. Yale Law School officially admitted female students in 1919, the same year as Columbia University Law School in New York.

Women began petitioning Harvard Law School for admittance in 1871. When Harvard Law opened its doors to female students in 1950, historians note that it was several decades behind most law schools in the country.

Ada Kepley is generally acknowledged as the first woman to graduate from an American law school, today's Northwestern University School of Law in Chicago. Kepley earned her law degree from that institution in 1870. When she graduated, however, she was barred from legal practice due to a state law denying women a license to practice in what it called the "learned profession." Kepley died in poverty in 1925.

Arabella Mansfield is cited as the first woman admitted to a state bar in the United States. She did so after taking the Iowa bar exam despite a state law restricting the bar exam to males. Mansfield took it anyway and earned high scores. Although Mansfield opened the door for women in the legal profession, she never practiced law.

Myra Bradwell passed the Chicago bar exam, but when she petitioned the Illinois Supreme Court to join the bar, she was denied on the grounds that as a married woman, she could not be bound by contracts. Years later, Bradwell was finally admitted to practice law and was even approved to practice before the U.S. Supreme Court, but she died without ever having the chance to do so.

Ruth Bader Ginsburg was getting ready to follow in the footsteps of those pioneering women. She would prepare for a career as an attorney at

Harvard Law, one of the most elite and selective law schools. But Cambridge, Massachusetts, in the Boston metropolitan area, was a world away from the windswept prairie of Fort Sill, Oklahoma. After spending two years away from the East Coast, she and Marty had to become reacclimated to life amid the swirling tide of an urban center in mid-century America.

WHILE YOU WERE GONE

During 1954–1956, the two years when Ruth and Martin Ginsburg were at Fort Sill, American culture was undergoing a dramatic transformation. The couple no doubt kept up with current events and probably discussed them with each other as well as friends on the base. But it was difficult for anyone to see into the future and comprehend what those current events would mean to America and the world.

In 1954, Ruth turned 21, and she completed her undergraduate studies. By the end of the year she would be married, settle in as an Army wife, and would soon be a mother. While those events in her life were transpiring, the year 1954 was when the song "Rock Around the Clock" was recorded by Bill Haley & His Comets. Its release ignited the national craze for rock and roll music, especially when it was used on the soundtrack of the movie *Blackboard Jungle* about rowdy teens, or "juvenile delinquents," then a hot topic. Like most Americans, Ruth and Marty could not have foreseen how rock and roll would conquer the world. In any case, they both preferred the classical orchestrations of opera.

Also in 1954, in a faraway Southeast Asian country called Vietnam that few Americans could find on a map, the town of Dien Bien Phu fell to Communist forces, a decisive event leading to North Vietnam and South Vietnam becoming separate states, inciting a civil war. After that happened, it would not be long before most Americans became very familiar with the name and location of Vietnam.

The year 1954 also saw the landmark *Brown v. Board of Education* decision in which the Supreme Court ruled that the concept of "separate but equal" public schools for black students and for white students was unconstitutional and by extension, was unconstitutional in other public entities as well.

With the help of the National Association for the Advancement of Colored People's Legal Defense Fund, civil rights attorney Thurgood Marshall argued in front of the Supreme Court that school segregation was a violation of individual rights guaranteed in the Constitution. After winning the fight, Marshall later went on to become the first African American to serve on the Supreme Court.

Historians have stated that Chief Justice Earl Warren met with his fellow Supreme Court justices to determine if the court could issue a unanimous ruling on this watershed decision. The justices agreed that "separate but equal" denied the Constitution's 14th Amendment guarantees of equal protection under the law. The Supreme Court vote in favor of *Brown* was indeed unanimous, although it was soon followed by billboards that sprouted up in certain parts of the country proclaiming "Impeach Earl Warren!" Warren was not impeached, and the *Brown* decision set a course for the nation's future. In later life, Ruth Bader Ginsburg would become extremely familiar with the precedent set by the *Brown* decision in seeking equal rights for all Americans regardless of race, gender, or other qualifiers.

There were other events during that time that some considered to be a "landmark." If they had followed sports as closely as opera, something that would have been close to the heart of both Ruth and Marty, being fellow

---

Brown v. Board

In the 1950s, racial matters in the United States that had simmered since the Civil War ultimately came to a boil. A major turning point in civil rights took place with the U.S. Supreme Court's landmark *Brown v. Board of Education of Topeka, Kansas* ruling in 1954. That decision struck down a previous Supreme Court decision from 1896, *Plessy v. Ferguson*, which upheld racial segregation in public facilities as long as the segregated facilities were said to be equal in quality. *Plessy* became popularly known as the "separate but equal" doctrine. Even in the Atomic Age of the 1950s, the races were segregated as in the past: public places, public schools, and public transportation as well as through daily reminders like separate public drinking fountains labeled "whites only" and "colored." Opponents of "separate but equal" claimed the facilities may have been separate but were rarely equal, especially in blacks-only schools where students made do with sub-par buildings, equipment, and books. Often, just getting to the black schools was a challenge. The landmark case of *Brown v. Board* was brought by African American pastor Oliver Brown on behalf of his daughter Linda. The third-grader had to travel a long distance, including through dangerous train yards, to her segregated black elementary school while a whites-only school was just a few blocks from their home. The *Brown* decision was argued successfully in front of the Supreme Court by attorney Thurgood Marshall, who later joined the high court as the first African American Justice. His victory in *Brown* did not arrive until Linda was in junior high school, but she went on to attend Kansas State University and continued her life-long advocacy of equal access to education. Before Linda Brown died in 2018 at the age of 75, she was able to see the black school she was forced to attend in Topeka declared a national landmark.

Brooklynites, was when baseball's Brooklyn Dodgers beat the New York Yankees in 1955, winning their first and only World Series. Then, two years later, the Dodgers moved to Los Angeles. Much of America seemed to be moving west in the 1950s, with California becoming known as the nation's trendy cultural center.

In 1955, Disneyland, Walt Disney's amusement park in Anaheim, California, opened to the public and was an immediate hit. That same year, the Disney dream factory produced "Davy Crockett," a serial on the *Disneyland* television series, setting off a nationwide craze among American children for coonskin caps and all things Crockett. For their older brothers and sisters, 1955 saw musician Elvis Presley signing a recording contract with RCA Records, skyrocketing to fame as rock and roll icon.

Toward the end of 1955, seamstress Rosa McCauley Parks of Montgomery, Alabama, was jailed for not giving up her seat on a city bus to a white man as required by local law. This small act of defiance by Rosa Parks triggered civil rights protests across both Alabama and the nation that lasted for many years.

The face of the nation in the 1950s was America's avuncular president, Dwight Eisenhower. Nicknamed "Ike," he won the second of two terms as U.S. president in 1956, once again heading the Republican ticket that defeated Democratic candidate Adlai Stevenson as he had also done four years earlier.

In 1956, there were two "Graces" who had an impact on the culture of the nation. That year Academy Award–winning American actress Grace Kelly married Prince Rainier of the tiny country of Monaco amid media frenzy, setting the tone for all media frenzies to follow. In addition, New England housewife Grace Metalious published her best-selling novel *Peyton Place* that same year, shocking many Americans with its steamy realism, denunciation of small-town hypocrisy, and scandalous portrayal of female sexuality.

Contrary to popular opinion, conservative Boston did not actually ban *Peyton Place*. However, a young law student in Boston was stung by what she considered to be another type of hypocrisy, small town or otherwise.

THE MENAGERIE

Before her marriage, "Miss Ruth Bader" had been accepted at Harvard Law School. However, when she returned to the East Coast in the autumn of 1956 after the two-year hiatus due to Marty's military service, she was a married woman named "Mrs. Ginsburg" who had to reapply.

For the hierarchy of Harvard Law, Mrs. Ginsburg's marital status brought forth yet another matter. Now she was asked to provide financial statements from her father-in-law, ostensibly as proof of fiscal security. Ruth is said to have felt that married male students would not have been asked to provide financial statements from *their* in-laws.

Nevertheless, the situation had a silver lining. Although Morris Ginsburg knew his son Marty would be a good provider for the young family, Ruth's father-in-law offered to pay Ruth's tuition at Harvard Law outright, which was no small investment. Marty's parents also helped financially with apartment rent and a gasoline credit card. Her mother-in-law, Evelyn, offered to help with babysitting whenever she was needed.

Marty enjoyed his legal studies, realizing that he liked working with the tax code, thereby finding his particular calling in the law. Ruth managed to juggle the rigorous first-year schoolwork at Harvard Law along with making time to care for her husband and toddler.

Erwin Griswold, a distinguished attorney, was serving as dean of Harvard Law School when Ruth arrived. His tenure would last for more than 20 years, holding that office between 1946 and 1967. While some have painted Griswold less than kindly, it must be noted that in the early 1950s, he was one of the few to denounce Senator Joseph McCarthy. Griswold considered McCarthy to be trampling on the Constitution's Fifth Amendment, with Griswold writing a book that examined the constitutional protection against self-incrimination. From 1961 to 1967, Griswold was a member of the U.S. Civil Rights Commission, having been appointed by President John F. Kennedy, a Democrat, while Griswold himself was said to be a moderate Republican. It was an appointment that some observers felt spoke well of Griswold's even-handedness.

In 1946, just after Erwin Griswold took the office of dean at Harvard Law School, Soia Mentschikoff was appointed Visiting Professor, the first woman faculty member in the history of Harvard Law. Griswold said that in 1948, he began trying to convince the Harvard Corporation, the institution's overseeing board, to allow the enrollment of female students in the Law School. He stated that the Harvard Corporation had previously overruled several attempts to admit women, efforts that dated back to 1890.

When the Fall 1950 semester began, Harvard Law history was made when the first female students were admitted. There were about a dozen women in the Harvard Law School Class of 1953, which numbered around 500 students. After Harvard's Graduate School of Education and the institution's Medical School, the Law School was the next graduate school at Harvard to admit women.

According to Hope et al. (2003), the Law School had a lack of women's bathrooms, which had been a major stumbling block every time the subject of admitting females came up. The cost of adding a ladies' restroom was said by the powers-that-be to be "astronomical" (81), with a figure of $80.00 most often cited. Finally, a basement janitors' closet was converted,

> ### CLASS OF '53
>
> In 1953, out of about 500 students, a dozen women graduated from the first class at Harvard Law School in which female students were admitted. By way of comparison, in 2018, there were 280 women earning degrees from Harvard Law, about equal to the number of male graduates arriving at Harvard Law in 1950, six years before RBG, the women of the Class of 1953 were the first females to be enrolled there. During the years between 1953 and 2018, Harvard Law School saw other changes, such as having more than just one women's bathroom among its various buildings. Another significant event happened at Harvard Law exactly 50 years after the first women graduated in the Class of 1953. In 2003, Elena Kagan was named the first female dean of Harvard Law School. Kagan left Harvard in 2009, on her way to becoming a colleague of RBG on the Supreme Court. She was followed by another female dean at Harvard Law, Martha Minow, who served until 2017 and was herself among those considered for a Supreme Court appointment. But those events took a half century to arrive. In 1953, students heard a panel of speakers at the Harvard Law School Forum which included newspaper columnist Earl Wilson, who aired his belief that "American Girls" should dress up more, making his point by using the example of a nudist colony. Another speaker, cartoonist Al Capp, spoke vehemently against women wearing blue jeans. Whether those first women graduates of Harvard Law School in 1953 took those comments to heart is unknown. But it is known that one pioneering member of Harvard Law's Class of 1953, Frederica Brenneman, was appointed to a Connecticut judgeship in 1967, only the second woman on the bench in that state's long history. Her daughter Amy Brenneman, also a Harvard alumna, became executive producer and star of the hit television series *Judging Amy*, based on her mother's career. It is unclear if Judge Brenneman ever wore blue jeans under her judicial robes.

necessitating "quite a sprint [for the women], especially during exams, when every minute counted" (82).

Later in life, Erwin Griswold was quoted as saying that as he recalled it, more than a third of the Law School faculty opposed the admission of women. Facilities of any kind for female students were not a priority. In a policy that was the opposite of Ruth's experience at Cornell, female students were not permitted to live in the dorms at Harvard Law School, so they had to find housing elsewhere and make their way to campus each day. It was 27 years before Harvard College itself fully admitted women as undergraduates, which it did in 1977.

Although a few women students had been present at Harvard Law since 1950, Ruth Bader Ginsburg was quoted as saying that when she arrived in

1956 as one of 9 women in a class of over 500, the feeling was still that they were like exotic animals in a menagerie.

The book *Particular Passions* by Gilbert and Moore (1981) illustrates this. It includes a first-person account by RBG written around the time she was nominated for a judgeship in the federal appeals court and before there were any women on the U.S. Supreme Court. She says that she and the other 9 women entering Harvard Law in 1956 amid more than 500 men wondered why there were so few female students. One apparently well-meaning faculty member stated that it was certainly *not* discrimination. He said that the Law School tried to select individuals who had a little something different, something to set them apart. "If you are a bull fiddle player, for example, you would get a plus," he said, "and if you're a woman you would get a plus" (5). It therefore put half the human race on a par with bull fiddle players, suggesting to RBG "that women in the law were strange, unusual" (6).

THE DINNER PARTY

Soon after Ruth Bader Ginsburg started at Harvard Law School, one of the most famous incidents, as she has recounted publicly, was the Griswold dinner party. It was hosted by Erwin Griswold, dean of the Harvard Law School, and his wife at their home. The first-year women, including Ruth Ginsburg, dined with the dean and several of their professors. After dinner, as recounted in Hope et al. (2003), Griswold asked each of the 9 women out of a class of more than 500, "Why are you at Harvard Law School taking the place of a man?" (105). It is unknown if Dean Griswold ever asked any of the male first-year students why they occupied a space that could have gone to a woman.

According to the movie *On the Basis of Sex*, which was written by Ginsburg's nephew, Daniel Stiepleman, the female student who spoke first said she hoped to join her father's law firm. Another said she thought it would be a good place to find a husband. Ruth Ginsburg stated that her husband was in Harvard Law School's second-year class, and she was at Harvard Law to learn more about his work, so she could be a more understanding wife.

Whether she presumed it was the kind of answer that was expected and whether she or anyone else anyone believed it is unknown. As noted in the *Stanford Lawyer* (Fall, 2013), RBG stated that decades later, around the time of her appointment to the U.S. Supreme Court, Griswold said "he didn't ask the question to be unkind. He said there were still Doubting Thomases on the faculty who thought it was unwise to admit women. So the dean wanted to be armed with stories from the women themselves, about what use they would make of their legal education, so that he could satisfy his dubious colleagues" (n.p.). He was also quoted by other sources as saying it was meant as a joke.

COMIC RELIEF

The women at Harvard Law School, dressed in their 1950s-era skirts and sweaters, were far more conspicuous than the men dressed uniformly in their dark suits. First, there was their rarity. They stood out. Male students who might not have been well prepared on a given day could simply blend into the crowd or sit in the back of the lecture hall to avoid being called upon.

But when, as was often the case, there were only two women present in a particular class, they were obvious and in plain sight wherever they sat. Today's students, both male and female, might be dressed in similar-looking jeans and T-shirts, with hair pulled back in a ponytail. When RBG was a law student, women were very much on display.

In *Particular Passions*, RBG is quoted as saying that women students in her day had to be on their guard constantly in a way that current female law students are not, as today there are often over 100 women in each class. She has publicly described the so-called Ladies Day at Harvard Law School when, on designated days, the few female law students in class were asked complex questions that were designed to humiliate them in front of the surrounding sea of men. In interviews, RBG has described the feeling that all eyes were on you and that if a female student did not perform well, she felt she was failing not only herself but for all women. It was a sentiment echoed by a woman law student of that era in Hope et al. (2003): "Because there were so few of us, I felt that if I was wrong, every other female there afterwards was going to be considered wrong by everyone in the whole darned class" (90). The kinds of questions the women were asked "seemed designed to amuse the men—and embarrass us" (90). Female classmates of that era recall that some professors would ask the women leading questions designed to make them respond with embarrassing, off-color answers.

One incident by a male was especially frustrating for RBG. In a bureaucratic regulation that was said to be symbolic of the old days, Harvard kept a periodicals room in the library as "Men Only." It was therefore closed to women, even if the woman was a full-time law school student with proper identification. In keeping with her usual working hours, near midnight Ruth had to check a legal reference prior to a looming deadline. Because she was a woman, the library guard would not allow her to enter. She then offered to stand outside the door if he could just bring her the legal journal so she could quickly check the reference. Still, he refused. Ultimately, she had to leave and go find a man at midnight to go check the citation. She later publicly called it one of "an accumulation of small instances."

LAW REVIEW

Despite those instances in which her gender worked against her, a major achievement came when Ruth Ginsburg was invited to join the *Harvard Law Review*.

A law review is a scholarly journal focusing on legal issues, with a primary function of publishing in-depth scholarship in the field of law for jurists and attorneys. The articles found in law reviews are usually lengthy, comprehensive treatments of subjects written by law professors, judges, or noted legal practitioners, as well as pieces written by law students who have been invited to join the law review board. Earning a spot on a law review is a high honor reserved only for the very top students. Martin Ginsburg often jokingly predicted that Ruth would be asked to join the *Harvard Law Review*, but he himself would not. He was correct.

On top of their other classwork, members of law reviews spend many hours each week doing legal research, writing, and editing. Being a law review board member makes the individual a highly attractive candidate for job opportunities in the legal field. To potential employers, it signals that if hired, law review candidates will arrive on the first day of work with skills that will set them apart from other new hires who lack similar experience.

Individuals named to the *Harvard Law Review* who went on to become Supreme Court justices include Stephen Breyer, Felix Frankfurter, Elena Kagan, John Roberts, Antonin Scalia, and Ruth Bader Ginsburg. RBG served as editor at Harvard's *Review* before transferring to Columbia Law School where she was quickly named to the *Columbia Law Review*. In doing so, RBG became the first person to be named to both the Columbia and Harvard law reviews.

Another of the small indignities to which Ruth Ginsburg has referred took place at the annual *Harvard Law Review* banquet. As a member of the *Review* board, Ruth had hoped to bring her ever-supportive mother-in-law, Evelyn, to the prestigious event. However, women guests were not permitted. Like banning women from the law library, it was another of what she called "an accumulation of small instances" that were iron-clad but made no sense apart from gender-specific pettiness.

LIFE AND DEATH ISSUES

While it was a great honor to be named to the *Harvard Law Review*, it was also extremely time consuming. That would pale compared to a life-and-death hurdle that Ruth and Marty had to face during her second year at Harvard Law.

Even with the added challenge of raising a toddler, the couple had settled into a comfortable routine. Each day was consumed with taking classes and studying until 4:00 p.m. At that time, Ruth would go home to their apartment in Cambridge, where a nanny cared for Jane during the day. After the sitter left, Ruth played with her daughter, fed her, and did the kinds of things that are done to nurture a small child. Ruth later said it was an enjoyable respite from the grind of law school work and helped her to keep things in perspective. Marty was happily finding his way through the maze of tax codes, believing that he had found his life's work in becoming a tax attorney. Then the life he was building became precarious when his doctor found a cancerous tumor.

For Ruth, it must have been a devastating reminder of her mother's death from cancer. With Celia Bader's passing, Ruth lost the person she had loved the most growing up. Now Ruth faced the specter of cancer taking her beloved husband, Marty, the person she adored in her adult life. With characteristic determination, she set out to prevent that from happening.

Marty was told he had about a 5 percent chance of survival. The couple chose new kinds of experimental treatment to combat his testicular cancer. The surgery and six-week radiation therapy left him in a chronic weakened state. He slept most of the day, unable to attend all but his first two weeks of classes.

Ruth organized his most conscientious classmates to make carbon copies of their class notes or attended his classes by herself in addition to going to her own classes. After visiting Marty at Massachusetts General Hospital, she would transcribe his class project paper for him at night in addition to keeping up with her own coursework, *Law Review* obligations, and caring for their baby. Although RBG has acknowledged the help she received from friends and a housekeeper, no one else could help with her own coursework.

Sometimes Marty's classmates would stop by to discuss points of corporate law with him, visits that cheered him enormously. But for the most part, he slept most of the day, usually waking around midnight. It was only then that he was able to eat, consuming whatever Ruth fed him, although she later described her efforts in the kitchen as lacking. She would go back to her own schoolwork around 2:00 a.m., setting the pattern for the rest of her life in which she worked through the night, operating on very little sleep.

Ruth refused to consider a life without Marty, nor did she allow him to concede being defeated by the disease. But, like other women in her situation, she had to face the potentially unhappy prospect of having to make a living as a single mother so that she could raise her daughter on her own.

After an unsatisfying meeting with Dean Griswold in which the Ginsburgs were denied a hardship exception to be made for Marty's final grades due to his devastating illness, she simply told Marty that everything was fine. She pretended that the meeting went well, that the pressure was off, and that he could just do the best he could on exams. Bolstered by her confidence, he did; he passed.

HAIL, COLUMBIA

In 1958, a now-healthy Martin Ginsburg graduated magna cum laude with the rest of his Harvard Law School class. He was offered a job as a tax attorney with the top-tier law firm of Weil, Gotshal and Manges in New York City. For a pair of New Yorkers like Ruth and Marty, it meant returning home.

But there was a snag. Ruth still had one more year of law school to complete before receiving her degree. Once again she went to Dean Griswold. She asked if a hardship arrangement could be made to transfer credits from her final year of law school elsewhere to Harvard Law in order to get a Harvard degree. Once again, she was turned down.

Although it meant dropping out of Harvard Law, she would follow husband, Marty, to New York. Like Marty, she'd had her heart set on a degree from Harvard, but for reasons of policy, it was not to be, even for one of Harvard Law's top students. Around the time RBG was nominated to the U.S. Supreme Court, the then-current dean of Harvard Law said that after Ruth left, the law school adopted exactly the kind of hardship policy she had sought. Under those new rules, someone in her situation would indeed be granted a Harvard diploma. Throughout her years of service on the U.S. Supreme Court, RBG was repeatedly offered Harvard degrees. As of this writing, those offers have been politely declined with the rationale that history cannot be rewritten. In numerous interviews, RBG has said that she did accept an *honorary* degree from Harvard in 2011, adding that she holds a law degree from Columbia and an honorary degree from Harvard, which suits her fine.

In 1958, RBG transferred to New York's Columbia University Law School, where she would be one of 12 female students in a class of about 500. De Hart (2018) states that the word flew among her Columbia classmates that "the smartest person on the East Coast was going to transfer, and [they] were all going to drop down one point" (74). True to form, Ruth soon earned a spot on the *Columbia Law Review*, thus becoming the first to serve on the *Law Review* at both Harvard and Columbia.

In May 1959, RBG graduated from Columbia Law School, tying for first in her class. She was admitted to the New York Bar soon after. Then, as a top-ranked student who had made history by being on the *Law Review* at both Harvard and Columbia, the next step for Ruth Bader Ginsburg was to look for a job.

SOURCES

"At the U.S. Supreme Court: A Conversation with Justice Ruth Bader Ginsburg," *Stanford Lawyer*, November 11, 2013, Fall 2013, Issue 89. https://law.stanford.edu/stanford-lawyer/articles/legal-matters/.

De Hart, Jane Sherron. *Ruth Bader Ginsburg: A Life*. New York: Knopf, 2018.

Gilbert, Lynn, and Gaylen Moore. *Particular Passions: Talks with Women Who Have Shaped Our Times*. New York: Clarkson Potter, 1981.

Hope, Judith Richards, et al. *Pinstripes & Pearls: The Women of the Harvard Law Class of '64 Who Forged an Old Girl Network and Paved the Way for Future Generations*. New York: Scribner, 2003.

4

Academia: The Swedish Connection

In May 1959, when Ruth Bader Ginsburg graduated from Columbia Law School, she was at the top of her class, tying for first place with a male student. Most top-ranked graduates who had made history by being on the *Law Review* both at Harvard and at Columbia would normally be assured of a good job.

In addition, the year 1959 was an exciting, forward-looking time for America. There was every reason to feel optimistic. The Eisenhower era was coming to an end, with intriguing new presidential candidates on the horizon. One of the most talked-about was the attractive young Senator John F. Kennedy of Massachusetts. The following year, Kennedy would run for the presidency and win the election of 1960.

In April 1959, the month before Ruth graduated from law school, the National Aeronautics and Space Administration (NASA) announced its selection of the first U.S. astronauts, called the "Mercury Seven." They were treated like superstars as America aimed for the skies.

The country itself was still growing. During the summer of 1959, Alaska and Hawaii were admitted to the Union, as the 49th and 50th states, respectively.

Two events on either side of Ruth's graduation seemed to bookmark American history. In March 1959, the last documented Civil War veteran died at age 111. In July, the first documented American servicemember was killed in the Vietnam War.

In some ways, the United States seemed on the verge of a new and more inclusive society for the future. Two months before Ruth graduated from law school at Columbia, a new play opened to great acclaim on Broadway. Called *A Raisin in the Sun*, with the title coming from the poem "Harlem" by African American writer Langston Hughes, it starred a charismatic black actor named Sidney Poitier. The drama was a searing portrait of the African American experience seen through one family's attempt to move to a predominantly white neighborhood. *A Raisin in the Sun* was the first play written by a black woman to be produced on Broadway, as well as the first with a black director—Lorraine Hansberry and Lloyd Richards, respectively. The New York Drama Critics' Circle named it the best play of 1959.

As much as many people wanted to see those developments as a growing trend toward a more equitable future for all Americans, some things were still firmly rooted in the past.

With her usual meticulous planning, Ruth Bader Ginsburg had always been looking ahead to the job market well before law school graduation. She signed up to be considered for summer internships and job interviews with every firm that did not post "Men Only" on the position announcements she saw on the Law School's bulletin board.

At one firm, the man who interviewed Ruth quickly hired her to be an intern for that summer. While on the surface, it seemed to be flattering, Ruth later discovered the reason: the firm had made up its mind to accept a woman that summer and she was "it." She worked hard to fulfill the usual custom that law firms hired their summer associates but was disappointed not to receive a job offer.

She found out the reason later. The firm hired a fulltime associate who was both female and African American. In the parlance of the day, to meet the perfunctory standard of appearances by hiring women and minorities, a black woman was often considered "two for one." In this case, the woman was named Pauli Murray who would later become friends with RBG.

Of the firms that posted sign-up sheets for job interviews on the Columbia bulletin board, only two would even invite Ruth to stop by for a meeting. Her mother-in-law, Evelyn, bought Ruth a very professional-looking dark suit for interviews that added to Ruth's appearance of confidence and competence as she answered their questions. Yet, despite her impeccable credentials, neither of the two firms that interviewed her followed up by offering a job. According to McNeil (2018), one response was "we hired a woman last year, we don't really need you" (66).

THREE STRIKES

RBG later said that she had three strikes against her: she was female, she was Jewish, and she was the mother of a young child. In the latter 1950s, some law firms were slowly starting to thaw their restrictions against Jewish people and women. But her ultimate downfall came when all were convinced that Ruth's child would be her top priority, to the detriment of the long, arduous hours that new hires were expected to devote to the firm.

Some of the excuses Ruth heard included the statement line that they once hired a woman and she didn't work out. It was never revealed how many male hires "didn't work out" either. Some rationalized that potential clients would not accept a woman lawyer to handle their business, thereby diminishing her capacity as a rainmaker, someone who attracts profitable clientele to a law firm. Some said that their all-male staff would not be comfortable having a woman around as sometimes the men liked to "kick off their shoes."

With no legal recourse by women who felt they faced blatant discrimination, the law firms were quite open with their excuses not to hire her, if they bothered providing any reason at all.

After exhausting possibilities at the high-paying private firms where there might be the chance to someday become a partner, Ruth tried her luck in the public sector. There, she discovered that ironies abounded. At the U.S. Attorney's office, she learned that women were considered "too soft" to prosecute the hardened criminals with whom they came into contact. On the other hand, the low-paying Legal Aid office hired a number of women as defenders, putting them in much closer contact with hardened criminals than the U.S. Attorney prosecutors.

LEARNED HAND IN THE LEARNED PROFESSION

A legendary jurist much admired by Ruth Ginsburg was a federal judge named Learned Hand. He sat on the bench from 1924 when he was nominated by Calvin Coolidge, until the Eisenhower era of the 1950s. Judge Hand was known as a pioneer of modern approaches to the interpretation of legal statutes as well as for issuing legal opinions that were strong on clarity and judicial craftsmanship, traits later ascribed to Ruth Bader Ginsburg

Learned Hand was said to believe in bold legislation to address social and economic problems, which would have been attractive to RBG, and she sought a clerkship in his office. He was also said to believe in the protection of free speech. As it turned out, that especially included his own.

Decades earlier, when he was a student at Harvard, Learned Hand had felt the sting of exclusion. Due to what some speculate was due to his deficient social skills and strict Calvinist leanings, he was not chosen for any of the social clubs that dominated campus life. That rejection was said to have remained with him for the rest of his life. Therefore, some may say he might have considered extending a helping hand to someone who was being excluded from the "learned profession" as Ruth was.

> ### LEARNED HAND, DEAD DODO
>
> After Lydia Learned married Samuel Hand, they had a son, Billings Learned Hand (1872–1961) who went on to become an iconic American figure on a scale with others of the era with colorful names like federal judge Kenesaw Mountain Landis. Abbreviating his name to Learned Hand, the jurist went on to serve on the U.S. District Court for the Southern District of New York and later the U.S. Court of Appeals for the Second Circuit. Historians note that Learned Hand has been quoted more often by the U.S. Supreme Court than any other lower court judge. Admirers often lobbied for Hand to be nominated for the Supreme Court, a distinction that never quite came about. Hand had attended Harvard Law School and was named to the *Harvard Law Review*, although he resigned because it took too much time (as opposed to Ruth Ginsburg who stayed on the *Review* in addition to caring for a husband and a child). As early as 1947, even before the most vitriolic period of McCarthyism in the early 1950s, Judge Learned Hand used the phrase "witch hunters" to describe those who were propelling the nation's bitter anti-communist campaign. At that time, Hand was considered a defender of civil liberties. However, by 1954, he was attacking the Supreme Court's *Brown v. Board* civil rights decision, criticizing the high court for overruling local Jim Crow segregation laws. Learned Hand wrote approximately 4,000 often-quoted judicial opinions during his career that were admired by legal scholars for their astute analysis, clarity, and precision. However, Supreme Court Justice Felix Frankfurter predicted that Learned Hand's decisions "will all be deader than the Dodo before long." Yet, both Hand and Frankfurter *did* agree on one thing: neither would hire the brilliant Ruth Bader Ginsburg as their clerk.

However, his years at Harvard Law School found Hand rooming at a boarding house with a group of fellow law students. According to Gunther (2010), "they regaled themselves with philosophical and literary banter, and with bawdy tales" (37).

Apparently, that bawdy collegiate humor carried over into Hand's professional life as an adult. His rationale for rejecting Ruth Ginsburg for a clerkship was because he liked to use foul language in the office and would thus be uncomfortable having her around.

CARROT AND STICK

Someone like Ruth, with her stellar credentials and top-rated class standing, would have had every reason to remain optimistic about securing some sort of judicial clerkship. Those positions lasted a year or two and usually involved working with distinguished jurists on legal research and in drafting opinions. It was a plum assignment for any newly minted attorney and was often a significant career move.

Gerald Gunther, one of Ruth's professors at Columbia, admired her capability, intelligence, and tenacity. He often recommended top students to Federal Judge Edmund Palmieri of the U.S. District Court for the Southern District of New York. Judge Palmieri had a long and distinguished career, serving on the federal bench from his appointment in 1954 until his death in 1989.

Like his fellow jurists, Judge Palmieri's first response to being offered a woman as law clerk was not favorable, even though he had always unquestionably accepted clerks recommended by Gunther. It was not simple discrimination, as Palmieri was among the few judges who would appoint women as law clerks in the 1950s. He had recently accepted a female clerk from Yale Law School's Class of 1955 and was also familiar with professional women, having a sister who was a physician.

The problem was motherhood. When Ruth was recommended to Judge Palmieri in 1959, he was said to be concerned that, having a small child at home, she would not be able to meet the heavy workload required for the job. There was also the matter of appearances in terms of how it might look for a family man like himself to be working late, alone in the office with an attractive young woman.

Unbeknownst to Ruth, Professor Gunther countered with an offer that has been characterized as the "carrot and stick." If she did not work out, Gunther said that a top-notch male graduate would be supplied to replace her in Palmieri's chambers with no questions asked. On the other hand, if Ruth was not given a chance, Gunther is said to have vowed that he would never again recommend clerks for Palmieri. There have been various interpretations of this story, although the principals have stood by the facts as stated here.

Neither carrot nor stick proved necessary. Ruth Ginsburg performed far above expectations for a legal clerk, working nights and weekends as well as taking work home with her. At one point, Judge Palmieri was about to rule in court when Ruth found a precedent that neither he nor the attorneys had discovered. If Palmieri had ruled without being aware of the precedent that RBG uncovered, he could have been found in error on his decision by an appeals court, something no jurist ever wants.

Judge Palmieri later said she was one of the best clerks he ever had. After Ruth moved on, he continued hiring women as law clerks.

In an oft-repeated footnote, Palmieri was friends with a neighbor, Judge Learned Hand. Palmieri often gave both his clerk Ruth Ginsburg and Judge Hand a ride home from the federal courthouse in his car. RBG, who greatly admired Judge Hand, has said that in the car, Learned Hand would give full rein to his collegiate-era "bawdiness," making risqué comments or singing off-color songs. In an interview with Saulnier (2013), Ginsburg said she once asked Hand why he spoke so freely during those rides but would not hire her as a clerk because her presence would supposedly inhibit him. From his perch in the front seat, Hand is said to have replied that in the car, he was not looking her in the face.

FRANKFURTER'S STAND

As her time with Judge Palmieri wound down in 1961, one of Ruth's former Harvard professors, Albert Sachs, remained highly impressed by the 28-year-old Ginsburg. Sachs recommended her to be a law clerk at the very top: the U.S. Supreme Court, working for the legendary Justice Felix Frankfurter.

Since the time when the first law clerks were hired for the Supreme Court in 1882, they have assisted the justices in doing extensive legal research. Clerks might suggest questions for their justice to ask during oral arguments, draft legal opinions, and even propose rationales about what cases for the Court to accept on its docket. Usually, each justice employs three or four law clerks per term. Most clerks are recent law school graduates who typically ranked at the top of their class. Serving as a Supreme Court clerk is considered by many to be the ultimate entry-level position for an attorney and is usually a stepping-stone to lofty heights in the legal profession.

Felix Frankfurter shared some common background with Ruth. He was an immigrant who had grown up on New York City's Lower East Side, was a graduate of Harvard Law School, and later returned there to teach. After World War I, he helped found the American Civil Liberties Union (ACLU), which describes itself as an organization that works to defend individual rights.

Following the civil rights victory in the Supreme Court's 1954 *Brown v. Board of Education* decision, it was Frankfurter who coined the phrase "with all deliberate speed" regarding the timetable for schools to desegregate racially. Even before that landmark ruling, Frankfurter employed the first African American to serve as his Supreme Court law clerk, which he did in 1948 when he hired William Thaddeus Coleman.

Frankfurter was much admired by progressives for championing the concept of judicial restraint, the concept of judges limiting the exercise of their power in striking down legislation, usually progressive laws, unless they are clearly unconstitutional. According to Feldman (2010), "judicial restraint was Frankfurter's most important intellectual accomplishment" (32). It would become "the unofficial constitutional philosophy of the movement that would itself become known as American liberalism" (32).

> ### WALLA WALLA TO WASHINGTON
>
> If Ruth Bader Ginsburg had been accepted as a Supreme Court clerk when she sought a job in 1961, she would not actually have been the first woman to serve as a clerk at the high court. It took World War II to bring about that milestone. Lucile Lomen (1920–1996) was not only a female but also did not have a degree from an elite Eastern law school. She attended Whitman College in Walla Walla, Washington, which happened to be the alma mater of Supreme Court Justice William O. Douglas. Because East Coast law schools like Harvard did not accept women in 1941, she went to the University of Washington law school, an institution that enrolled women from the time it opened in 1899. As one of three women in her law school class, Lomen was *Law Review* editor and graduated first in her class. In 1944, with the United States fighting World War II and young men on the homefront being scarce, Supreme Court Justice Douglas agreed to hire Lomen, a woman, as his clerk. After completing her year-long clerkship in 1945, Lomen returned to the state of Washington to work as an assistant state attorney general. It was not until 1966 that the next female law clerk was hired at the Supreme Court, when Justice Hugo Black hired Margaret Corcoran. Then, in the go-go 1970s, Justice Douglas hired two: Carol Bruch (1971) and Janet Meik (1972). In 1998, during a speech at Wellesley College, Ruth Bader Ginsberg stated that Lucile Lomen's *Law Review* note on the Fourteenth Amendment in 1943 had what RBG called remarkable staying power. By that time, Ginsburg, who was not seen fit to be a Supreme Court clerk in 1961, was a Supreme Court justice herself.

Considered a progressive liberal, and having hired the first African American Supreme Court clerk, there was every possibility that Frankfurter, nearing the end of his Supreme Court term in 1962, might hire a woman as a clerk.

Frankfurter was never known to have rejected a clerk recommended by a colleague like Sachs whose opinion he respected. As Frankfurter himself was Jewish, he could hardly have held Ruth Ginsburg's faith against her. But the thought of Ginsburg being a woman apparently tipped the scales against her.

Even after one of his male clerks who had admired Ruth in law school spoke up in her favor, Frankfurter was adamant. He cited excuses that were patently false, such as that she had several children and her husband was ill. He also claimed that he worked his clerks relentlessly and that he liked to swear in the office. Neither argument is confirmed by former clerks.

Some felt that Frankfurter, a scion of jurisprudence who helped found the American Civil Liberties Union, appeared to believe that civil liberties might be fine in principle, but not for equal employment opportunities regardless of gender.

> **DISAPPEARING FRANKFURTERS**
>
> Felix Frankfurter (1882–1965) served on the U.S. Supreme Court from 1939 to 1962. He helped found the American Civil Liberties Union (ACLU) to defend individual rights and liberties. Frankfurter also hired the first African American, William Thaddeus Coleman, to serve as a Supreme Court law clerk. The world may never know why none of his human rights credentials prepared him for the concept of a human being who happened to be female serving as one of his law clerks. The answer is not to be found among his correspondence. Frankfurter's Supreme Court papers, which were donated to the Library of Congress, contained more than 250 boxes of diaries, letters, and other documentation. However, in 1972 came the shocking discovery that more than 1,000 items from the Frankfurter archives had been stolen from the Library of Congress. Those papers were in the process of being catalogued; therefore, no accurate record was available. It was, however, known that they included almost a decade of Frankfurter's diaries as well as his correspondence with U.S. president Lyndon Johnson, Supreme Court Justice Hugo Black, and Chief Justice Charles Evans Hughes. The theft was followed by a year-long FBI investigation, a grand jury empanelment, and a highly publicized offer to accept the safe return of the Frankfurter papers with no questions asked. However, there were no credible leads. Then, the investigation was suddenly abandoned. The thief was never caught and a half century later, the Frankfurter papers are still missing. Ironically, in 1941, after Supreme Court Justice Louis Brandeis donated his own papers to the University of Louisville in Kentucky, Felix Frankfurter stormed into that library one day and asked for the file in the Brandeis collection labelled "Frankfurter." He removed nearly everything out of it, hauling those papers out the door with the pronouncement that they pertained to him and he was taking them back. Like the papers from Frankfurter's own archives, they were never returned.

THROUGH THE SIDE DOOR

After two years of clerking for Judge Palmieri, Ruth earned rave reviews from her boss about the caliber of her work. A few job interviews were granted to her as the doors to some private law firms slowly began to open. However, it was a side door that changed her life.

In 1961, she accepted an invitation to have lunch with Hans Smit, a distinguished professor at Columbia. Like Ruth, Dutch-born Smit had graduated first in his law school class at Columbia. He was well known as a leading scholar and practitioner in the field of international law. At the time when he invited Ruth to dine with him, Smit was the director of Columbia University's Project on International Procedure. As its name suggests, the project was intended to look at legal systems around the world so that they might be compared with the United States Code, especially pertaining to international cases.

For their lunch meeting, the pair planned to meet at New York City's Harvard Club, which dated back to 1894. Members of the exclusive club, open to Harvard alumni, met in a landmark building in mid-town Manhattan. Its members have included U.S. presidents John F. Kennedy, Franklin D. Roosevelt, and Theodore Roosevelt. In 1940, a side door called the "Ladies Entrance" was added to allow female guests of male members to enter. In 1973, when female alumni were admitted as full members of the Harvard Club, the Ladies Entrance was removed. But in 1961, Ruth had to enter through the side door.

Over lunch, Smit told her about his work with the Columbia Project on International Civil Procedure. Members of the project conducted onsite research in foreign countries. Civil procedure is the system of rules governing how a court tries a civil case, as opposed to a criminal trial. This procedural structure determines the rules for the kind of motions, orders, and pleas that are allowed in a civil trial, as well as how to handle depositions and discovery by the attorneys.

Members of the Project on International Civil Procedure would record their findings, which could be utilized for possible changes of conduct in the U.S. system of litigation, especially as it pertained to cases involving foreign countries in the ever-expanding global economy of the postwar era. Smit is said to have stirred Ruth's interest by asking if she would like to write a book about it. Researching and writing about legal scholarship was something she was very interested in doing.

If Ruth accepted, her assignment would be the Scandinavian country of Sweden, in northern Europe. Smit said that there were men who were willing to go to plum locations like France or Italy. But the Swedish assignment was less desirable to some because it would involve the intensive study of the Swedish language, a relatively little-used tongue compared to French or Italian. It would also entail going to the chilly northern region of Scandinavia rather than the sunny Mediterranean.

RBG has said that she was especially intrigued by the thought of writing a book. She was also not averse to the thought of living by herself, something she had never done. Her husband, Marty, was working hard for a partnership at his law firm, but he was supportive if she chose to go. With household help, he would care for six-year-old Jane, who by this time had entered school.

Apart from her European honeymoon with Marty, the farthest Ruth had been from either New York or Massachusetts was the two-year sojourn for her husband's military service in Oklahoma. Going to Sweden would be an opportunity to see the wider world and be immersed in it as someone other than a tourist.

SMALL WORLD, WIDE HORIZONS

On a broader canvas, as someone who had grown up during World War II, Ruth no doubt recognized that the postwar world was getting smaller. As the century progressed, there would be more international contact rather than less. The prewar concept of American isolationism based on the alleged protection of its "twin moats"—the Atlantic and Pacific Oceans—was no longer realistic.

She also recognized that good ideas might possibly come from someplace outside the United States. As a scholar, she advocated learning from a variety of sources if the knowledge was worthwhile. Obviously, decisions made in foreign courtrooms were not binding in the United States, but there might be new ideas and strategies to be discovered elsewhere. In addition, matters of international law were becoming more commonplace. It was vital for the United States and other countries to learn how each other operated in case a situation should arise, such as an international trade issue that was key to both their interests.

The postwar world was getting smaller, but Ruth's horizons were expanding. Amazingly for the time, Smit was not only willing to hire a woman but to pay Ruth the same salary that the males were being paid.

Columbia was able to help by providing a Swedish tutor who offered intensive language training. The tutor was a former principal dancer with the Royal Swedish Ballet who provided not only grammatical rules but tips about Sweden's cultural scene. Ruth learned enough Swedish to be able to translate Sweden's code of civil procedure into English. She could also converse and understand conversational Swedish as well as dialogue in movies like those of up-and-coming Swedish director Ingmar Bergman.

Ruth Ginsburg flew to the Swedish capital of Stockholm in the spring of 1962. Marty and Jane planned to join her when Jane's school was out for the summer.

Ruth's work initially took place at Sweden's University of Lund, which was situated in the 1,000-year-old city of Lund on Sweden's southern tip. The University of Lund is one of the largest in northern Europe and is rated among the top 100 universities in the world. In 1969, the school would go on to award Ruth with an honorary degree for her outstanding work in the comparative civil procedure project.

Before she left America for Sweden, Ruth was coached by Hans Smit not only in the project's goals but also in developing her personal confidence, which had been badly shaken by the overwhelming rejection in her futile job search. In addition to Ruth being a researcher for the project, he named her the program's associate director. He also invited her to lecture in his civil procedure class at Columbia for a week, a taste of the direction her career's next phase would take. Although her mother Celia had encouraged Ruth to become a teacher, student teaching at a local high school as a Cornell undergraduate had left Ruth uninterested in that career path. Her perception of academia, particularly at institutions of higher learning, would ultimately change.

SWEDISH RIPPLE EFFECT

Arriving in Sweden during the spring of 1962, Ruth was greeted at the airport by a distinguished Swedish jurist, Anders Bruzelius, who had at first assumed he would be meeting a woman who was older than the 28-year-old Ruth. Bruzelius had a daughter who was roughly Ruth's age and who would go on to attend Columbia. Once he and Ruth connected, they formed a firm bond.

It was a good time for a legal scholar to be in Sweden. Just 14 years before, in 1948, Sweden had adopted a new code of civil procedure as the way in which their courts would operate. The Swedes, known for their civility, felt it combined the best of traditional European procedures with relevant points of American and British common law.

Starting in 1962, Ruth spent two lengthy stays in Sweden, returning stateside in 1963. During that time she not only observed but also, thanks to her newly acquired language skills, was able to fully comprehend the Swedish court system. She and Anders Bruzelius worked well as coauthors of the book *Civil Procedure in Sweden*, which was published in 1965 and is still available online. It was billed as the first of the series from Columbia's Project on International Procedure, a tribute to their prompt work compared to the rest of the group. The book on civil procedure in Italy was not published until later that year, and the civil procedure in France volume was published in 1967.

Ruth Ginsburg's work in Sweden had a very positive ripple effect on her professional life. Her mentor Hans Smit, who had brought her aboard on the International Civil Procedure project, encouraged her to publish articles in legal journals. This led to a newfound higher profile for Ginsburg and increased respect from colleagues for her scholarly contributions. She was invited to join the editorial board of the *American Journal of Comparative Law* as well as the American Bar Association's Europe Committee and the board of directors of the American Foreign Law Association.

Those were valuable accolades, but even more important was that the time Ruth spent in Sweden would prove to be significant, not only to her personal life and professional career but also to the evolution of the United States as a whole.

SWEDISH TIMES A-CHANGIN'

Even apart from professional advantages came personal benefits and an expanded outlook that may have been equally important. Underscoring her philosophy of gleaning knowledge from the wider world, Ruth Ginsburg herself was learning from what was happening in Sweden.

In 1963, folksinger Bob Dylan wrote a hit song called "The Times They Are a-Changin'" that went on to become an American anthem. However, across the ocean in Sweden, the times had already changed.

During World War II, Sweden was unscathed by the scourge of the Nazis who had controlled its neighboring countries of Denmark, Finland, and Norway. The Swedes avoided the fate of their Scandinavian neighbors by proclaiming Sweden to be neutral and managed to stay that way until the war ended in 1945.

While the rest of Europe remained devastated for a number of years after the war, Sweden enjoyed an exceptional period of prosperity that began in 1946. Having that economic comfort zone also inspired a period of social advances that included the role of women in Swedish society.

Still, there was work to be done. In 1961, just before Ruth Ginsburg's arrival in Stockholm, a Swedish intellectual named Eva Moberg confronted gender issues in Sweden head-on. That year, she published an article translated into English as "Woman's Conditional Release" that became an instant classic. Moberg argued that despite societal advances, women were still expected to see their purpose in life as marrying, giving birth, and caring for children. Her defining argument was that although women are the only gender capable of giving birth, there is nothing biological that requires her to be the one who feeds, diapers, and cares for offspring until they become adults. Moberg stated that married women have two jobs—one outside the home and, at the end of that workday, another job that starts at home—while males have only one. She believed that both males and females have but one role, "that of being people," and having the same obligations toward society.

A concept of Moberg's that was to have profound impact on Ruth, and therefore ultimately on American society, was the notion of not only seeking equality for women but also that of men. One of Moberg's oft-quoted statements, which became the title of her lecture tour, was "Men are better than the patriarchy." Under patriarchy, males control the power over their society, whose members are conditioned to believe that men are superior to women.

Stockholm's daily newspaper carried the ongoing debate over Moberg's ideas that were well known when Ruth arrived in Sweden during 1962. She was intrigued to note that 20–25 percent of Swedish law students that year were women, as opposed to about 4 percent in the United States. She also noted that Moberg's concepts were the talk of all the cocktail parties she attended in Sweden.

FLASHPOINTS

Ruth spoke conversational Swedish with ease, so amid the cocktail party chatter it would have been obvious to her that the discussion of Eva Moberg's philosophy was a serious one in Sweden, but not in the United States. In America, gender issues often became punchlines for comedians as well as flashpoints for social conservatives.

In the 1950s, an American named George William Jorgensen became better known in a new identity as Christine Jorgensen. George Jorgensen, who had served in the U.S. Army during World War II, was the first person to become widely recognized in the United States for having sex reassignment surgery. George Jorgensen was known to have headed to Sweden, where the only doctors who performed the surgery were located. The procedure was eventually performed in Denmark due to Jorgensen's personal connection with a Danish endocrinologist.

Returning home to the United States in 1953 as Christine Jorgensen, some Americans of the Eisenhower era were shocked and some were outraged. Others had perplexed conversations about gender identification. The *New York Daily News* ran a front-page story under the headline, "Ex-GI Becomes Blonde Beauty." Jokes abounded, such as one in the parlance of the day using terminology that referred to women: "Jorgensen went abroad, and came back a broad." "Going to Sweden" became a comedic shorthand reference to switching genders.

Far from shunning the limelight, Jorgensen embarked on a nightclub act that included a rendition of the song, "I Enjoy Being a Girl." In 1967, *Christine Jorgensen: A Personal Autobiography* became a best-selling book. A film, *The Christine Jorgensen Story*, premiered in 1970.

At the time when Ruth was in Sweden, another American became the subject of public debate over a private issue involving that country. Unlike Jorgensen's case, it definitely did not become a laughing matter among pundits. But like Jorgensen's, it also became a flashpoint for social conservatives.

In 1962, a married woman named Sherri Finkbine from Arizona became the topic of enormous controversy. She sought to terminate her pregnancy after discovering that the drug thalidomide, which she had been taking for morning sickness, caused severe fetal deformity. Her physician recommended a therapeutic abortion but refused to perform the procedure as it was illegal in the United States.

However, the procedure was legal in Sweden. In 1962, the Swedish Medical Board granted Finkbine's request for an abortion on health-related grounds, with the operation taking place at a hospital in Stockholm the following day. Afterward she was told that the fetus would likely have died, lacking arms and legs, as was the case with most "thalidomide babies." It was so badly deformed that even its gender could not be determined. Her story made newspaper headlines across America, she lost her job at a Phoenix, Arizona, television station, and she and her husband received death threats.

This was the atmosphere when Ruth Ginsburg arrived in Sweden. That country was in the forefront of many people's minds for matters involving gender, specifically pertaining to women.

SWEDISH INVASION

By agreeing to go to Sweden, which male colleagues preferred not to do, Ruth Ginsburg was ahead of the curve. In the past, if most Americans thought about the Scandinavian country at all, it was in connection with Swedish meatballs or smorgasbord, a kind of buffet that originated in Sweden. However, that would soon change. At the time Ruth arrived, Sweden, with its cold temperatures, was "hot" culturally.

When Ruth left the United States in 1962 to begin her civil procedure assignment abroad, John F. Kennedy was U.S. president. He and his wife Jacqueline infused America with a sense of excitement that was compounded that same year when astronaut John Glenn became the first American to orbit the earth.

America was about to be consumed by the "British Invasion" when the Beatles and all things British were in vogue. But in 1962, Sweden seemed to be at the top of the charts as a global trendsetter and cultural center.

Swedish boxer Ingemar Johansson made headlines by holding the world heavyweight title through 1960, becoming only the fifth heavyweight champion of all time to be born outside the United States. Johansson later parlayed his fame into the movies.

Swedish film director Ingmar Bergman became world renowned in the early 1960s. In other kinds of movies, Sweden became a leader in what was called the sexual revolution with hit films of the 1960s such as *I Am Curious (Yellow)* that became must-sees, especially when American celebrities like Johnny Carson were known to have attended the sexually explicit yet socially acceptable film.

Apart from popular culture, in Sweden itself, the early 1960s saw many more women entering professional fields than in the past, including the clergy. In later interviews, Ruth Bader Ginsburg said that her time in Sweden caused her to think strongly about women's equality.

She saw women serving as judges. This included a visit to one Stockholm courtroom where the presiding judge quite visibly appeared to be in the final stages of pregnancy, which would have been unthinkable in the United States at the time. She also pondered Eva Moberg's question of why women, if they worked outside the home, had two jobs while men had only one.

With those thought processes being stimulated in Sweden, she came back home and saw things she considered unjust in America, and what she considered to be things that needed to change. She could not have known how integral she would become in making those changes.

EVENTFUL YEAR

By the time Ruth Ginsburg returned fulltime to the United States from Sweden in 1963, the country was beginning a series of cataclysmic events that would roil the rest of the decade. Some might state that the events of that year had an impact not only on the 1960s but on American life well into the next century. Certainly, they would greatly affect Ruth Bader Ginsburg.

In February 1963 came the publication of a groundbreaking book by author Betty Friedan, *The Feminine Mystique.* Its study of the general discontent among American women launched a critical look at the status of the female half of the population, along with the stirring of actions to attempt to generate improvements.

In April 1963, civil rights leaders including Dr. Martin Luther King Jr. were jailed in Birmingham, Alabama, during a protest regarding the treatment of African Americans. The highly publicized arrests increased momentum for the civil rights movement. A few months later, in September 1963, much of the nation was appalled when the bombing of an African American church in Birmingham killed four little girls.

The killings of civil rights leaders, such as the murder of Medgar Evers on June 12, 1963, presaged the assassination of the president of the United States that November. A month before JFK's death, a significant event took place in October 1963 when the Presidential Commission on the Status of Women issued its final report to President John F. Kennedy.

PRESIDENTIAL COMMISSION

The commission had been established in late 1961 to study and make recommendations about issues concerning women in the United States. Former First Lady Eleanor Roosevelt chaired the commission, although she died the next year. On October 11, 1963, on what would have been Mrs. Roosevelt's 79th birthday, the commission issued its report, entitled *American Women.*

> ### FOURTEENTH AMENDMENT
>
> The Fourteenth Amendment was adopted in 1868 and was added to the U.S. Constitution as one of what were considered the Reconstruction Amendments. It concerns citizenship rights and equal protection under the law. The amendment was proposed regarding the status of formerly enslaved people following the Civil War. It includes a number of clauses that give a broad definition of citizenship. In doing so, it nullified the Supreme Court's *Dred Scott* decision of 1857 maintaining that people descended from African slaves could not be citizens of the United States. But the Fourteenth Amendment goes further, declaring, "No State shall deny to any person within its jurisdiction the equal protection of the laws." From that phraseology, the amendment has become one of the most-cited portions of the Constitution, including landmark decisions such as 1954's *Brown v. Board of Education* regarding racial segregation and *Obergefell v. Hodges*, the 2015 decision regarding same-sex marriage. The Fourteenth Amendment also formed a basis for legal arguments proposed by RBG in defense of gender equity [for full text of the Fourteenth Amendment, see PRIMARY SOURCE DOCUMENTS].

While acknowledging the importance of women's traditional gender roles as mothers and homemakers, the report criticized inequalities facing women in America. Significantly for the later career of Ruth Bader Ginsburg, the report stopped short of endorsing an Equal Rights Amendment at that time. Instead it stated that constitutional equality between men and women was essential and should be achieved through a Supreme Court decision holding that women were protected by the Fourteenth Amendment's equal protection clause.

The committee's membership included a number of men, including Attorney General Robert Kennedy, brother of the president. Cynthia Harrison (1989) suggests that the creation of the commission was not entirely altruistic. In his presidential administration, John Kennedy "neglected appointments of women but he was protected from charges of indifference by the establishment of the President's Commission on the Status of Women and administration pursuit of equal pay legislation" (87). The commission worked quickly, submitting their report in October 1963. But Kennedy was unable to respond before being assassinated the following month.

Immediately after Kennedy's assassination, his successor Lyndon Johnson was sworn in on Air Force One by Sarah Hughes of Dallas, the first female federal judge in Texas.

Johnson vowed to continue Kennedy's programs, which included progress in civil rights and presumably women's issues. According to Harrison, in January 1964, Johnson told a *Washington Post* reporter that he intended

> ### Sarah Hughes
>
> It would not have escaped Ruth Bader Ginsburg's notice that Sarah Tilghman Hughes (1896–1985) was the *female* Texas jurist who administered the presidential oath to Lyndon Johnson on Air Force One in Dallas after John F. Kennedy was assassinated in 1963. The photograph of Hughes administering the oath to Johnson is often cited as the most famous photo ever taken aboard Air Force One. After graduating from law school in 1922, Hughes, like Ruth Ginsburg, had great difficulty finding a job. Eventually, a small Dallas law firm took her on, referring some cases to Hughes in exchange for her services as a receptionist. In 1962, she was nominated for a federal judgeship in the Dallas district by longtime friend Lyndon Johnson when LBJ was Kennedy's vice president. Hughes was the only female judge appointed by President Kennedy. She was the first female federal judge in Texas, and only the third woman to serve as part of the federal judiciary in the nation's history. A year after her appointment to the federal bench in Dallas, Judge Hughes was getting ready to go to a banquet honoring Kennedy on November 22, 1963. Instead, after Kennedy's assassination, Hughes was called upon to administer the oath of office to his successor, Lyndon Johnson. The presidential oath is something usually administered by the Chief Justice of the Supreme Court. As of this writing, Sarah Hughes is the only woman in American history to have sworn in the president of the United States.

to appoint 50 women to significant policy-making decisions within the month. The story garnered good press, appearing on the front page. Harrison says that eventually there were 27 total appointments in various federal departments like Health, Education, and Welfare, with "the number of women serving in the administration [rising] from thirty in 1963 to fifty-two in 1968" (174). However, like Kennedy before him, no women were named to LBJ's presidential Cabinet.

That was where the highest echelon of America's leadership stood regarding women's issues in late 1963, a time when Ruth Ginsburg was pondering issues of her own.

RUTGERS

With the completion of her project for Columbia University's Project on International Procedure and the publication of her book, Ruth Bader Ginsburg had time to consider options for the next step in her career.

Private law firms were not entirely as unwelcoming to her as they had previously been. Yet, perhaps seeing Marty's all-consuming quest for a partnership at his law firm, the reality of going to a private firm might have seemed somewhat less attractive. In addition, there was always pressure at private firms to bring in new business. A soft-spoken, self-effacing, introspective person would find that kind of salesmanship requirement to be a challenge.

Ruth's experience studying civil procedure in Sweden had only increased her fondness for legal research. After her return to the United States in 1963, she became aware of a position teaching law at the Rutgers University Law School in Newark, New Jersey, discovering that the institution was not averse to hiring a woman.

That path came about as the result of a coincidence. From her work on the Swedish project, Ruth recognized her interest in legal scholarship. She had added her name to a questionnaire from Harvard Law about former students who might be interested in teaching. A professor from Columbia Law saw her name included among the list of Harvard responses and asked *why*—as a Columbia graduate—she was on *Harvard*'s list. The professor then told her of an opening, not at Harvard or Columbia, but at the Rutgers Law School in Newark, New Jersey.

Rutgers University is the largest institution of higher education in the state of New Jersey. It has a long and impressive history. Originally chartered in 1766, it was one of only nine colleges established before the American War of Independence. After the Revolution, its original name, "Queen's College" in honor of English royalty, was tactfully replaced by "Rutgers College" in honor of a Revolutionary War hero, Colonel Henry Rutgers. Soon after the renaming, Colonel Rutgers presented his namesake school with a bond equivalent to over $110,000 in today's dollars as well as a commemorative bell that still hangs on campus. With that financial security, the college was off to a good start. Also called "The State University of New Jersey," Rutgers has three campuses, in the towns of New Brunswick, Camden, and Newark. The latter was where the Law School was housed.

At the time of the professor's conversation with Ruth, Rutgers Law School had recently lost its minority faculty member, an African American male. He had taught civil procedure, the rules governing how courts process civil cases. This was the topic Ruth had studied for the project in Sweden. The only other "minority" on the faculty was a woman who had been hired the previous year. Ruth met with the female faculty member and was assured she would be welcomed if she took the job. Like Ruth, the other woman also lived in New York City and stated that the daily commute back and forth to Newark was workable.

TENURE TRACK, SUBWAY TRACKS

Although Ginsburg later said she wondered if the job was offered to her only because Rutgers could not find another African American, she accepted. The position was what was considered "tenure track," the academic path to promotion and job security. At the time, there were only 18 women who held tenure, or protection from unfounded dismissal, in all of the nation's law schools combined.

After discussing it with Marty, Ruth Ginsburg accepted the position, although she discovered a troubling fact: at the Rutgers Law School, she would earn a lower salary than males with similar—or lesser—qualifications. When she questioned it, the dean said Rutgers was a state university with a limited budget, and after all, she had a husband who made a good salary. Males, he said, had families to support. At that time, she chose not to ask about bachelors on the faculty who did *not* have to support families. It is not known if any of those males receiving higher salaries had graduated at the top of their class in Ivy League law schools like Harvard and Columbia, or if any had made history by being the first person to make *Law Review* at both top-notch schools. Still, they enjoyed a higher pay scale than the woman who did both.

As would be her strategy throughout her career, Ruth chose the best time to make a well-reasoned legal argument against inequality. After just having been hired by Rutgers, she believed it was not the time. Moreover, she would be on an annual contract at Rutgers that might or might not be renewed when it expired each year. And, as would be the case with many women before and since, she needed the job.

Ruth Bader Ginsburg started teaching at Rutgers September 1963, making the long daily commute between Manhattan and Newark. From the Ginsburg apartment on the Upper East Side, she had to change subway trains three times to get to work. Any delay along the way would cause her to miss connections. She used the time to study her daily lesson plans and stay up to date by reading legal journals.

That first year was challenging in the sense that everything was new. Along with finding her way among the faculty, which in academia can be a minefield, she had to develop brand-new lecture outlines and find way to keep her students engaged. At least she had her solid background in research on civil procedure from her time in Sweden.

According to Kanefield (2016), students in her classes at Rutgers "saw her as quiet, intense, and ultra-focused" (58). She dressed impeccably, wearing her hair in a no-nonsense ponytail secured with attractive scarves. At the end of Ruth's first year of teaching, the students performed skits poking fun of the faculty members. Kanefield says, "The actress playing Ginsburg read civil procedure while a male student approached from behind, unzipped her dress, and pulled it down to her ankles" (59). Standing in her underwear, the actress playing "Professor Ginsburg" in the skit "kept on lecturing, entirely oblivious to the fact that she was being undressed" (59).

It is not known if male professors were portrayed in similar skits, being stripped down to their underwear, before having to return to the classroom in real life with their half-naked image in the minds of many students.

FRIEDAN'S *MYSTIQUE*

In 1963, early in RBG's academic career at Rutgers, a groundbreaking book was published by author Betty Friedan titled *The Feminine Mystique*. Like RBG, Friedan had attended an elite college—in Friedan's case, the all-female Smith College. Also like RBG, the married Friedan was dismissed from her first job after graduation when she became pregnant, in Friedan's case while writing for a trade newspaper. Friedan then took on freelance jobs, which ultimately gave her time to research what became *Mystique*, one of the bestselling and most influential books of the century.

Friedan shared stories of postwar American women who married right after graduation or who gave up their own education—and their dreams—to put their husbands through college. The women became housewives and mothers, often isolated in suburbia. In middle age, some women found themselves left high and dry due to widowhood or divorce, perhaps with children to support and no work experience to help them find the kind of job that would enable them to do so.

Friedan (2013) stated her case: the "problem that has no name" lay unspoken in the minds of American women. It was a sense of dissatisfaction that each woman felt she struggled with alone as she made beds, cleaned house, and tended children. That woman was afraid even to form the thought in her own mind: "Is this all?" (57)

Many historians believe that Friedan's *The Feminine Mystique* was the impetus for the wave of women's causes that swept the United States in the 1960s, ultimately reshaping the course of the nation. It certainly influenced the students in RBG's classes, as well as the work of RBG herself.

... AND BEAUVOIR'S *SECOND SEX*

French writer Simone de Beauvoir (1908–1986) also wrote a groundbreaking work about women and their place in society. *The Second Sex* was published in France in 1949 but became virtually required reading for many American women in the late 1960s, which is when RBG recalls reading it. In the book, de Beauvoir discusses the treatment of women throughout history and then looks at science and sociology, arguing that males are considered the default gender, whereas women are considered the "other," or "second" sex, subordinate to the one primary group: males.

Presenting the lives of children from birth, the upbringing of girls and boys are contrasted. De Beauvoir (2011) states that a girl is taught to be a woman by having her "feminine destiny" (15) imposed on her by society. In the book, she describes the painful realization when a female discovers that men are masters of the world, which modifies her consciousness of herself. Most shockingly to many, de Beauvoir stated that in women, there is actually no "'maternal instinct,' innate and mysterious" (296).

She found that the concept of "mankind" is male, with women only defined in relation to males. Ironically proving her point, in most reviews when the book arrived in America, de Beauvoir was described in terms of her lifelong relationship with the male French philosopher Jean-Paul Sartre.

SURPRISE

Ruth, at this point 32 years old, successfully completed the 1963–1964 academic year at Rutgers. She returned for the 1964–19165 term, conveniently able to use some of the lesson plans she had developed during her first year. Just when she started to get comfortable with the teaching arrangement, she was in for a huge surprise.

In early 1965, Ruth and Martin Ginsburg learned that against all odds, they were going to be parents again. During the mid-1950s, the testicular cancer that had devastated Marty in their law school days had been treated with massive doses of radiation. They had been told that Jane would be their only child. Now, having miraculously conceived another, they had reason to be concerned whether the fetus would be affected.

As happy as the couple was, there was also another concern. Ruth had not forgotten the result of announcing her pregnancy at work when they were at Fort Sill during Marty's military service. She had been demoted and then dismissed.

At Rutgers, she was still on a yearly contract that could be terminated at any time, for any reason. Rather than risk losing her job, she took another course of action, one that began in her mother-in-law's closet. Ruth borrowed some of Evelyn Ginsburg's clothes, which were larger than her own. With luck, the bulk of her pregnancy would take place during the summer months when she was not working. With more luck, the baby would arrive just before classes began for the following Fall semester—*after* she signed a new contract.

Everyone's luck held. On September 8, 1965, before classes started, a healthy baby boy, James Steven Ginsburg, was born.

SANDWICHED

During this time, with a newborn baby boy, a growing ten-year-old girl, and new classes to teach at Rutgers, came another development. It is said that Ruth's father, Nathan Bader, had never fully recovered from the death of his wife, Celia. Around this time in Ruth's life, he was badly injured in an auto accident. Having been living alone after Celia's death, he needed care.

Ruth moved her father, Nathan, into the Ginsburg apartment, having to turn daughter Jane's bedroom into a hospital room. Even with as much household help as possible, it was a difficult time for Ruth. Once again, she was ahead of the curve. In the coming years, Baby Boomers, or people born roughly between 1946 and 1964, would become known as the "Sandwich Generation." Many people, particularly women, would find themselves sandwiched between the needs of both growing children and aging parents, having to care for both at the same time. Ruth got even less rest than before but did not dare ask for a leave of absence at Rutgers. As well as jeopardizing her own chances for promotion and tenure, she recognized that such a request would further reinforce negative perceptions about the priorities of *all* women in the workplace: that their home life was more important to them than the job.

As crushingly difficult as it was to deal with demands of her extended family at home, make the grueling daily trip back and forth to New Jersey, prepare to teach new classes, and write scholarly articles in academia's "publish or perish" hothouse atmosphere, Ruth Ginsburg made it through. Much was due to supportive husband, Martin Ginsburg. Being stretched thin and usually exhausted, RBG was often a somber presence at the dinner table. According to de Hart (2018), Marty enlisted daughter Jane into a game of seeing how often they could amuse Ruth. Keeping a record of those moments, Jane "produced a booklet called *Mommy Laughed*" (97).

Ruth's father, Nathan, recovered from his injuries sufficiently enough to be able to take his grandchildren for weekend walks in the park. But on June 20, 1968, he died at age 71.

Nathan Bader had lived long enough to see his daughter become a teacher—a university professor, no less—one of the cherished goals of his generation. He saw his only child happily married and become a mother herself. The life journey for this immigrant boy who had no formal education and spoke no English when he arrived in America had not been an easy one. He had suffered business reversals and the devastating loss of his wife. Now he would once again be at Celia's side, buried at Mount Carmel Cemetery in Queens. His portion of the double headstone that he shares with Celia reads: "Beloved Husband | Devoted Father."

In 1969, Ruth was offered tenure at Rutgers. It was a year too late for Nathan Bader to enjoy seeing his daughter receive the ultimate accolade: permanent job security. In the United States, tenured educators are legally protected from dismissal without just cause, even if they espouse unpopular ideas. Tenure is granted only to professors who have proven to be exceptionally productive in their academic careers. Ruth Bader Ginsburg certainly met those criteria.

Around that point, she accepted an offer to teach a part-time class at Columbia University in New York City in addition to her work at Rutgers. She felt it would be a foot in the door at Columbia; perhaps an offer for a fulltime position there might someday be forthcoming.

She was correct about that, although the fulltime job offer at Columbia did not come her way until 1972. She accepted the position at Columbia Law School, becoming the first woman to join the school as a tenured faculty member.

It was also around this time that in along with everything else, she added an additional item: volunteering at the ACLU. It would change her life and the course of American history.

SOURCES

De Beauvoir, Simone. *The Second Sex.* New York: Vintage Edition, 2011.

De Hart, Jane Sherron. *Ruth Bader Ginsburg: A Life.* New York: Knopf, 2018.

Feldman, Noah. *Scorpions: The Battles and Triumphs of FDR's Great Supreme Court Justices.* New York: Twelve Books, 2010.

Friedan, Betty. *The Feminine Mystique.* New York: Norton, 50th anniversary edition, 2013.

Gunther, Gerald. *Learned Hand: The Man and the Judge.* New York: Oxford University Press, 2nd edition, 2010.

Harrison, Cynthia. *On Account of Sex: The Politics of Women's Issues, 1945–1968.* Berkeley: University of California Press, 1989.

Kanefield, Teri. *Free to Be Ruth Bader Ginsburg: The Story of Women and Law.* San Francisco, CA: Armon Books, 2016.

McNeil, Liz. "Ruth Bader Ginsburg: Her Great Love Story," *People*, December 31, 2018, pp. 65–67.

Saulnier, Beth. "Justice Prevails: A Conversation with Ruth Bader Ginsburg '54," *Cornell Alumni Magazine*, November/December 2013. http://cornellalumnimagazine.com/justice-prevails/.

5

ACLU: The Litigator

From the vantage point of 1969, the year when Ruth Bader Ginsburg earned tenure at Rutgers, the span of the 1960s that preceded it almost appeared to be three separate decades in one. Perhaps no decade in American history so clearly exemplified a phrase that would have been known to Ruth from her enjoyment of the classic literature class she took with Marty at Cornell: "It was the best of times, it was the worst of times," the opening phrase from Charles Dickens's *A Tale of Two Cities* (1859).

In the 1960s, so much happened so quickly and in only ten short years. When the decade began in 1960, there was still squabbling in the United States about whether the country really needed an Interstate Highway System. By the end of the decade in 1969, American astronauts were walking on the moon. It was indeed one giant step.

The early part of the decade pulsed to the good vibrations of California's Beach Boys and buzzed with the excitement of the Kennedy "Camelot" years. It all came to a halt in November 1963 with the Kennedy assassination. A kind of national malaise set in.

Mid-decade saw all things English take over America with the "British Invasion," culminating in 1967's hippie-clad "Summer of Love." Then, the final few years of the decade arrived, when Chappaquiddick eclipsed Camelot, flower children transformed into the Manson family, and peaceful Woodstock turned into lethal Altamont. At the end of the decade in 1969, Americans were walking on the moon but also marching in the streets.

During the final few years of the 1960s, the nation seemed to be consumed with race riots and Vietnam War protests across the country. But there were some hopeful signs in terms of granting rights to all American citizens. In 1967, ruling on the case of *Loving v. Virginia*, the U.S. Supreme Court declared that state laws prohibiting interracial marriage were unconstitutional. Later that same year, civil rights attorney Thurgood Marshall, who had won the landmark *Brown v. Board of Education* decision, was sworn in as the first African American justice of the Supreme Court.

However, occasionally in the 1960s, it seemed a case of "one step forward, two steps back" as riots and ugliness continued unabated, reaching a boiling point in 1968. Civil rights leader Martin Luther King Jr. was assassinated, sparking riots in major American cities that lasted for several days. One of the few cities where riots did not occur was Indianapolis, Indiana, after a conciliatory speech by presidential candidate Robert F. Kennedy. Two months later, he too was assassinated.

On September 7, 1968, about 150 women arrived in Atlantic City, New Jersey, to protest the Miss America Pageant for being exploitative of women. What was called the Women's Liberation Movement gained traction and media coverage. Less than a year later, in June 1969, the Stonewall riots in New York City spurred America's modern gay rights movement.

Civil rights were in the forefront of people's minds. It was a fortuitous time for attorney Ruth Ginsburg to begin her groundbreaking work with the ACLU.

THE ACLU

The America Civil Liberties Union, more commonly known as the ACLU, states that it is a nonprofit, nonpartisan organization that works through litigation and lobbying. It evolved from the National Civil Liberties Bureau (CLB) founded in 1917, which focused on freedom of speech, primarily antiwar speech in the wake of World War I. After that war ended, the CLB reorganized in 1920 under a new name, the American Civil Liberties Union. Its intent was not to represent any particular group or a single theme but to uphold civil liberties when the organization considered them to be in danger.

In the 1920s, the ACLU found a number of issues to be within its mission. At that time, the nation's "Comstock Laws" mandated the routine confiscation of magazines and other publications, even pamphlets, for subjects considered obscene. By an act of the U.S. Congress, contraceptives were banned and condemned as obscene, making it a federal offense to distribute birth control information through the mail or across state lines.

> ## Monkey Trial, Part II
>
> *McLean v. Arkansas Board of Education* was a legal case in the state of Arkansas during 1981–1982, more than a half century after the original Scopes "Monkey" Trial. While Joan Jett's "I Love Rock N' Roll" hit the top of the charts and *E.T.* dazzled film-goers at that same time, the Arkansas case seemed to be a throwback to the 1920s. It began when the Arkansas legislature passed an act proposed by a fundamentalist religious group requiring "creation science," or the literal Biblical version of the seven-day creation story, to be taught in Arkansas public schools. When the ACLU and others filed suit, they argued that creationism was an explicitly religious doctrine with no scientific basis. National headlines ensued. The news media called *McLean v. Arkansas* a Monkey Trial sequel. Based on the Constitution's First Amendment regarding separation of church and state, the Arkansas law was ruled unconstitutional, finding that creationism is religion, not science. In a footnote, the Arkansas governor at the time was a Republican banker named Frank White who admitted he had not read the creation science bill before signing it. White was elected after unseating the previous governor who had irked the electorate by raising auto license plate fees, but who easily returned to the governor's office in the next election: Bill Clinton. Ten years later, after being elected president of the United States, it was Clinton who nominated Ruth Bader Ginsburg to the U.S. Supreme Court.

In other areas, the government often denied permits for labor rallies. Virtually all antiwar or antigovernment literature was prohibited. Activities promoting labor unions were denounced as un-American by social conservatives.

The ACLU did not have many successful efforts until 1925. Then suddenly it became a household name. The organization defended public school teacher John Scopes, who taught evolution in his high school science class, breaking a Tennessee state law. Americans across the country followed the Scopes "Monkey" Trial, so named in the media because some religious groups objected to the idea that humans evolved from monkeys and apes. In the spotlight of publicity, the ACLU became known nationwide, even being endorsed by major newspapers.

CRITICS FROM BOTH SIDES

Through the years, the ACLU has supported freedom of speech and other causes. The organization is not without critics from both sides of the political spectrum. The phenomenon depends on what kind of issue the organization is supporting. The ACLU has been criticized by conservatives in instances when it argued against mandatory prayer in public schools. But when the ACLU supported entities like the National Rifle Association, the ACLU was commended by conservatives. Conversely, ACLU has been praised by liberals for supporting affirmative action and human rights but opposed from the left during times when it defended neo-Nazis and the Ku Klux Klan on the basis of freedom of speech.

Its efforts in women's rights were enhanced by the ACLU's Women's Rights Project (WRP), which was created in 1971.

TENURE AND TURMOIL

Earning tenure at Rutgers in 1969 was a plus for Ruth Ginsburg among other positive things during that time. While she was still having nightmares about missing connections on the trains she needed to ride during her daily commute to Newark, her family life had settled into a comfortable place.

In 1969, she was able to see her children growing up, happy, and healthy. James, born in 1965, was four years old and attended nursery school. Jane, age 14, was an adolescent. Husband, Marty, secure at his law firm, was highly respected in the field of tax law. In 1967, Marty had been invited to teach at New York University Law School as an adjunct faculty member, which he did for the next decade in addition to working as a partner at his law firm.

At the time Ruth Ginsburg was granted tenure in 1969, her family life may have stabilized, but the country was in turmoil. One Vietnam War protest alone attracted almost a half million people. Students were staging sit-ins on college campuses to protest the war, Reserve Officers' Training Corps (ROTC) programs, and the lack of what students considered relevant coursework.

A group of Native Americans occupied Alcatraz Island in 1969 to call attention to Native American issues. That same year, the Stonewall riots in New York City underscored the inequities faced by the nation's gay people. Some African Americans turned to the Black Power movement.

Groups of Americans who had been marginalized were demanding their rights as citizens of the United States. One of those groups was the nascent women's movement.

The National Organization for Women (NOW) had been founded in 1966, garnering headlines for events like a protest at the Miss America pageant. They also endured trivializing mockery from male pundits about so-called Women's Lib. Often the male humor, as quoted by Strebeigh (2009), was along the lines of one U.S. Congressman who said that in his home, he had the last word: "Yes, Dear" (113).

> ### Help Wanted Male/Help Wanted Female
>
> In her book *The Feminine Mystique*, Betty Friedan argued that women are as capable as men for any type of work, despite traditional ideology to the contrary in education, mass media, and society as a whole. Many young people today find it hard to believe that in 1967, the year of the freewheeling hippie "Summer of Love," most newspapers across the country listed their want ads for jobs separately as "Help Wanted-Male" and "Help Wanted-Female." The jobs for men were advertised in terms of skills and opportunities. On the female side, jobs were almost always lower-paying, subordinate positions specifying that applicants must be attractive and well-groomed, attributes that were never required in the ads for men. In 1967, protesters picketed the classified ad office of the *New York Times*. Some carried signs like "Women can think as well as type." The response from the *Times* was that the ads were gender-segregated for the convenience of readers. Furthermore, they contended, doing it any other way would mean fewer jobs for women because men would apply for them. The reverse was unspoken. A year later, in 1968, a decision by the federal Equal Employment Opportunity Commission (EEOC) ruled that gender segregation was unlawful under the Civil Rights Act. The *Times* and other newspapers eventually integrated their listings after strongly protesting the decision.

NO REST FOR RUTH

In academia, a lot of effort goes into earning tenure. In exchange for job security, applicants must prove their value by showing an outstanding commitment not only to teaching but also developing new courses, intellectual research, and publishing scholarly works in addition to serving the campus and community in demonstrable ways. One of the most critical factors is the applicant's relationship to other faculty members, especially those on the tenure committee. The applicant must walk a fine line between the "traditionalists" who espouse the tried-and-true way of doing things and the "modernists" who champion new directions.

For a woman on the faculty of Rutgers Law School, there was already an aura of something new. It was much like the sense of being "singular and unusual" that Ruth experienced when she was herself a law school student. With the late 1960s being a time of tremendous social change in the United States, many Americans were feeling threatened. While it was important for a person in Ruth's situation on a quest for tenure to be on the "right side of history," it was also important not to appear to be a radical.

With her characteristic attention to detail, impeccable work ethic, and intellectual authority, Ruth Ginsburg avoided the pitfalls that can often trip up a faculty member when facing a tenure committee. In 1969, at age 36, she earned tenure at Rutgers Law School. For the first time in her working life, she was not subject to being dismissed at a moment's notice for any reason, with or without cause.

She was only later to discover that it had not been a unanimous vote of the tenure committee. But, in any case, she had overcome this important hurdle after attempting to prove her worth over the six years she had been at Rutgers. As it was not in her nature to rest on her laurels, even after attaining this newfound sense of security, Ruth Bader Ginsburg turned to new challenges.

THINGS ADD UP

Rarely does a person decide at one specific moment to change the course of their life. Usually, it comes after an accrued series of life experiences that have built up over decades. Perhaps without articulating them, the slights for Ruth Ginsburg added up: Not being allowed to join mourners for her beloved mother because only males could be part of the religious ritual. Losing a job after sharing the happy news of expecting a baby. Having to justify a place in school that could have been taken by a male. Being banned from a much-needed area of a library because she was a woman. Graduating at the top of the class but seeing lower-ranked males hired immediately after graduation. Suffering rejection after rejection after rejection by employers who quite openly said it was for reasons of gender. Being rebuffed for clerkships by much-admired, legendary scions of justice for spurious reasons. Being paid less than men for doing the same job at an institution of higher learning. Miraculously expecting another child and having to hide the "condition" for fear of being fired.

In professional settings, she was often introduced as a "wife and mother of two" rather than by her impressive legal credentials with which any male would have been introduced. She had to miss meetings that were held at "Men Only" facilities. She offered ideas that were ignored until a male brought the same idea forward, receiving acclaim for his contribution.

For someone like Ruth, being told "that's just the way things are" became both unpalatable and untrue after seeing progress in a vibrant society like that of Sweden. There, she saw that the vision of a more equitable society was not just a pipe dream but was being practiced daily as both genders strove toward the goal of simply exemplifying "human beings."

An especially strong motivator for many people, those of any race, religion, or gender, is being the parent of an intelligent child who most likely will be denied opportunities for the same discriminatory reasons if things stay the way they are. These are the kind of things that add up.

THE NORA SIMON CASE

Given the spirit of the activism of the time, it was not surprising that students at Rutgers approached Ginsburg about offering a new course. Like many undergraduates nationwide, law school students were demanding the types of classes that they felt to be more relevant, including those focusing on the law's relation to what were seen as underserved groups like minorities.

By the year of her tenure in 1969, Ruth had begun volunteering her legal services for the New Jersey affiliate of the ACLU. She took on a case that may have resonated strongly, given her own past history: a woman who was denied a career due to marriage and pregnancy.

Nora Simon had enlisted in the Women's Army Corps during the Vietnam War as a medical specialist. As an army lieutenant, Simon was commended and promoted for her work, but before long, she was also pregnant after marrying a male army officer in 1968. Per army regulations, Simon received an honorable discharge and was told that being the mother of a child, she would not be eligible for reenlistment. Meanwhile, her husband kept his rank and position in the army. Nothing in his life had changed, while everything in *hers* had.

By 1970, Nora Simon's marriage had been annulled and her baby given up for adoption. Then she tried to reenlist in an attempt to serve her country during the Vietnam War. The request was denied even though at that point she was neither a married woman nor a mother. Believing her civil rights were being violated, she turned to the ACLU.

In accepting Simon's case, ACLU volunteer Ruth Ginsburg went forward in a manner that was low-key and logical. In her argument, she pointed out that Simon had "no child dependent on her for care and support. Her legal status is in all respects that of a single woman without issue." In other words, Simon was at this point exactly the kind of skilled, motivated recruit the military would presumably want.

Ginsburg underpinned it with a pointed reference to the Civil Rights Act of 1964 "with respect to equal opportunity for women." She put her complaint in the form of a letter rather than a lawsuit and waited for a response from the Pentagon. None was forthcoming. She then formatted her letter in the form of a legal complaint and sent it to the army's general counsel as well as the U.S. Secretary of Defense. Ginsburg won Simon's bid for reinstatement under what the army called a "special dispensation."

As gratifying as winning the Nora Simon case was, Ginsburg recognized that the "special dispensation" granted by the military was for that one particular instance. It did not affect long-term policy, either for the military or the nation's women as a whole. That was about to change, and Ruth Ginsburg would make it happen.

SPIRIT OF THE TIMES

Ultimately the military revised its policy affecting women like Nora Simon. Ruth Ginsburg's victory in the Simon matter led to other "women's issue" cases being brought to her attention from the ACLU. One involved a teacher who had been forced to take unpaid leave when her pregnancy started to show, with no guarantee of getting her job back, a policy followed by most school boards across the country at the time, and one that would have resonated with Ruth.

Another matter concerned a female employee of Lipton Tea where the health insurance plan offered better benefits than her husband's employer. When she tried to enroll her spouse and family in the plan at Lipton, as male employees were able to do, she was denied. Female employees, she was told, could only enroll themselves, not their families—something male employees did as a matter of course.

Having an intelligent adolescent daughter herself, Ginsburg was also sympathetic to parents of girls wishing to enter a summer enrichment program in engineering at Princeton University that was open to sixth graders, but only those who were male. Girls, it was said, would be too distracting for sixth-grade boys.

Even at the nation's law schools, self-described bastions of knowledge and justice, inequities persisted. One popular class at Yale Law School was held at an all-male club. The best scholarship at NYU Law offered full tuition to 20 students each year but was limited to males only, for the official reason that men were the ones who were "future public leaders."

Once again, the spirit of the times influenced the events that took place in the late 1960s. In 1968, law schools suddenly found that they had a powerful incentive to admit more women. It did not involve a moral obligation or an attempt to redress inequity. In the midst of the Vietnam War, the nation's Draft Board changed its rules.

Young men who were teachers continued receiving a deferment from being drafted. However, male law school students no longer did. Males who preferred not to go to Vietnam sought teaching jobs or options other than law school. Enrollment in law schools dropped, tuition payments were down, and revenue suffered. Empty seats had to be filled. Admitting a greater number of women to law school became more attractive in the face of budgetary constraints.

Most of the women who applied to law school probably did not have to justify taking the place of a male, because males were not applying. Female enrollment in law schools nationwide grew on average to 40 women per 500 men. It was not a staggering jump, but it was at least some progress considering that Ruth Ginsburg was one of only 9 women in her law school class of more than 500.

The number of female students in law schools slowly continued to grow, although it would take the coming of the next century for the number of male and female students to be equal.

ON THE BASIS OF NUDITY

The aforementioned full-tuition scholarship at the NYU Law School that was offered to 20 males each year as "future public leaders" was called the Root-Tilden. It was named for attorneys Elihu Root and Samuel Tilden, both of whom had distinguished legal careers. When female students at NYU banded together to form a Women's Rights Committee, their representative went to see the law school's dean to protest the exclusion of women from being considered for the Root-Tilden award.

She was told that the Root-Tilden scholarship was a "sacred trust" that included building the attribute of male camaraderie. Strebeigh (2009) says this male bonding among our nation's future public leaders included "throwing water balloons at each other while running nude through the all-male Root-Tilden residence" (17). The dean fully endorsed nakedness as part of the sacred trust.

After a lengthy, arduous course of action that included threatening to sue their own law school for discrimination, in late 1968 the female NYU students gained success. The Root-Tilden scholarship was opened to women. It is not known how this may have affected the male bonding through nudity that was felt to be vital for future public leaders.

WOMEN AND THE LAW

Female students at other schools who had complaints about discrimination were finding it just as difficult as the NYU women had. In attempting to address through legal processes what they felt were injustices, female law students were unable to find much in the way of legal precedent, the procedure upon which much of the law is generally based. There were no courses on women and the law where they might learn if any precedents actually existed.

With the lack of material on women's rights fresh on their mind and wishing to know more about the subject in general, the NYU women sought the addition of a course on women and the law. Strebeigh states that one male professor responded by trivializing their request, stating that the inevitable next step "would be to teach the law of the bicycle" (19).

The first course on women and the law at NYU began in the fall semester of 1969. Those women who had fought for the NYU course had friends at other law schools. At Rutgers, a student who had taken a class with Ruth

> ### LIKE A FISH NEEDS A BICYCLE
>
> When the male professor compared a course on women and the law to teaching a class on "the law of the bicycle," it was an interesting analogy. When bicycles became popular in the United States during the 1890s, critics bemoaned the fact that bike-riding females would be able to escape the narrow confines of their homes. Even worse, they could do it by themselves without male supervision. With the addition of baskets on bikes, women could free their arms from carrying bulky packages. Bicycles were lightweight and affordable. They provided fresh air, fitness, and freedom that were exhilarating for women. Soon, to ride with greater ease, there came less restrictive clothing for women such as "bloomers," loose trousers gathered at the ankles. Critics attacked those garments as bringing about the doom of American society. The hit song of the decade was "A Bicycle Built for Two" in 1892. It popularized the concept that couples—even unmarried ones—could ride away together, escaping watchful eyes. The critics felt that was another blow against keeping women in their rightful place, with the bicycle presaging the downfall of civilization. Perhaps coincidentally, in the late 1960s, about 75 years later, T-shirts appeared with the slogan, "A woman needs a man like a fish needs a bicycle."

Ginsburg as well as being a fellow ACLU volunteer approached RBG in 1970 to develop a similar course there. Apart from the NYU class that the woman had fought for, there was no other course on women and the law anywhere else in the country.

At the time, there was a widely quoted reference in a textbook that caused dismay among many women. According to Vanderheiden (2012), Columbia University law professor Curtis Berger was considered an expert on real estate law, taught classes in property law, and was the author of a textbook called *Land Ownership and Use* (1968). Vanderheiden cites the passage that aroused consternation among female law students: "The more central concern of the article—land—is captured in an unguarded aside of our colleague, Curt Berger: '... after all, land, like woman, was meant to be possessed'" (288).

Amid that atmosphere, in the Spring semester of 1970, Ruth Ginsburg taught her first class on women and the law.

WOMEN'S RIGHTS LAW REPORTER

Ruth Ginsburg, who by this time had tenure at Rutgers, had been intrigued by the students' passion for a course on women and the law. As someone who valued legal scholarship, RBG set out to research the materials that were available, seeking out court decisions and articles in scholarly legal journals. Finding precedent and scholarly material would also help in her volunteer work for the ACLU, so both efforts dovetailed with the other.

However, there was simply not much. Seeking out legal journals and court decisions, it took her less than a month to find all the pertinent documents that were there was to find.

Characteristically, Ginsburg endeavored to improve the situation. In 1970, she cofounded the *Women's Rights Law Reporter* (WRLR), the first law journal in the United States to focus exclusively on women's rights law. This quarterly journal of legal scholarship was published by Rutgers law students with Ginsburg as faculty advisor to explore law and public policy relating to women's rights and gender issues.

At first, they found office space in an old building. But in 1972, WRLR was moved onto the Rutgers campus, becoming formally associated with Rutgers University in 1974. Along with examining judicial doctrine, legislative developments, litigation strategies, and pertinent state and federal court cases, *Women's Rights Law Reporter* also examined the careers of women jurists, advances for women in the legal profession, and relevant areas of public policy relating to women's rights.

THE '60S BECOME THE '70S

By 1970, Ruth had attained tenure at Rutgers but after seven years, was also still enduring the nightmarish commute to Newark. But there was a new spirit in the air as the 1970s began, which made a difference not only in her daily commute but in the next step of her career.

It wasn't just the commute that caused Ginsburg to think about making a move. Rutgers was a fine institution. However, New York City's Columbia University was Ivy League, along with other schools considered to be an "Ivy" like Brown, Cornell, Dartmouth, Harvard, Princeton, University of Pennsylvania, and Yale.

Beyond its prestigious status, a bonus was that Columbia was much closer to her home. That alone could help alleviate the stress that prompted friends to express concern that Ruth always looked exhausted.

In 1970, the mood of the country was shifting. After the tumultuous years of the late 1960s, Republican Richard Nixon was U.S. president after winning the 1968 election although Democrats controlled both houses of Congress. There were still protests against racial injustice and the Vietnam War, including one that turned deadly on May 4, 1970, when National Guardsmen opened fire on war protestors at Ohio's Kent State University.

For women, there were some rays of hope toward gender equality. In June 1970, the first female generals in the U.S. Army were named: Anna

Mae Hays and Elizabeth Hoisington. On a larger scale, August 26, 1970, saw the Women's Strike for Equality in New York City when 50,000 women marched down New York City's Fifth Avenue, not far from the Ginsburg apartment. The women linked arms, blocked a major thoroughfare during rush hour, and attracted widespread media attention.

Media attention was exactly the goal of the National Organization for Women (NOW), which organized the march. It started as an idea that was first put forward by NOW cofounder Betty Friedan in her book *The Feminine Mystique*. The original goal was a national work stoppage when women would not perform their usual cooking and cleaning tasks in order to spotlight the unequal distribution of domestic labor. It was expanded into a protest march to demonstrate the status of women in American society. Other related events took place that day around the country, including a women's march in Washington, D.C., that attracted about 1,000 protestors, marching behind a banner reading, "We Demand Equality."

Nixon and his advisors already had the status of women in their sights, creating the Women's Task Force on Rights and Responsibilities. In June 1970, the committee released their report titled "A Matter of Simple Justice." It recommended that an Equal Rights Amendment (ERA) be added to the U.S. Constitution. The report also advocated an increased level of civil rights and equal opportunity for women along with recommending that more women be appointed to high-level positions in the Nixon administration.

Two months later, in August 1970, future U.S. Senator Daniel Patrick Moynihan distributed a memo to White House staff making the case for female equality becoming a major cultural and political force in the 1970s. Writing to President Nixon, Moynihan said, "The essential fact is that we have educated women for equality but have not really given it to them."

CAMP REUNION

Around this time, Ruth Ginsburg had a visitor in her office at Rutgers. It was Melvin Wulf, who had dropped by the campus from Manhattan to meet with another Rutgers colleague. Ruth had known Wulf at Camp Che-Na-Wah. There, the two had shared a love of the operas of Gilbert and Sullivan.

As a fellow alumnus of Columbia Law School, Wulf had since become legal director for the ACLU. In the atmosphere of the era, when marginalized groups of Americans were demanding their full rights, the ACLU was taking on a number of causes that were increasingly being resolved by litigation.

Litigation is also known as "going to trial." Litigation attorneys, called litigators or trial lawyers, debate their arguments in open court. Trial lawyers are the type of attorneys most often seen in movies, TV shows, and books like the best-selling legal thrillers of John Grisham. Other types of attorneys, like tax lawyer Martin Ginsburg, do much of their work outside a courtroom, researching complex legal codes and documents to seek a solution to a client's problem, often within their own office. Litigators, on the other hand, go to court. Neither Melvin Wulf nor the ACLU was reluctant to go to court.

At the time of the reunion between former campmates Ginsburg and Wulf, the ACLU was planning to begin a new unit within the organization to be called the Women's Rights Project (WRP). It would specifically address the kind of issues that Moynihan alluded to in his memo to Nixon: women were making gains as a cultural and political force but had not yet received equality in American society. The ACLU was prepared to fight for their rights in a court of law. To do so it needed a director for the WRP and a skilled litigator to argue their cases at trial.

REED V. REED

During the Spring semester of 1970, Ruth Ginsburg taught Rutgers University's first class on women and the law. She was also still volunteering for the ACLU. In that capacity, she approached her Camp Che-Na-Wah buddy Mel Wulf about coauthoring a brief together that was destined for the Supreme Court of the United States. It would be her first, but not the last.

The case, *Reed v. Reed*, questioned an Idaho court's decision that was based on a statute from 1864. It required a father to be preferred over a mother in administering the estate of a deceased child. In this situation, the parents, Sally Reed and Cecil Reed, were divorced. The teenage son had lived with his mother after the abusive father deserted the family. In a unanimous opinion, the Idaho court rejected Sally Reed's plea to act as administrator of the son's small estate after he died, including a college savings account she had started for him. Cecil Reed's legal argument was that Sally Reed was "too dumb" to administer the boy's small estate. The Idaho court agreed with a law written over 100 years earlier, during the Civil War, that men were better qualified to act as administrators than women.

Sally Reed's case was appealed to the U.S. Supreme Court in a brief written by ACLU legal director Mel Wulf and volunteer Ruth Bader Ginsburg. Its docket cover shows that it was filed with the Supreme Court on June 25, 1971—the anniversary of Celia Bader's death. If Celia had lived, she would have been 69 years old when her daughter's legal case was accepted for argument at the Supreme Court of the United States.

Reed v. Reed was the first major case that addressed discrimination based on gender. When the Supreme Court handed down its opinion in *Reed v. Reed* in November 1971, the decision made headlines across the country. It ruled that the Idaho law was unconstitutional because it denies equal protection, in this case, to a particular gender.

It was the first time since the Fourteenth Amendment (see PRIMARY SOURCE DOCUMENTS) had gone into effect in 1868 that the Supreme Court struck down a state law on the ground that it discriminated against women in violation of the Equal Protection Clause. Scores of state laws were changed after the decision, which set a major precedent for gender bias cases to follow. It also raised hopes among some women's rights advocates that a federal Equal Rights Amendment, which at the time was working its way through Congress, would pass.

In addition to the historic nature of the case and the irony of it being filed with the Supreme Court on the anniversary of Celia Bader's death, the *Reed v. Reed* brief was also remarkable for the front cover of its legal brief. Along with Sally Reed's original Idaho lawyer, the "Brief for Appellant" listed the attorneys for her appeal as follows: Melvin L. Wulf, American Civil Liberties Foundation; Ruth Bader Ginsburg, Rutgers Law School; Dorothy Kenyon, New York, New York; and Pauli Murray, Boston, Massachusetts.

Because of a remarkable request by Ginsburg, Dorothy Kenyon and Pauli Murray were recognized as coauthors of the brief, giving the women credit even though they did not help on it. Ruth wanted to acknowledge the debt she owed them for their work in the past, efforts that had created a basis for her successful arguments.

DOROTHY KENYON

Who were Dorothy Kenyon and Pauli Murray to whom RBG felt she owed so much? Born in 1888, Dorothy Kenyon was an attorney and women's rights activist. After graduating from the elite Smith College, she spent a year in Mexico where she observed the effects of injustice and poverty on women who were often burdened with more children than they could care for. Returning to New York City, Kenyon worked as a law clerk. In the 1920s, she was known for her support of birth control at a time when providing information about contraception was considered obscene, immoral, and illegal.

In 1930, with Dorothy Straus, she established the law firm of Straus and Kenyon, working for the advancement of women. New York mayor Fiorello

LaGuardia appointed Kenyon to the city's Municipal Court bench in 1939, after which she became known for the rest of her life as Judge Kenyon.

After World War II, she was a member of the United Nations Commission on the Status of Women, a position from which she denounced the small role of women in the government of the United States. She was targeted by the McCarthy anticommunist "witch hunts" but struck back, calling Joseph McCarthy a coward by his taking shelter "in the cloak of congressional immunity." In more succinct terms, she also called him "an unmitigated liar." Kenyon was supported in an editorial by the *New York Times*, after which the Senate subcommittee dismissed charges against her. McCarthy then lost interest.

However, that experience tarnished Kenyon's reputation. Despite her credentials, she never received another political appointment. During the 1950s and 1960s, Kenyon prepared briefs for the National Association for the Advancement of Colored People (NAACP) and worked for the ACLU. As the only woman on the ACLU board for many years, she urged the organization to take a stand against gender inequality.

Kenyon worked with attorney Pauli Murray in preparing briefs to challenge discrimination. At age 83, she marched in the 1971 Women's Strike for Equality. She joined the movement calling for the enactment of an Equal Rights Amendment, working with much younger women.

By that time, however, she was already dying of stomach cancer although she kept it to herself, refusing to slow down. Kenyon died in 1972, just a month after Ruth Bader Ginsburg was heralded by the *New York Times* for RBG's historic hiring as the first female tenured professor by Columbia Law School. In the 2018 movie about RBG, *On the Basis of Sex*, Kenyon was portrayed by Academy Award–winning actress Kathy Bates.

PAULI MURRAY

Also credited on the *Reed* brief, although she too had not worked on it, was Pauli Murray. When Ruth had worked as a summer intern at a private law firm in 1959 after graduating from law school, she had hoped to be offered a full-time position. Instead, the firm hired someone who was both female and African American. To allegedly demonstrate that they were hiring women and minorities, a black woman was considered "two for one." The person they hired was Pauli Murray, who would later become a friend and inspiration to RBG, as acknowledged on the *Reed* brief.

Human rights activist Anna Pauline "Pauli" Murray was born in 1910. She was an attorney who also became the first African American woman to be ordained as a priest in the Episcopal Church. As a young woman in 1940, Murray sat in the whites-only section of a Virginia bus, moving up from the broken seats in the "black" section. She was arrested for violating state segregation laws. That incident led her to pursue a career as a civil rights lawyer.

Murray enrolled in law school at Howard University, a historically African American college, where she was the only woman in her law school class. On her first day, one professor remarked that he did not know why women went to law school. Thus, in addition to racism, at Howard she was exposed to the kind of sexism that she called "Jane Crow," in reference to racially discriminatory state laws termed "Jim Crow."

As a lawyer, Pauli Murray argued both for racial civil rights and women's rights. Attorney Thurgood Marshall, chief counsel for the NAACP, called Murray's book, *States' Laws on Race and Color*, a "bible" of the civil rights movement. Her approach, to challenge state segregation laws as unconstitutional, was influential in the NAACP's strategy of arguments in 1954's landmark *Brown v. Board of Education* decision.

In 1961, Murray was appointed by John F. Kennedy to serve on the Presidential Commission on the Status of Women. Murray continued her legal studies. In 1965, she became the first African American to receive a Doctor of Juridical Science degree from Yale Law School.

Pauli Murray and Dorothy Kenyon successfully argued *White v. Crook*, a groundbreaking 1966 case in which the U.S. Court of Appeals ruled that women have an equal right to serve on juries.

Murray taught law at Brandeis University in Massachusetts from 1968 to 1973. In addition, she introduced classes there on African American studies and women's studies, both firsts for Brandeis.

When Ruth Bader Ginsburg wrote her brief for *Reed v. Reed* in 1970, extending the Fourteenth Amendment's Equal Protection Clause to women, she added Murray and Kenyon as coauthors in recognition of the debt she felt she owed to their work.

In later years, Murray worked in a parish in Washington, D.C., where she focused on ministering to the sick. In 1985, at the age of 75, Pauli Murray died of pancreatic cancer. In 2016, her alma mater Yale University announced that one of two new residential colleges on campus would be named for alumna Pauli Murray. The other was to be named after Benjamin Franklin.

MORITZ

While Ruth was teaching at Rutgers and volunteering for the ACLU, her husband, Martin Ginsburg, had reached the point in his career when he was renowned as a leading tax attorney. He was also still devoted to his wife. Marty and Ruth had followed their original plan to enter the same profession, but their paths had diverged. Ruth taught law; Marty practiced it. Neither usually pursued their area of law into the courtroom as litigators. That would all change one evening at home at October 1970 when Marty brought a case to Ruth's attention that he thought she would find interesting.

He read about it in a journal pertaining to tax law but saw that it had potential implications for Ruth's work in gender inequity. Ultimately, *Moritz v. Commissioner of Internal Revenue* was the first gender discrimination suit argued in court by Ruth Bader Ginsburg. It was also dramatic enough to form the basis for the case portrayed in the Hollywood movie *On the Basis of Sex*.

They decided to work on it together. Marty agreed to handle the tax law portion of the case. Ruth asked Mel Wulf to secure the ACLU's sponsorship of the litigation, using phraseology derived from the Gilbert and Sullivan operas they had enjoyed performing at camp. Next, the Ginsburgs only needed convince their potential client, a man named Charles Moritz, to be their test case.

Charles Moritz was a traveling salesman from Denver, Colorado. The never-married Moritz was the sole caregiver of his 89-year-old invalid mother. He claimed a tax deduction for the cost of a nurse who he needed when he was out of town. The Internal Revenue Service (IRS) denied the deduction, allowing such a deduction only for women. The IRS ruling was upheld by the U.S. Tax Court in Washington, D.C.

To appeal that decision, Martin and Ruth Ginsburg represented Moritz with the support of the ACLU's Mel Wulf. Their strategy at the Tenth Circuit Court of Appeals for *Charles E. Moritz v. Commissioner of Internal Revenue* was to prove that the tax code conflicted with the Fourteenth Amendment's Equal Protection Clause. It was, they argued, therefore unconstitutional. They maintained that the caregiver deduction should be extended to never-married men as well as women because there was no rational basis for unequal treatment between males and females in this situation. Denying the deduction was discrimination based on gender, violating the constitutional guarantee of equal protection "to any person." It was a class, RBG stated, in which men and women share full membership.

In presenting their case during the oral arguments, Martin Ginsburg, the renowned tax attorney, spoke about tax law for about the first ten minutes. His cocounsel, Ruth Bader Ginsburg, then addressed the court on the constitutionality of the case. It was her first time as a litigator.

She had prepared the *Moritz* legal brief, one that ran for more than 40 pages. Drawing on her college class with novelist Vladimir Nabokov, she painted word pictures, allowing the court to see Mr. Moritz as a fellow human being in a particular situation. Although the monetary amount of the tax deduction was relatively small, about $300, he was an American citizen who faced discrimination.

It took more than a year for a decision to be made by the Tenth Circuit Court of Appeals, one of the highest courts in the land apart from the Supreme Court. In November 1972, the court ruled in favor of the Ginsburgs and their client Charles Moritz. Just as the Ginsburg argument had maintained, the court found that the tax code constituted "discrimination based solely on sex." It was the first time any provision of the Internal Revenue Code was declared unconstitutional. *Moritz v. Commissioner of Internal Revenue* was also the first gender discrimination suit argued in court by Ruth Ginsburg as a trial lawyer.

The *Moritz* decision of November 1972 took place exactly a year after the *Reed v. Reed* decision, handed down in November 1971. Both were based on Ruth Ginsburg's brief. Based on her slow and steady style, with *Moritz*, RBG now had two history-making cases decided in her favor but more importantly, in favor of equality. With *Moritz*, Ruth Ginsburg had also quietly become a litigator.

AFFIRMATIVE

During the early 1970s, events on the national level were occurring that were intertwined with Ruth's life as well as her involvement with the *Reed* and *Moritz* cases. With the burgeoning civil rights and women's movements, one took place in 1970, when President Richard Nixon extended affirmative action programs in the United States to include universities.

Affirmative action is a set of laws that are intended to correct the effects of discrimination. It especially focuses on equal access to education and employment, attempting to "level the playing field" by offering special consideration to historically excluded groups like minorities or women.

In 1961, President John F. Kennedy had first used the phrase by instructing federal contractors to take "affirmative action to ensure that applicants are treated equally without regard to race, color, religion, sex, or national origin." His administration also created the Committee on Equal Employment Opportunity, which later became the Equal Employment Opportunity Commission (EEOC).

Kennedy's successor, President Lyndon Johnson, expanded the scope of affirmative action to include any entities doing business with the federal government, directly or indirectly. In 1970, Nixon extended affirmative action to include universities that received federal funding.

In order to meet what the government called "reasonably attainable targets," colleges began an effort to recruit women and minorities so their numbers would be acceptable. The first to approach Ruth Ginsburg to teach for their school was Harvard. However, despite her class standing and *Harvard Law Review* credentials, the school did not offer her a full-time job. Instead, they invited her to serve as a "visiting professor" in the fall of 1971. In that way, she could be observed by the powers-that-be to determine if she was a good fit.

While Ruth continued commuting from her New York City home to New Jersey to teach her course load at Rutgers, she also began traveling to Massachusetts to teach as a visiting professor at Harvard. When Harvard asked the exhausted Ginsburg to teach again as a visiting professor during the Spring semester so they could continue sizing her up, she declined.

However, another option was on the horizon. It was RBG's alma mater, Columbia. As opposed to Rutgers in New Jersey and Harvard in Massachusetts, Columbia University in New York City was at least in the same state as her home.

COLUMBIA

On January 26, 1972, a headline in the *New York Times* read, "Columbia Law Snares a Prize in the Quest for Women Professors." The article by Oelsner (1972) called the hiring of Ruth Bader Ginsburg a major coup, marking the first time in the 114-year history of Columbia Law that the school hired a woman for a tenured position as full professor.

As noted by de Hart (2018), the fact that not one woman had been hired by the institution in more than a century was not seen in any way as an anomaly. Apparently without a trace of irony, one veteran member of the Columbia Law School faculty said, "It really wasn't sexism so much as just not wanting to change the club-like atmosphere that prevailed" (137). The club in question was, of course, Boys Only.

Ginsburg was asked how she planned to combine her teaching courseload when she arrived at Columbia the following Fall with her sex discrimination work in conjunction with ACLU. Referring to Ginsburg as the "38-year-old wife of a successful tax lawyer and mother of a girl, 16, and a boy, 6" (A39), Oelsner's article said RBG's response was that the only confining thing for her is time and that she did not plan to curtail her activities in any way.

Hans Smit, her mentor from the Sweden project, had suggested in the past that Columbia Law School hire Ruth Ginsburg, the woman who was being called a "major coup" for the school. According to de Hart (2018), RBG "was not on Columbia Law's short list of possibilities" (138). Even so, Smit distributed her résumé along with a letter of support from a Rutgers colleague. Many faculty members had been her professors while she was in law school at Columbia. She received an offer, and accepted.

But once again it came down to a particular issue: bathrooms. Columbia Law's dean decided to convert half of the extra-spacious men's room into a ladies' restroom for new women faculty.

Even before RBG started her term on the Columbia Law faculty in the Fall of 1972, she was approached by a group of students. They told her that Columbia was making budget cuts in a manner familiar to many business executives—firing the lowest-paid workers, usually women. Ginsburg was told that 25 women who were employed as custodial help at Columbia were being fired. No male custodians were affected. The women, almost all of them minorities, were often the sole support of their families. Much like the opposite policies about women and dormitories at Cornell and Harvard, this was the opposite of Ruth's experience at Rutgers where she was told she received lower pay because the males had families to support. In this case, the women were the breadwinners. Through a number of strategies that ran from collegial chats with university administrators to the threat of a lawsuit, ultimately not a single custodian, male or female, was fired.

THE WOMEN'S RIGHTS PROJECT

Ruth Ginsburg discovered that there were other gender inequities at Columbia. They ran the gamut from salary inequity to different dining requirements for males and females. Some athletic facilities were off limits to women, in one case requiring women's track athletes to run on the streets of upper Manhattan.

With the confidence that job security can bring, Ruth Bader Ginsburg, Columbia's much-heralded "major coup," was not reluctant to address unfairness wherever she saw it. She was also fortunate to have the power of the ACLU with her. The ACLU would soon find itself fortunate to have Ruth Ginsburg.

As the women's movement gained momentum in the early 1970s, the ACLU recognized that there was a role for the organization to play in guaranteeing the civil liberties of half the population, people who were female.

In 1972, concurrent with her faculty position uptown at Columbia, RBG was able to spend her afternoons downtown in the ACLU offices with the WRP. At first, the WRP had no office space, no staff, no files, and very little funding.

One source of financial support came from grants, including one from the Playboy Foundation, an offshoot of the men's magazine. When WRP mailings went out with an imprint of the familiar *Playboy* bunny, as required by the grant, outrage ensued. Some complaints may have been from women with long memories. Watts (2008) points out that a decade

Ruth and Ruth and Barbie

It is not known if RBG's daughter, Jane, ever owned one of the enormously popular Barbie dolls, nor is it known if Ruth Ginsburg ever crossed paths with the doll's creator, a fellow New Yorker named Ruth Handler. In 1959, within three months of Ruth Ginsburg's graduation from Columbia Law School at the top of her class, Ruth Handler unveiled a voluptuous fashion model doll called "Barbie" (named after her daughter Barbara) at the American International Toy Fair in New York City. By the early 1970s, the ACLU's leadership recognized that there was a change in the air for the women's movement, responding to it by placing Ruth Ginsburg at the head of a new division called the Women's Rights Project. But not all advances in women's rights happened in the courtroom; some were much more subtle. Starting in 1963, designer Carol Spencer created the iconic wardrobe for the Barbie doll. Spencer said that during the women's movement of the early 1970s, she and other Barbie designers belonged to the National Organization for Women, but didn't flaunt it. The Barbie doll moved from being a fashion model to Astronaut Barbie, athletic Gold Medal Barbie, and Surgeon Barbie. Thanks to the efforts of quiet heroines like Spencer—and Ruth Ginsburg—little girls playing with dolls in the 1970s began to realize there were other choices for their own lives than being solely somebody's wife and somebody's mother. They could be Barbie!

earlier, in 1962, before there were many—if any—gains in women's rights, *Playboy* gathered an eight-man panel to discuss a topic called "The Womanization of America." Most of the men on the highly publicized panel endorsed the view that women had become "more selfish, more greedy, less romantic, less warm, more lusty, and more filled with hate" (234). Hefner added the rallying cry, "We think it's a man's world, or should be" (234).

Playboy was also not known for leveling the playing field professionally. It did not publish female writers, and the only way it printed a 1969 piece by bestselling author Ursula K. Le Guin was billing her as "U. K. Le Guin."

Despite controversy and criticism, under Ruth's guidance, the small staff of women kept the WRP office organized, sorting out the issues that came their way. Although Ginsburg was as always focused on her work, she did her best to make the WRP office as friendly an environment as possible. Women with small children were permitted to bring them to the office, although males in other departments at the ACLU demanded their equal rights, in this case, to bring their pets to work. One of the major reasons for women to bring their babies to the office was to be able to breast feed them; no males were known to be observed performing the same function for their dogs.

By 1974, the Women's Rights Project had participated in more than 300 gender discrimination cases. As the WRP's general counsel, Ginsburg charted a strategy. Recognizing that some powerful elements of American society felt threatened by women having increased rights, she attempted to avoid a destructive, long-term backlash by trying to do too much too soon. As a legal scholar, she believed that the safest course was to utilize strategic cases as building blocks for the future, slowly but surely building precedent.

She chose cases carefully, picking battles she believed could be won. At times, they were cases involving male plaintiffs, situations that could demonstrate gender discrimination being harmful to both men and women. That strategy aroused harsh condemnation from some self-styled feminists for using male plaintiffs. Still, Ginsburg not only persevered in the face of criticism, she scored one historic victory after another in the cause of women's rights.

FIVE OUT OF SIX

Yet, in the early 1970s, as the criticism of Ginsburg by some factions foreshadowed, the women's movement was unraveling even as it gathered strength. Nora Ephron (1984) described the scene at the 1972 Democratic Convention in Miami, with the growing animosity of Betty Friedan (*Feminine Mystique*) toward Gloria Steinem (*Ms. Magazine*). At the press conference for the National Women's Political Caucus, Friedan was introduced as "the mother of us all" (58). But Friedan countered with the statement that she was sick and tired of that description because, as Ephron says, "in the women's movement, to be called the mother of anything is rarely a compliment. . . . [I]t was her movement. Was she supposed to sit still and let a beautiful thin lady run off with it?"(59).

Ruth Ginsburg weathered the criticism that she was doing too much/too little, or too quickly/too slowly, for women's rights. However the feminist movement played out in front of the cameras, she was making slow, steady, lasting changes. All she needed to do, and all she wished to do, was to keep her head down and do the work.

Between 1973 and 1976, as director of the ACLU Women's Rights Project, attorney Ginsburg argued six gender discrimination cases before the U.S. Supreme Court, winning five. In-depth details for each can be found at the *Oyez.org* legal websites cited below.

Her first case and first victory was 1973's *Frontiero v. Richardson*, which she won by challenging a military statute that denied female service members the right to claim benefits for a husband. Sharron Frontiero, a lieutenant in the U.S. Air Force, had applied for housing and medical benefits for her husband but was denied. Male service members could automatically receive the same allowance for a wife. Ginsburg convincingly argued that

> **WHO WAS SARAH GRIMKE?**
>
> When Ruth Bader Ginsburg gave her oral arguments to the Supreme Court in *Frontiero*, incorporating a quotation about men taking their feet off women's necks, it was a powerful moment that begged the question about the source of the quote. Sarah Grimké (1792–1873) of South Carolina was an abolitionist, lecturer, and early member of the women's suffrage movement. As a young woman, despite her obvious intelligence, Grimké was denied the education that her brothers enjoyed, thus preventing her from pursuing her dream of becoming an attorney. It was probably no great comfort to Grimké when her father said that if she had been a man, she would have been the greatest lawyer in South Carolina. The full quote was in a letter written by Grimké in 1837: "I ask no favors for my sex. I surrender not our claim to equality. All I ask of our brethren is that they will take their feet from off our necks, and permit us to stand upright on that ground which God designed us to occupy." In 1853, Grimke visited the U.S. Supreme Court when it was not in session. Writing to a friend, she noted that she had been invited to sit in the Chief Justice's chair, exclaiming that someday the seat may be occupied by a woman. In her letter, she said, "The brethren laughed heartily." The anecdote was related in a 1999 *Indiana Law Review* article by Ruth Bader Ginsburg, then in her sixth year as a Supreme Court justice. At that point, no one was laughing.

the statute treated women as inferior, doing it in a quiet, understated way that apparently captured the attention of the nine men on the high court bench. In fact, it was barely an argument at all—it was a lesson being taught politely by the experienced teacher that she was, one who respects her students but has important information to share about the subject. According to Carmon and Knizhnik (2015), lawyers are almost incessantly interrupted by questions from the Supreme Court justices while trying to make their case, often having trouble getting out a full sentence. On this day, however, "RBG spoke for ten minutes without a single interruption from the justices. She had stunned them into silence" (46).

The Supreme Court ruled 8–1 in RBG's favor. Only William Rehnquist dissented. It was during *Frontiero* that Ginsburg set the foundation for her legal arguments to follow, famously quoting Sarah Grimké: "I ask for no favor for my sex. All I ask of our brethren is that they take their feet off our necks."

The result of *Kahn v. Shevin* in 1974 did not go as well as RBG might have hoped. This case involved a Florida tax exemption for widows but no similar exemption for widowers. In a 6–3 decision, the Court ruled that single women face more hardship in the job market than single men, thus confirming the gender-specific policy. The Court itself brought this ruling into question in 1977 when RBG again faced the men of the high court.

She argued *Edwards v. Healy* in 1975 regarding jury exclusion for women. RBG can be seen to have won her point by virtue of the case becoming moot pursuant to changes in the Louisiana law that had originally instigated the matter.

Ginsburg scored a major Supreme Court victory in 1975, arguing the case of *Weinberger v. Wiesenfeld*. Stephen Wiesenfeld, represented by RBG, was a widower who had been denied survivor benefits under Social Security. The law permitted widows—but not widowers—to collect special benefits in order to care for their minor children upon the loss of a spouse. Ginsburg argued that the statute discriminated against male survivors by denying them the same protection as their female counterparts. This, she claimed, violated the constitutional right to equal protection. In addition, the contributions made by Wiesenfeld's late wife to Social Security were not treated on an equal basis to salaried men who would have been able to claim their contributions, thus demonstrating further discrimination. Eight of the nine Supreme Court justices who were present found in RBG's favor. Justice William O. Douglas, who retired from the Court that year because of health issues, did not participate in the discussion or decision of this case. As Ginsburg had carefully planned, the favorable *Wiesenfeld* decision stood on the building blocks she had put in place during earlier cases. The Supreme Court's written opinion stated that "the Constitution forbids the gender-based differentiation premised upon assumptions as to dependency made in the statutes before us in *Frontiero*."

During her argument in 1977's *Califano v. Goldfarb*, again concerning a widower who applied for survivor's benefits under the Social Security Act, RBG was asked twice by the high court justices whether she thought they had ruled wrongly *Kahn v. Shevin* in 1974. So as not to offend the jurists whose support she hoped to gain in *Califano v. Goldfarb*, RBG diplomatically sidestepped the question both times it was asked. Kanefield (2016) says, "Instead of answering directly, she distinguished the cases in *Goldfarb*" (184). Her diplomatic handling of the challenge scored another win for RBG.

The 1979 case of *Duren v. Missouri* regarding the automatic exemption from jury service for women upon request may have built on her diplomacy in *Goldfarb*. Part of Ginsburg's argument in *Duren* was that making jury duty optional for women essentially treated women's service on juries as less valuable than men's as well as discriminating against men who enjoyed no such exemption. The justices voted 8–1 in her favor, with Rehnquist again dissenting. After this victory, *Duren* became the final case that RBG argued before the Supreme Court as an attorney. It would not, however, be the final time she walked up the marble steps of the Supreme Court building.

ALPHABETICAL MALE

In 1974, while in the middle of winning cases before the Supreme Court, RBG added another book authorship credit to her résumé in addition to her 1965 work on Swedish civil procedure. The new one, called *Text, Cases, and Materials on Sex-Based Discrimination,* coauthored with Kenneth M. Davidson and Herma Hill Kay, was published in 1974. It was America's first casebook on gender discrimination, published five years after men landed on the moon.

At the time, Herma Kay was a professor at the University of California at Berkeley's Boalt Hall School of Law. Kenneth Davidson was an associate professor at the State University of New York in Buffalo. Like RBG at Rutgers, they had been asked by students to teach a course on women and the law but discovered there were no casebooks on the topic. Finding very little information, Davidson used his own mimeographed materials. Reaching out to each other, both Davidson and Kay thought of Ruth Bader Ginsburg, who directed the Women's Rights Project for the ACLU. They arranged to meet her at a conference called "The Law School Curriculum and the Legal Rights of Women," which RBG had helped to organize.

The three agreed to work together. According to the description in "Feminist Jurisprudence" issued by the Columbia Law Library, the book's topics included admission barriers in schools and universities, employment discrimination remedies, and family life without marriage. The review goes on to state that introducing those topics into the law school curriculum "gave a significant boost to the idea of equal rights for men and women and raised the consciousness of many law students on the effects of discrimination" (n.p.).

When the time for publication approached, their editor believed the book would have more market appeal if, as women, either Kay's or Ginsburg's name was given first place in the list of co-authors. According to Kay (2012), "Ruth, who had learned that ending sex discrimination begins at home, was adamantly opposed to the idea. The co-authors should be listed in alphabetical order, and no priority should be given to either of the female authors over their male colleague. . . . [T]he book was published as Davidson, Ginsburg, and Kay" (58).

Today, that book, which has undergone numerous updated editions since 1974, is considered a classic.

MILICENT TRYON MAKES HISTORY

During this era, Ruth Ginsburg worked at Columbia with a woman named Milicent Tryon who served as her secretary. Tryon had been an arts critic for a cultural magazine, but by the time she and RBG began working together at Columbia, the magazine had folded.

As related by Garner (2011), RBG stated, "When men see or hear the word *sex*, they think of only one thing. . . . For me it became altogether clear when my secretary at Columbia said, 'I'm typing these briefs and articles for you and jumping out all over the page is *sex, sex, sex*. Don't you know that for the male audience you are addressing, the first association of the word *sex* is not what you're talking about? So why don't you use a grammar-book term? Use *gender*. It has a neutral sound and it will ward off distracting associations.' Milicent Tryon was my astute secretary then, and from that day to this, I've used *gender*" (387).

As Ginsburg said, Tryon was indeed astute. From that time forward, RBG's strategic advocacy extended to the specific word choice in her arguments, favoring the use of *gender* instead of *sex*. Using the word *gender* became the preferred grammatical form according to reference books like Garner's *Dictionary of Legal Usage*, in which it is noted that "the shift [to *gender*] is now irreversible" (387).

In 1970, before Ginsburg and Tryon worked together at Columbia, congressional hearings began on what was called the ERA. The text of the proposed amendment read, "Equality of rights under the law shall not be denied or abridged by the United States or by any State on account of *sex*" [emphasis the author's].

By the end of the decade, although it had congressional support, the ERA did not gain enough of the required votes in state legislatures to pass. Some have wondered whether, if the text had been written using the word *gender* instead of *sex*, things might have turned out differently.

In any case, Ruth Ginsburg quietly continued drafting briefs for the ACLU's Women's Rights Project. Her studied approach and string of victories were exemplary. However, she recognized that the mood of the country was shifting yet again. She and her husband, Marty, began looking in other directions where meaningful, enduring change might be achieved.

SOURCES

Carmon, Irin, and Shana Knizhnik. *Notorious RBG: The Life and Times of Ruth Bader Ginsburg*. New York: Dey Street Books, 2015.
De Hart, Jane Sherron. *Ruth Bader Ginsburg: A Life*. New York: Knopf, 2018.
Ephron, Nora. *Crazy Salad Plus Nine*. New York: Pocket Books, 1984.
"Feminist Jurisprudence," *Columbia Law Library*. http://library.law.columbia.edu/rise_of_women/jurisprudence/sexbaseddiscrimination.html.

Garner, Bryan A. *Garner's Dictionary of Legal Usage, Third Edition.* New York: Oxford University Press, 2011.

Kanefield, Teri. *Free to Be Ruth Bader Ginsburg: The Story of Women and Law.* San Francisco, CA: Armon Books, 2016.

Kay, Herma Hill. "Claiming a Space in the Law School Curriculum: A Casebook on Sex-Based Discrimination," *Columbia Journal of Gender and Law*, Symposium Issue, 2012, p. 54.

Oelsner, Lesley. "Columbia Law Snares a Prize in the Quest for Women Professors," *The New York Times*, January 26, 1972, p. A39. https://www.nytimes.com/1972/01/26/archives/columbia-law-snares-a-prize-in-the-quest-for-women-professors.html.

Strebeigh, Fred. *Equal: Women Shape American Law.* New York: Norton, 2009.

Vanderheiden, Steve. *Environmental Rights.* New York: Routledge, 2012.

Watts, Steven. *Mr. Playboy: Hugh Hefner and the American Dream.* Hoboken, NJ: Wiley, 2008.

6

Federal Court: The Judge's Judge

In 1968, Republican Richard Nixon campaigned for the presidency as a supporter of women's rights. However, after he won the election that year, he was criticized for doing little to help women's causes, specifically the proposed Equal Rights Amendment (ERA), which was working its way through state legislatures during his administration.

During Nixon's term of office, which ran from 1969 to 1974, he made several appointments to the U.S. Supreme Court, which signified to many people a sharp move toward conservatism in judicial matters. Nixon appointed Warren Burger to replace Chief Justice Earl Warren, as well as naming Harry Blackmun, Lewis F. Powell, and William Rehnquist to join the highest court in the land.

MOVING TO THE RIGHT

For someone like Ruth Ginsburg, who followed legal developments closely, it was no surprise that the Supreme Court moved significantly to the right under Nixon's conservative appointees.

One Nixon appointee to the Supreme Court, William Rehnquist, would eventually preside over the 1998 impeachment trial of President Bill Clinton, a man who would play a major role in RBG's career. That was, of course, in the future.

> **FIRST SINCE HOOVER**
>
> Harrold Carswell and Clement Haynsworth were also nominated to the Supreme Court by Richard Nixon but those nominations were rejected by the Senate. Along with accusations of financial impropriety, Haynsworth was rejected for his previous rulings as a circuit court judge on union representation and school desegregation. Carswell, a district court judge, was not only shunned by civil rights groups for his earlier support of segregation, but earned a footnote in history when one apparently well-meaning Senator argued unsuccessfully for Carswell saying, "Even if he is mediocre, there are a lot of mediocre judges and people and lawyers, and they are entitled to a little representation, aren't they?" Nixon's failed Supreme Court nominations were the first to be rejected since the doomed Herbert Hoover administration in the 1920s.

Some in the legal field knew that as a past clerk to Justice Robert H. Jackson, as noted in de Hart (2018), Rehnquist "had drafted a memo arguing against *Brown v. Board of Education* and racially integrated schools" (166). Rehnquist also gave testimony to Nixon that was unsupportive of the Equal Rights Amendment, writing a memo stating that ERA supporters had a "virtually fanatical" distaste for the differences between a man and a woman as well as a "complete rejection of woman's traditional role" (167).

Even after having had almost half a dozen victories before the Supreme Court, an astute observer like Ruth Ginsburg could hardly ignore the direction in which things were going. They were unlikely to improve as Nixon's administration wore on.

Nixon was reelected in 1972, but his presidency became bogged down with a distraction of historic proportions: Watergate. In an attempt to spy on the opposition, the "Watergate Scandal" began with a burglary of the Democratic National Committee headquarters at the Watergate complex in Washington, D.C. The scandal consumed his administration from 1972 until 1974, when Nixon resigned.

At the time when Nixon resigned from the presidency in the wake of Watergate, Ruth Ginsburg was teaching at Columbia University and writing briefs for the ACLU in New York. She had no way of knowing how the Watergate complex would figure into her future.

FORD TO CARTER

After Richard Nixon resigned, Republican Gerald Ford finished out Nixon's presidential term. Ford, the former Speaker of the House, had risen to the vice presidency after Nixon's second term began due to the resignation of Nixon's original vice president, Spiro Agnew, who was accused of financial irregularities.

Upon Nixon's resignation, Ford became the only person in U.S. history to serve as both vice president and president without being elected. Therefore, as he did not have to campaign, he did not have to specify for the voters the kind of Supreme Court nominee he would favor.

During his time in office, President Ford made only one appointment to the Supreme Court, nominating John Paul Stevens in 1975 to replace the ailing William O. Douglas. While in Congress, Gerald Ford had attempted to impeach Justice Douglas for what Ford called the "liberal opinions" held by Douglas.

By the time of the 1976 election, some felt that the country was ready for a change after Watergate, Ford's unpopular pardon of Nixon, a stagnating economy, and the nation's unsatisfying exit from the Vietnam War. Evangelists from the Religious Right were bemoaning what they saw as the country's decline in patriotism and morality. A little-known Georgia governor, Democrat Jimmy Carter, defeated the Republican Ford in the 1976 election, but it was not by a landslide. Campaigning as a political moderate and Washington outsider, Carter won a majority of the popular vote, but only by 50.1 percent. Some said he carried the south because he was a southerner. Ford won 27 states, the most states ever carried by a losing candidate.

Therefore, when Carter took office, it was not by an overwhelming mandate. Ruth Ginsburg correctly observed that the Supreme Court had shifted to the right and showed little chance of moving toward a middle ground. The movement toward gender equity that she had successfully argued at the Supreme Court could not be expected to continue forever. Her career as a litigator might well face an uphill and ultimately unsuccessful battle. Ruth and Martin Ginsburg began to consider various options for the next phase of their lives.

EERILY FAMILIAR

During the presidential administration of Jimmy Carter, there were no vacancies that occurred on the Supreme Court. Carter completed his four-year term of office without the opportunity to make any appointments whatsoever to the Supreme Court.

On the other hand, there were some judicial appointments that *were* within his power to make. They will still significant positions, and they were underrepresented by women and minorities.

In 1976, when Carter was elected, only 11 women served on the federal bench among 505 judgeships. That number was eerily close to the situation

20 years before, when Ruth entered Harvard Law School in 1956 as one of 9 women in a class of more than 500 men. The United States had progressed in many ways between 1956 and 1976, including taking "one small step for a man" on the moon, but there had not been "one giant leap" for womankind onto the federal bench.

However, under Carter, there was a real possibility that things would change. In 1978, Congress passed the Omnibus Judgeship Bill that was intended to establish more than 100 new judgeships. They would address the increase in district court case filings and appeals court filings. Intended to relieve massive backlogs in federal court cases, it was the largest number of judgeships ever created by a single act of Congress. The bill required the president to establish standards and guidelines for the selection of judges on the basis of merit.

It could not have escaped Ruth Ginsburg's attention that at the White House signing ceremony for the Omnibus Judgeship Bill, Carter made a point of noting the scarcity of women and minorities on the federal bench. He also made a point of stating that his appointments would be more than token representation. Combined with the merit standard, that meant quality as well as quantity.

Carter was making good on his campaign promises to women, including one particular voter, his wife, First Lady Rosalynn Carter. By the time his one-term presidency came to an end in 1980, Carter had appointed 41 women to serve as federal judges.

BACKLASH

In 1977, Martin and Ruth Ginsburg enjoyed the chance to see the world beyond New York City by spending a semester at Stanford University in California. Marty taught a course in tax law as he had been doing at New York University (NYU) while Ruth earned a prized fellowship at Stanford's Center for Advanced Study in Behavioral Sciences. It was an interdisciplinary research program to study areas of anthropology, economics, political science, psychology, and sociology. The elite program annually hosted a small group of scholars who, like Ruth Ginsburg, studied ways to gain deeper insight into human behavior.

Even before her study at Stanford, someone as observant as Ruth would have noted what was happening around her. The historic victories she had won for gender equality were becoming the victim of backlash, from those who saw her as moving too slowly as well as others who saw her moving too fast.

There was dissention and fragmentation within the women's movement itself. Rumors were picked up by the news media and male pundits that

Betty Friedan clashed with Gloria Steinem over the group's leadership and direction the movement should take. Some women felt forced to take sides, while others tried holding their ground with a sense of "united we stand, divided we fall." The conflict within the movement was fanned by outside sources, gleeful that one of the criticisms of Gloria Steinem by other women was that Steinem was too attractive.

What Karbo (2018) calls "the common wrong-headed thinking" was that "only plain women want equal rights because they aren't hot enough to attract a husband" (47). Karbo goes on to ask what happened when a beautiful wife's husband died, divorced her, or was abusive. In 1974, a woman still could not get a credit card in her own name. There was no actionable recourse until 1977 if a boss demanded sexual favors from a woman in order to keep her job. Karbo (2018) cites the powerful editor of the *New York* magazine who said that child care was the only real problem for women: "If they just imported more nannies, everything would be fine" (47).

Someone as perceptive as RBG would have known there was change in the air amid the general resurgence of conservatism. Her project at Stanford was an account of her litigation for equal rights. However, she was aware that there was much more work to be done. Perhaps there was another way to do it.

HAPPY HOME

To some, Ruth appeared to be the calm at the center of the cultural storm that was swirling around her in the late 1970s. Apart from her usual quiet demeanor, there was indeed an added sense of serenity that stemmed from her personal life at this time.

Ruth's daughter Jane graduated from the University of Chicago with a bachelor's degree in 1976 and a master's in 1977. Like her mother, Jane then entered Harvard Law School, receiving her law degree in 1980. Unlike her mother who, as one of only nine women, was one of only 2 percent of her law school class to be female, the percentage by Jane's time in the late 1970s had risen to more than 15 percent, or about 75 females in a class of 500. In 1977, the *Harvard Law Review* named its first female editor, Susan Estrich. By 1978, the 23-year-old Jane Ginsburg earned her own spot on the *Law Review* as her mother had done, a historic landmark as the first mother and daughter to do so.

After graduation from Harvard Law in 1980, Jane was hired as a clerk for the U.S. Court of Appeals in Philadelphia. Carving out a distinguished career as an expert in copyright law, Jane later taught at Columbia Law School, becoming the first mother/daughter duo to serve on the same law

> ### THE PARENT TRAP
>
> Ruth Ginsburg was teaching at Columbia University, running the ACLU's Women's Rights Project, and in her spare time, litigating cases in front of the U.S. Supreme Court. She also had an 11-year-old son, James, who attended an elite New York City school. His brand of spirited behavior occasionally prompted calls to her from school officials. One day, James acted on a dare by taking off in the school's manually operated elevator by himself, an infraction that was forbidden to students. After having stayed up all night writing a legal brief, Ruth Ginsburg received a call in her office at Columbia from James's school, wanting her to appear in person to discuss his transgression. She informed them that the boy had two parents, and to please alternate calls between herself and her husband. There were no quick changes in the boy's behavior but the number of calls from school officials dropped dramatically since they were presumably reluctant to interrupt busy fathers at *their* jobs.

faculty in the United States. The Ginsburgs had reason to be proud of their daughter settling into the "family business."

James Ginsburg, Ruth and Marty's son, attended elite private schools in New York City. Growing up, he was showing signs of enjoying the classical music that Ruth and Marty adored, having begun collecting records of classic music at an early age. James would later go on to be the founder of his own classical record label, Cedille Records, based in Chicago, where he attended college. Apart from some youthful antics as a boy, he was a source of energy in the household and a joy to his parents.

By the late 1970s, Ruth and Martin Ginsburg had been happily married for more than a quarter of a century. Marty still treated Ruth like she was a treasure he had won because, in his unassailable confidence, he felt he was entitled to the top prize. As a partner at the law firm of Weil, Gotshal and Manges, Marty had risen to the top of his field. Although he was respected nationwide as a tax attorney, he enjoyed his part-time teaching at NYU as well as his visiting professorship at Stanford during 1977–1978. It appeared to some that he might not have been averse to making a change, even joining a law school faculty on a regular basis.

SOMETHING DIFFERENT

When the new judgeships under Jimmy Carter opened up in the late 1970s, Martin Ginsburg was as always a cheerleader for the possibility of Ruth's attaining one, even if it meant making a move toward something different.

When a position appeared on the horizon at the U.S. Court of Appeals based in New York City, Ruth submitted her name as a prospect. If she was granted that position in 1979, there would have been some delightful symmetry as it was at the same courthouse where Ruth had clerked for Judge Palmieri in 1959, a full 20 years earlier.

Friends and colleagues wrote strong letters of support for her. When Ruth arrived for her interview with the deciding panel, she had a measure of confidence that, based on merit, she stood a good chance to be selected.

What she could not have anticipated was that the all-male panel consisted of men who were Wall Street corporate attorneys asking questions about securities law. It was a field in which Ruth Ginsburg claimed no expertise. Nor, if she was selected as a judge, would securities law be the only area in which she would have to adjudicate. She answered to the best of her abilities, but the panel called an abrupt halt to the interview, berating Ruth for her lack of expertise in their area of the law.

Ruth experienced an awkward echo from the past. In 1959, working as a summer intern at a private law firm after she graduated from law school, she had hoped to be offered a job. Instead, the firm had hired Pauli Murray, who was African American as well as female, the firm's "two for one."

Twenty years later, in 1979, the Wall Street lawyers who were interviewing for the federal judgeship on the New York Appeals Court were under pressure by the Carter administration to nominate women and minorities. They tapped Amalya Kearse, an African American woman who worked at a major corporate law firm. She was the first woman and second African American (after legendary civil rights advocate and future Supreme Court Justice Thurgood Marshall) to serve on the New York Appeals Court.

THE D.C. CIRCUIT

In 1979, RBG received an interesting invitation from former U.S. Senator Joseph Tydings of Maryland. As a respected attorney, he was chairing the selection committee for two judicial posts under the Carter-era Omnibus Judgeship Bill on the U.S. Court of Appeals for the District of Columbia Circuit, often abbreviated simply as the D.C. Circuit. Another member of the selection committee was none other than Erwin Griswold, former dean at the Harvard Law School when RBG was a student.

As a lawyer, Tydings had argued *Eisenstadt v. Baird* before the U.S. Supreme Court in 1972. In what has been called one of the most influential Supreme Court decisions of the twentieth century, Tydings successfully argued for the legalization of birth control for single persons—something that had been denied in many states.

Once again, Ruth's friends and colleagues wrote strong letters of support for her nomination. She made the list of finalists, but the night before the decision was made public, Tydings phoned her to say that the vacancies went to other people. However, he assured her that there would be other posts available on the D.C. Circuit if RBG was still interested, which she was.

The U.S. appeals courts are powerful and influential, deciding appeals from federal district courts. They are able to set precedent, and are often the final step in the judicial process before the U.S. Supreme Court. Like Supreme Court justices, federal appeals court judges are nominated by the president of the United States and confirmed by the Senate. Also like the justices of the Supreme Court, judges in the U.S. courts of appeals have lifetime tenure.

Apart from the D.C. Circuit's jurisdiction in Washington, federal appeals courts can be found geographically across the country, serving districts in Boston, New York City, Philadelphia, Richmond, New Orleans, Cincinnati, Chicago, St. Louis, Denver, and San Francisco.

SUDDEN DEATH PLAY-OFF

When another vacancy on the D.C. Circuit occurred in late 1979, President Jimmy Carter nominated an African American, Harry T. Edwards. However, in November 1979 there was a sudden death among the judges, creating an unexpected vacancy. Carter's advisors met to discuss possible nominees, including Ruth Ginsburg. However, one top-level advisor heard that Ginsburg had been turned down for the Circuit Court in New York, expressing the opinion that if she was not good enough for New York, she was not good enough for D.C.

Ultimately, Ginsburg supporters prevailed but the news of her probable nomination leaked to the media, angering Carter's Attorney General who delayed the announcement process. At the same time, in late 1979, there were other issues that the Carter administration was facing: gasoline shortages, spiraling inflation, the Russian invasion of Afghanistan, and even competition from Ted Kennedy against Carter for the Democratic Party's presidential nomination in the 1980 election.

On top of those troubling situations, a shocking event blindsided both President Carter and the rest of the country. Beginning on November 4, 1979, it was something that aroused tremendous media attention as well as the nation's ire: the Iran Hostage Crisis. Muslim extremists stormed the U.S. Embassy in Tehran, holding 52 Americans as hostage for 444 days. As 1980 began, it was not the best time for the Carter administration.

Nor was it a good time for supporters of Ruth Ginsburg's nomination to the D.C. Circuit. Going into an election year, there were rumblings that Jimmy Carter might not be reelected. The winner of the presidency might well be a conservative Republican who would nominate someone from the right wing, with Ginsburg frozen out.

IT'S ALL POLITICAL

As the calendar turned from 1979 to 1980, Ruth Ginsburg continued with her teaching work at Columbia, although she was moving away from her involvement with the ACLU. A solid staff at the Women's Rights Project, the majority of whom she had recruited, was carrying on the ACLU's work in the field of gender equality.

After the news leak about Ginsburg's possible appointment to the D.C. Circuit, storm clouds gathered over Washington. Matters were made far worse by Carter's delay in officially naming her. Being dependent on presidential nomination, a federal judgeship on the D.C. Circuit was considered a political appointment. The problem with political appointments is simply that they are *political.*

Criticism of potential nominees will surface not necessarily because of qualms about the qualifications of the individual but in order to hurt the person who champions the nomination. In this case, going into an election year, that person was Jimmy Carter. His delay in making his selection for the judgeship official meant that opposition forces had a lot of time to gather strength.

Even women's groups launched a few broadsides against Ginsburg, a woman who had so ardently fought for gains in gender equality. Some felt

---

Bad Tydings

At this time, RBG was being attacked from both sides, either for being too liberal or too conservative. No one knew how it felt to be assaulted from both the left and the right better than Senator Joseph Tydings (1928–2018), the man who invited her to apply for the D.C. Circuit. In his quest for reelection to the Senate in 1976, Tydings was attacked by left-wing liberals for his support of a District of Columbia crime bill that was perceived as repressive against African Americans. On the other hand, he also sponsored a firearms licensing act that would have required the registration of weapons. Although Tydings was himself an avid hunter, the latter aroused ire from right-wing conservatives, the gun lobby, and the National Rifle Association. Assailed from both the left and the right, Tydings was defeated in the race against Congressman Paul Sarbanes, who went on to serve as U.S. Senator from Maryland for more than a quarter of a century.

she had not done enough, or that it was too little, too late. Some were livid that Ginsburg had chosen to argue cases that had *male* plaintiffs. The president of the National Organization for Women (NOW) issued a press statement about Jimmy Carter's perceived lack of support for women's issues. She declared her refusal to endorse his bid for reelection, a move that infuriated Carter. Politically astute Ginsburg supporters were aghast, fearing RBG's nomination would be derailed.

Therefore, Ginsburg supporters were thrilled and relieved when she was eventually nominated officially by President Jimmy Carter to a seat on the U.S. Court of Appeals for the District of Columbia Circuit on April 14, 1980, a few months before the presidential election. But any celebration was premature, as she had yet to be confirmed by Congress.

SECRET WEAPON

On Capitol Hill, where Ruth's nomination would have to be ratified, the opposition was lying in wait. News media regularly reported on the drama of their mounting hostility. Some members of Congress were angry at Jimmy Carter. They saw his previous nominees for judgeships as being too liberal in general and they did not want another.

Ohio congressman John Ashbrook labeled her a "militant feminist" who could hardly be expected to judge impartially. Philip Crane of Illinois predicted that, as a judge, Ginsburg would bring about a "vast revolution" in American society.

There were two individuals who were especially critical to her confirmation. Republican South Carolina Senator Strom Thurmond, usually described to his delight as an archconservative, claimed Ginsburg was a "one-issue woman," dismissing her candidacy.

The other was Democrat Ted Kennedy of Massachusetts, who chaired the Senate Judiciary Committee. He might have been seen as a strong ally for Ginsburg with the committee, but he was busy campaigning for the Democratic presidential nomination against fellow Democrat Carter, who had put Ginsburg's name forward.

However, Ruth had a secret weapon: Martin Ginsburg. Friends said he would have been outraged if his smart, talented wife was not considered. He enthusiastically spread the news that Ruth received the highest rating from the American Bar Association. He also noted that individuals on his client list as a tax attorney might be in a position to help. Some were friends with congressmen, and they arranged things like private luncheons to meet Ruth as a person rather than see her as simply a name on a résumé. After meeting informally, most came away recognizing her commitment to gender equality as well as being scholarly, fair-minded, and interested in other issues as well as they pertained to the point of law.

In June 1980, during her confirmation hearing for the D.C. Circuit, Ruth emphasized the strong relation between an appellate judgeship and legal scholarship. On the bench there would be ample time to study, consider the matter at hand, and make a sound judgment after conferring with colleagues. She minimized her past association with the ACLU and maximized her work in academia. She made it clear that she was far more comfortable in the role of a researcher than a litigator.

There was testimony against her from groups that claimed to be family-oriented, declaring that on the bench, Ruth Ginsburg would put families in danger. But on June 17, 1980, the committee's vote was 8–1 in RBG's favor with Thurmond as the only dissenter. Full congressional ratification soon followed.

Ruth Bader Ginsburg was confirmed for a seat on the U.S. Court of Appeals for the District of Columbia Circuit on June 18, 1980, receiving her commission later that day.

At age 47, Ruth Ginsburg, the top-ranked law school student who couldn't get a job, was now a federal judge. When she met with President Carter to receive her commission, she wore her mother Celia's circle pin.

MAKING A MOVE

In 1980, Ruth and Marty, finding it to be a good time for their family, were both comfortable making a move to Washington, D.C. Daughter Jane, having earned her law degree at Harvard, was on her way to a clerkship in nearby Philadelphia. Son James was 14 and was accepted at the Georgetown Day School, an elite prep school that was founded in 1945 as the first racially integrated school in Washington, D.C. Georgetown Day School, running through the 12th grade, is noted for having educated the children of high-ranking government officials, including the son of Supreme Court Justice Thurgood Marshall.

As a partner in the top-notch New York law firm of Weil, Gotshal and Manges, Martin Ginsburg was able to transfer his affiliation to the law firm of Fried, Frank, Harris, Shriver, and Jacobson, often abbreviated as Fried Frank. The firm had offices in Washington, D.C., as well as in New York City. Marty would go on to implement a tax department at Fried Frank, contribute to the development of tax policy, and earn further recognition as one of the nation's top tax lawyers.

Widely quoted as telling friends that his wife had gotten "a good job in Washington, D.C.," he and Ruth just needed to find a place to live.

HOME SWEET WATERGATE

Some call it the second most famous address in Washington, after the White House. Originally called Watergate Towne and designed as a self-sufficient city within a city, the name "Watergate" became synonymous with the Nixon-era scandal that consumed much of the nation's energy and newsprint between 1972 and 1974.

There was another "gate" tied to the Watergate, this one during Bill Clinton's presidential administration. The so-called Monicagate scandal of 1998 involved a young White House intern named Monica Lewinsky who was the next-door neighbor of Bob and Elizabeth Dole. When the grounds of the Watergate began swarming with reporters, Ms. Lewinsky moved out. Neighbors said the young woman wrote notes apologizing for any inconvenience she may have caused.

For some residents, it may have echoed the media barrage at the Watergate that accompanied the Nixon-era burglary at the former Democratic National Committee headquarters located on the sixth floor of the office complex. However, no notes of apology were known to have been received at that time.

THE "JUDGE'S JUDGE"

On June 30, 1980, Ruth Bader Ginsburg began her term serving as a federal judge of the U.S. Court of Appeals for the District of Columbia Circuit. On that day, the D.C. Circuit heard an average case with an average title: *State of New Jersey, Department of Environmental Protection, Petitioner, v. United States Environmental Protection Agency and Douglas M. Costle, Administrator, Respondents, state of Missouri, Environmental Improvement Division of The New Mexico Health and Environment Department, Department of Pollution Control and Ecology of the State of Arkansas, Department of Environmental Quality Engineering of The Commonwealth of Massachusetts, District of Columbia, State of Maine, W. Edward Wood, Director of Department of Environmental Management of the State of Rhode Island And Providence Plantations, Peter A. A. Berle, Commissioner of Environmental Conservation of the State of New York, State of Connecticut Department of Environmental Protection, The Agency of Environmental Conservation of the State of Vermont, State of Georgia, Department of Natural Resources, Division of Environmental Protection, City of New York, Intervenors.*

It was by no means the longest-titled case the court would hear throughout RBG's tenure on the D.C. Circuit.

A small sample of other cases heard by the judges soon after RBG took her place on the D.C. Circuit included such titles as *Kennedy for President Committee, Petitioner, v. Federal Communications Commission and United States of America, Respondents, American Broadcasting Companies, Inc., CBS Inc., National Broadcasting Company, Inc., and Public Broadcasting Service, Intervenors* on August 6, 1980. Another was *Morton H. Halperin, Appellant, v. Central Intelligence Agency* on August 7, 1980.

One that concerned matters in the court's back yard soon after RBG became a resident of the nation's capital was *Don't Tear It Down, Inc., Appellant, v. Pennsylvania Avenue Development Corporation et al* on October 2, 1980.

During her time as a judge on the D.C. Circuit, Ruth Ginsburg often confounded observers as she worked to find consensus with colleagues, including conservatives Robert Bork and Antonin Scalia. She quietly earned a reputation as a cautious jurist and a moderate. As reflected in Senator Joseph Biden's acknowledgment of RBG when she became a nominee for the Supreme Court in 1993, she earned the reputation of being a "judge's judge."

WALKING THE WALK

Whatever Ruth Ginsburg did not know about the issues arriving at the D.C. Circuit, she characteristically set about learning as quickly as possible. This entailed long hours at the office that went far into the night. Meanwhile, the ever-patient Marty and less patient son James waited at their apartment to have dinner with her. According to her son, the dinner hour was usually around 9:00 p.m., after Marty called her office repeatedly, trying to extricate her from work in order to come home.

She found that the judges of the D.C. Circuit worked each case in panels of three, all trying to persuade other members of the panel to join their opinion on each case. The judges had clerks, and Ruth set out to establish a friendly tone in her office as she had done at the ACLU. Impeccable work ethic, high standards, and dedication to the job at hand were expected as standard operating procedure for her clerks, but those requirements were leavened with kindness, sensitivity to their personal lives, small gifts, and to some, the best part: gourmet treats from Chef Martin Ginsburg.

Marty did more than just cook. He attracted an impressive group of clients to his tax practice at Fried Frank. But he also found that his expertise in tax law was matched, if not exceeded, by his enjoyment of teaching. He joined the faculty of Georgetown University Law Center in 1980, focusing his emphasis primarily on the Internal Revenue Code.

On the court, Ruth was highly ranked among legal sources, proving to skeptics among both liberals and conservatives that she was a moderate. She was a defender of equal rights for minority groups as well as free speech and freedom of information. Defending the separation of church and state, she supported religious freedom.

Her support of equal treatment for minority groups was not simply a case of "talking the talk" from the bench. She and Marty also "walked the walk" by resigning from a prominent Washington-area country club that changed its rules so that African Americans could not belong. In this case, the exclusion concerned a fellow D.C. Circuit judge, African American Harry Edwards and his wife.

To some observers, her friendship with conservatives like Judges Bork and Scalia proved baffling. But she enjoyed their wit and intelligence even if she did not always agree with their opinions. Ginsburg's cheerful willingness to cross ideological lines helped secure of reputation as a centrist who showed respect for colleagues and careful consideration of issues across the board. Critics who had labeled her a "militant feminist" who would bring about a "vast revolution" in American society found that they had little to complain about.

NOT JUST BUSINESS AS USUAL

On July 7, 1981, about a year after Ruth Ginsburg took the bench as a federal judge, the day began with business as usual for the D.C. Circuit. They would be hearing the case of *Refrigerated Express Lines (a/Asia) Pty., Ltd., Petitioner, v. Federal Maritime Commission and United States of America, Respondents, Hamburg-Sudamerikanische Dampfschiffahrts-Gesellschaft, Eggert & Amsinck, Farrell Lines Incorporated, Associated Container Transportation, Ltd., et al., Australian Meat and Livestock Corp., Intervenors.*

Before the day was over, however, President Ronald Reagan dropped a bombshell, making good on a campaign pledge. During his 1980 run for president, he had promised to appoint a woman to the U.S. Supreme Court for the first time in its 200-year history. On July 7, 1981, he announced that his choice for the newest Associate Justice of the Supreme Court would be Judge Sandra Day O'Connor who was then serving on the Arizona State Court of Appeals

After the announcement, Reagan formally nominated O'Connor on August 19, 1981. Several Republican senators claimed they would not support her nomination. Nonetheless, she was confirmed by the U.S. Senate on September 21, 1981, with a vote of 99–0, including those who said they would oppose her. One senator who was absent that day later sent O'Connor an apology for missing the vote.

> ### BURGER'S BEEF
>
> Republican senators who claimed they would not support Reagan's appointment of Sandra Day O'Connor as the first woman named to the Supreme Court appeared to rethink their position when it came down to the vote. Justice O'Connor was confirmed unanimously by the Senate. Those legislators were not the only ones who made threats about where they stood regarding female appointees. According to *Sisters in Law* by Hirshman (2016), back during the Nixon administration there was some talk around Washington of the political gain to be scored by appointing a woman to the Supreme Court. Warren Burger, Chief Justice at the time, threatened "to resign if the president polluted the court with a woman" (47). Not only did Burger fail to resign but on September 25, 1981, Sandra Day O'Connor is seen in photographs being sworn in to the Supreme Court by none other than Chief Justice Warren Burger. Apparently Burger had put his threat on the back burner.

"WOW" FACTOR

Bill Clinton was sworn in as president of the United States on January 20, 1993. Less than a month later, on February 11, he selected Janet Reno as the first woman to serve as U.S. Attorney General, which seemed a hopeful sign to many.

But by that time, Clinton had already been begun experiencing problems. Prior to choosing Reno, his nominations for Attorney General, Zoe Baird and Kimba Wood, were derailed in what came to be called "Nannygate" when it became known that there were irregularities by both nominees in paying Social Security taxes for household help.

At this time, Supreme Court Justice Byron White announced his impending retirement. White, with more than 30 years on the Court, had been appointed in 1962 by President John F. Kennedy and by 1993, was the only one of the nine justices then serving on the Court who had been appointed by a Democratic president. Clinton had the chance to name the first Supreme Court nominee by a Democrat since Lyndon Johnson appointed Thurgood Marshall.

According to de Hart (2018), Clinton "wanted to hit a home run with his nominee—a person to whom people would respond with 'Wow'" (302). The "Wow" factor finalists included District Judge Richard Arnold, Secretary of the Interior Bruce Babbitt, federal judge Stephen Breyer, New York governor Mario Cuomo, Senate Majority Leader George Mitchell, and South Carolina governor Richard Riley—all white males. For many observers, the response was not an enthusiastic "Wow."

Clinton eventually decided none would do. In one case, a background check showed the individual had not paid Social Security taxes for a housekeeper. It was exactly the kind of thing that had caused Clinton embarrassment a few months earlier when he had to withdraw the names of his nominees for Attorney General in "Nannygate."

And according to Carmon and Knizhnik (2015), "Mario Cuomo, Clinton's favorite, backed out mere minutes before the president was about to offer it to him" (78).

WOMEN AGAINST HER

Then a name was brought to Clinton's attention: Federal Judge Ruth Bader Ginsburg. According to de Hart (2018), at age 60 Ginsburg was considered by some to be too old as well as too "remote and bookish" (305).

But she also had advocates. Some noted her role as a consensus builder on the D.C. Circuit, often being a swing vote between conservatives and liberals. Others pointed out that her landmark legal victories in the 1970s had left such a lasting imprint on American society that by 1993, they were taken for granted. The latter point was meant to combat attacks on Ginsburg from women's groups who felt she had not done enough to militantly further their cause. Still, their complaints got back to Clinton, leading him to state, "The women are against her" (de Hart 2018, 316).

Then, unsolicited documents arrived at Clinton's office that could only be called "blasts from the past." One was from New York's powerful Senator Daniel Patrick Moynihan. It contained a strong letter of support for Ginsburg from her former dean at Columbia Law School, Michael Sovern, who had since become president of Columbia University. The other was a copy of a speech by Erwin Griswold, her former dean at Harvard Law School, who had spoken at a Supreme Court event recognizing three advocates for their contribution to changing the law: the NAACP's Charles Houston and Thurgood Marshall for race relations, and Ruth Bader Ginsburg for her work in the field of gender equality.

Once again, RBG's secret weapon worked behind the scenes. Martin Ginsburg reminded friends, colleagues, and high-profile tax clientele that his wife Ruth had earned the highest possible rating from the American Bar Association. As many of his tax clients were Republicans, he underscored her appeal by pointing out that in 1991, Ruth was named as one of the nation's leading centrists in the *American Lawyer* magazine. He also wrote articles and had breakfast meetings with leaders of women's groups, refreshing their memories on all Ruth had done for their cause over the past two decades.

On Friday, June 11, 1993, the D.C. Circuit was hearing cases including *Gold Coast Restaurant Corporation d/b/a Bryant & Cooper Steakhouse, Petitioner, v. National Labor Relations Board, Respondent.* When the judges returned after the weekend, on Monday, June 14, they would be hearing *Federal Labor Relations Authority, Petitioner, v. United States Department of Justice, Immigration and Naturalization Service, United States Border Patrol, San Diego, California, Respondent.*

Between those two sessions of the D.C. Circuit, Ruth Bader Ginsburg had a life-changing meeting with Bill Clinton.

SUNDAY BEST

RBG has stated publicly that she had an idea she was in the running as a Supreme Court nominee. But she and Marty had gone to Vermont for a weekend wedding after being told by White House staffers that they were free to do so while Clinton was considering his choices. Then she received a call in Vermont from White House staff on Saturday evening, June 12, asking her to come to Washington immediately. As she was in Vermont, she asked if the meeting could be held the next day, on Sunday morning.

Staffers agreed, telling her to come immediately from the airport to the White House. This concerned Ginsburg, who said she would not have time to change out of her traveling clothes. She was told by staff that it was no problem as Clinton would be coming directly off the golf course. As it happened, Clinton had decided to go to church that morning and, according to Ginsburg, he walked into the interview "dressed in his Sunday best."

However, she says, the president put her at ease. Late that night, she received a phone call from Clinton offering her the job of Associate Justice of the U.S. Supreme Court.

When a White House team later came to the Ginsburgs' Watergate apartment to check out their finances, Marty made lunch for them. The investigators found the couple's taxes and financial information to be in perfect order. There was no unpaid Social Security for household help nor were there any undocumented workers, issues that had tripped up Clinton's nominees for other positions. The investigators said they never saw anyone as well prepared as the Ginsburgs, crediting tax lawyer Marty with keeping such meticulously accurate records. In truth, it was Ruth Ginsburg who handled the family's finances.

On Monday, June 14, 1993, President Bill Clinton officially nominated Federal Judge Ruth Bader Ginsburg to the Supreme Court.

OTHER SIDE OF THE COIN

That day, the public nomination ceremony was held in the sunny Rose Garden of the White House. Ruth Bader Ginsburg was dressed in a cobalt blue suit adorned with her mother Celia's circle pin. (The full text of her speech can be found in this book in the PRIMARY SOURCE DOCUMENTS.)

Among the general comments and expressions of appreciation, there was one significant passage that proved memorable to those in attendance. "I have a last thank-you," she said. "It is to my mother, Celia Amster Bader, the bravest and strongest person I have known, who was taken from me much too soon. I pray that I may be all that she would have been had she lived in an age when women could aspire and achieve, and daughters are cherished as much as sons."

The other side of the coin was that RBG still had to undergo Senate confirmation. If that did not go well, she would remain a judge on the D.C. Circuit, never making it to the Supreme Court. And Senate confirmation hearings did not always go well.

Many people vividly recalled that two years before, the confirmation hearings of the most recent previous Supreme Court nominee, Clarence Thomas, had turned into a lurid media circus. With a vote of 52–48, Thomas was barely confirmed by the Senate. Six years before, in 1987, the Senate rejected Supreme Court nominee Robert Bork.

SUPREME REJECTION

As a student of legal precedent, RBG would have recognized that until she was officially sworn in as a Supreme Court justice, nothing was certain. She might have remained in relative obscurity on the D.C. Circuit. Some nominees almost made it to the high court bench before being -rejected by the Senate. Some who were rebuffed include Alexander Wolcott, who was nominated by President James Madison in 1811, John C. Spencer (Tyler, 1844), George Woodward (Polk, 1845), Jeremiah Black (Buchanan, 1861) Ebenezer Hoar (Grant, 1869), William Hornblower (Cleveland, 1893), Wheeler Peckham (Cleveland, 1894), John J. Parker (Hoover, 1930), Clement Haynsworth (Nixon, 1969), Harrold Carswell (Nixon, 1970) and Robert Bork (Reagan, 1987). Wheeler Peckham was rejected after a powerful senator lobbied against him. When the opposing senator fell out of favor the next year, President Cleveland nominated Wheeler Peckham's own brother, Rufus Peckham, who was quickly confirmed. Bork's name entered the national lexicon as a synonym for being damaged by harsh political opposition. Most quietly recovered from the Supreme snub, joining each other in the pantheon of "Footnotes to History."

Only days before the Rose Garden ceremony for Ruth Ginsburg, Clinton had been forced to withdraw his nomination of Lani Guinier for Assistant Attorney General due to what were called her controversial writings. The Guinier situation had followed close on the heels of the debacles that had involved nominations of two other high-profile women, Zoë Baird and Kimba Wood, for Attorney General.

On July 20, 1993, Ruth Bader Ginsburg's first day of Senate hearings began. Although she appeared to be calm, nothing was certain. In the contentious world of political appointments, she could well have been going back to the D.C. Circuit due to factors beyond her control.

SWARMED

A curious thing happened as Ruth Ginsburg walked through the halls of the Capitol. With her distinctive appearance, she was recognized by tourists who swarmed around her after seeing her on the news at Clinton's nomination ceremony. As politicians are usually not known to be reluctant about being part of a positive photo opportunity, another group joined the throng, Senators began clustering around Ruth, wanting their pictures taken with her.

At RBG's side was her life partner, Martin Ginsburg, who had played a huge role in her career to this point. Their daughter, Jane, and her husband, Paul Spera, who she had married in 1981, were with them that day, along with Ruth's grandchildren, Paul and Clara Spera.

As the family watched, Ruth Bader Ginsburg took her place in front of the Senate Judiciary Committee. Chaired by Senator Joe Biden, it consisted of Democrats and Republicans. Two women, Democratic Senators Dianne Feinstein and Carol Mosely Braun, had been added to the committee since the time when it had been an all-male group interrogating Anita Hill during the Clarence Thomas hearings. Also on the committee was Republican Senator Strom Thurmond who had dismissed Ruth Ginsburg's candidacy for the D.C. Circuit back in 1980 by calling her a "one-issue woman."

For four days, from July 20 through July 23rd, Ruth was questioned. She remained composed in her response to questions. Some observers characterized her as looking like a small, watchful bird. She politely declined to answer a few questions, as they concerned issues that had the potential to come before the Supreme Court, stating it would be inappropriate for her to comment in advance of seeing all the evidence. (Excerpts from RBG's hearing can be found in the PRIMARY SOURCE DOCUMENTS.)

Among pundits, some expressed a fear that she would go back to being a "liberal activist." Others were afraid she would go the other way, coming under the sway of her friend Antonin Scalia, a conservative who was then sitting on the Supreme Court.

In the end, Ruth Bader Ginsburg won the unanimous vote of the Judiciary Committee. The confirmation vote in the full Senate was 96–3 in her favor. With Senator Donald Riegle absent, only three conservative lawmakers voted against her. They were Jesse Helms, Robert C. Smith, and Don Nickles. Nickles had earned an unwelcome political footnote when, during a 1986 campaign rally, President Ronald Reagan accidentally called him Don Rickles, the comedian.

Until the moment when the Senate vote was formally finalized, Ruth's nomination for the Supreme Court was not a sure thing. But after the vote was announced, it was official, and she left the D.C. Circuit where she had served for 13 years. Ruth Bader Ginsburg of Brooklyn was now the 107th justice of the Supreme Court of the United States.

As quoted by newscaster Joel Brown, RBG asked, "What is the difference between a bookkeeper in New York's Garment District, which my mother was, and a Supreme Court justice? And my answer is, one generation."

It is hard to imagine what her mother, Celia, the former bookkeeper, would have thought.

SOURCES

Brown, Joel. "Hundreds Line Up to Hear Justice Ruth Bader Ginsburg Speak in Raleigh," *abc11*, September 23, 2019. https://abc11.com/politics/hundreds-line-up-to-hear-justice-ruth-bader-ginsburg-in-raleigh/5562079/.

Carmon, Irin, and Shana Knizhnik. *Notorious RBG: The Life and Times of Ruth Bader Ginsburg.* New York: Dey Street Books, 2015.

De Hart, Jane Sherron. *Ruth Bader Ginsburg: A Life.* New York: Knopf, 2018.

Hirshman, Linda. *Sisters in Law: How Sandra Day O'Connor and Ruth Bader Ginsburg Went to the Supreme Court and Changed the World.* New York: Harper Perennial, 2016.

Karbo, Karen. *In Praise of Difficult Women: Life Lessons from 29 Heroines Who Dared to Break the Rules.* Washington, DC: National Geographic Books, 2018.

"Nixon," *American Experience Films*, Aired October 15, 1990. https://www.pbs.org/wgbh/americanexperience/films/nixon.

7

Supreme Court: The Great Dissenter

On August 10, 1993, Martin Ginsburg held the Bible with an expression on his face that, as seen in photographs, can only be described as "beaming." At the White House ceremony, with President Bill Clinton looking on and dignitaries in the audience, Chief Justice William Rehnquist performed the swearing-in of Ruth Bader Ginsburg as an associate justice of the U.S. Supreme Court.

According to Kalb (1993), looking out among the attendees, RBG "singled out her mother-in-law, Evelyn Ginsburg, for particular praise, telling her she was 'overjoyed' by her presence at the ceremony" (3). Perhaps because Ruth's late mother, Celia, could not be there, having the always-supportive Evelyn was some recompense. Evelyn Ginsburg died the following year at age 86.

Kalb states that dignitaries included former chief justice Warren Burger. He was noted by Hirshman (2016) as having threatened to resign during the Nixon administration "if the president polluted the court with a woman" (47). Apparently, Burger overcame his dread of pollution because in 1981, it was he who had sworn in Sandra Day O'Connor, the first female justice, and on this day in 1993, he also attended Ruth Ginsburg's swearing-in. He passed away before any other women were appointed to the Court.

After prolonged applause and a few remarks by RBG, she was about to embark on a new journey. As part of the Supreme Court in 1993, she would be joining Chief Justice Rehnquist and fellow Associate Justices Harry

Blackmun, Anthony Kennedy, Sandra Day O'Connor, Antonin Scalia, David Souter, John Paul Stevens, and Clarence Thomas.

THIRD BRANCH

The mission of the Supreme Court is to be the defender and interpreter of the U.S. Constitution. Subsequent to the Judiciary Act of 1869, the number of Supreme Court judges, called "justices," is set at nine, of which five form a majority.

Therefore, only five people in the United States determine what is and is not constitutional.

Since 1935, the justices of the Supreme Court meet in a four-story white marble Corinthian-style building at 1 First Street NE, in Washington, D.C. The Supreme Court building is located one block away from the U.S. Capitol. The Court was originally housed in cramped office space within the Senate wing of the Capitol. The Founding Fathers may have smiled when a separate building was approved for the Court. That detachment, literally and figuratively, was the effect they were aiming for.

At the 1787 Constitutional Convention, the framers of the Constitution debated the separation of powers between the executive and legislative branches of government. Then they broke with the English tradition that they had roughly followed in establishing a government for the new American nation. They created a third branch to serve as the nation's highest judicial authority, keeping a balance with the other two portions of government, the legislative and executive, or in other words, Congress and the presidency.

The inscription engraved over the main doorway to the Supreme Court Building—EQUAL JUSTICE UNDER LAW—is not derived from the Constitution or any significant legal pronouncement. The Fourteenth Amendment to the Constitution containing the Equal Protection Clause states that no person shall be denied "the equal protection of the laws." However, with the size of the letters to be used, the words designated to be carved there by the building's architectural team led by Cass Gilbert was a matter of spacing: the shorter phrase fit perfectly into the allotted spot on the pediment over the main doors.

Another short phrase is often used in current jargon as an abbreviation referring to the Supreme Court of the United States: SCOTUS. According to the Merriam Webster dictionary, the suffix "OTUS" was first used in telegraphic code during the late 1800s as an abbreviation for "Of The United States" in order to save space when denoting governmental offices. SCOTUS was the earliest to appear, as listed in an 1879 telegraphic code just after "scndrl" (short for "scoundrel"). There is no record of POTUS, for "President of the United States," being used until 1895.

According to the Supreme Court website, the building that houses the high court is open to the public during normal business hours. But despite that level of accessibility, much of the work of the Court is not generally accessible or known to the public. According to Toobin (2008), "the Court by design keeps its operations largely secret from the outside world" (3).

Woodward and Armstrong (2005) go a step further in their book about the Court, thanking the *Washington Post* and publisher Simon & Schuster for support, stating that no other newspaper or book publisher would have been "willing to assume the risks inherent in a detailed examination of an independent branch of the government whose authority, traditions, and protocols have put it beyond the reach of journalism" (XIII).

SECRET HANDSHAKE

Since around 1800, it is traditional for justices to wear black robes while in Court, which is meant to convey dignity and seriousness of purpose. However, the justices have occasionally been known to personalize them, such as Chief Justice William Rehnquist's addition of four gold stripes on the sleeve or Ruth Bader Ginsburg's addition of her "jabot," an ornamental decorative collar.

In a nod to the earliest days of the court, white quill pens are placed on counsel tables each day that the Court sits for oral arguments. Many attorneys keep their quills, prizing them as souvenirs of their day at the Supreme Court. Under the watchful eye of U.S. Marshals, the attorneys and visitors to the Court wait patiently in the courtroom for oral arguments to begin promptly at 10:00 a.m.

Before the justices enter the courtroom from the Robing Room comes the "Judicial Handshake." Each justice shakes hands with each one of the other eight individuals. This has been a tradition since the late 1800s as a reminder that they are colleagues and that differences of opinion on the Court do not preclude overall harmony of purpose. Then, in three groups of three, the justices enter the courtroom through openings in the heavy red drapes.

BEHIND THE SCENES

There are a number of staffers behind the scenes at the Supreme Court who are unknown to most Americans. It even has its own law enforcement agency, the Supreme Court of the U.S. Police, established when the Court moved to its own building in 1935 in order to protect justices, employees, and visitors.

Supreme Court justices each hire an average of four law clerks to help with the volume of work. Clerks generally serve for one or two years. After leaving, to have the Supreme Court clerk credit on a résumé usually means a stepping stone to a bright career. Most law clerks are high-ranking and highly recommended recent graduates of top tier law schools and often served on the law review. It was the kind of position Ruth Bader Ginsburg had been well prepared for and hoped to find after attaining all of those distinctions—top graduate, exemplary recommendations, and law review—but did not due to open gender bias.

SUPREMES' GREATEST HITS

Ruth Bader Ginsburg knew that when she arrived at the Supreme Court for the session that officially began in October, she would no doubt be a part of history. What she probably did not anticipate was arriving at her chambers to find her secretaries in what Kanefield (2016) calls "a panic" after receiving "a phone call from a woman who said, 'Tell Mrs. Ginsburg she will not live to sit on that Court'" (235).

Despite that, the weekend before she was due at the Court, RBG spent several days very publicly celebrating family events, albeit guarded by U.S. Marshals. One occasion was a ceremony at Harvard with her daughter, Jane. Another was celebrating her granddaughter Clara's third birthday at the Supreme Court building. Children's birthday parties are not usually held at the Supreme Court, but as an adult, Clara has said publicly that her grandmother wanted her to know from an early age that a seat at such an imposing edifice—indeed, any position, anywhere—was possible for a little girl like her. As she had done when she was juggling Harvard Law School, Marty's illness, and caring for their toddler Jane, RBG may have welcomed the time spent with her family as a life-affirming respite in the face of unpleasantness like death threats.

JUST ENOUGH

Having argued six cases at the Supreme Court, Ruth Bader Ginsburg was no stranger to the courtroom when she arrived at the Court's marble temple as a high court justice herself. When her first term sitting on the Supreme Court bench began on October 4, 1993, she found that there were more than 1,600 cases for review and over 45 cases with which she had to be familiar immediately.

She selected second-floor office space that overlooks a quiet, sunny interior courtyard away from the busy street. Books and photos line much of RBG's available space. A picture of her late mother, Celia, occupies a place of honor on the desk.

Situated prominently at her Supreme Court office is the biblical imperative that was imprinted in her mind as a young girl, the phrase from Deuteronomy 16:20: "Justice, justice shall you pursue."

Ruth Bader Ginsburg has said publicly that Sandra Day O'Connor was especially helpful to her as a new arrival. After spending a dozen years as the only woman on the Court, Justice O'Connor offered advice that RBG has said was "just enough" to help her navigate those early days without being overwhelmed.

When it came time for RBG to be assigned her first opinion for the Court, she was dismayed to find it was not a decision with which she could ease her way as a newcomer into the demands of the job, but a complex matter on which the Court was split. Going to Justice O'Connor for guidance, RBG was told to do it as quickly and as well as possible before the next round of assignments by the Chief Justice, or face a similarly dreadful one next time. When RBG read her first, difficult opinion aloud from the bench, according to Carmon and Knizhnik (2015), Justice O'Connor passed her a note saying, "This is your first opinion for the Court. It is a fine one, I look forward to many more" (113). Those authors add that in years to come, RBG carried on the same tradition of approval and support for female justices Sotomayor and Kagan.

When RBG arrived, there was one critical need that needed to finally be addressed at the highest court in the land. It was a situation that was not unfamiliar to Justice Ginsburg, going back to law school days. In the Justices' Robing Room just off the courtroom, the only bathroom was labeled "Men." For 12 years as the only woman on the Court, Justice O'Connor had to make other arrangements when the need arose. RBG has said publicly that after her own arrival, "they rushed through a renovation. They created a women's bathroom equal in size to the men's." She said she saw it as a good sign that women were there to stay.

Both of the female justices knew that they were being scrutinized. RBG has noted publicly that she once unintentionally asked a question before Justice O'Connor followed up on one of her own, thinking O'Connor was finished. RBG apologized for inadvertently stepping in, whereupon Justice O'Connor said it was no problem, that the male justices did it to each other all the time. Yet the headline in a national newspaper the next day read, "Rude Ruth Interrupts Sandra."

It became fairly commonplace for attorneys arguing before the Court to address RBG as "Justice O'Connor" as there had been only one female voice on the Court for a dozen years. A short time after RBG joined they Court, both female justices were honored by the National Association of

> ### BATHROOM HUMOR
>
> When RBG arrived at the Supreme Court, the only restroom in the Justices' Robing Room, located near the courtroom where they worked, was for men. It was a recurring theme for Ginsburg and other pioneering women who stepped out into the world. In a positive development, between the time Ruth was at Harvard Law School in 1953 and more recent years, there have been changes such as having more than just one women's restroom among the various buildings at Harvard Law. At Columbia Law School, the bathroom issue came up again for RBG, both as a student and later as a professor. Since she was a prized faculty recruit, the dean of Columbia Law converted half of the spacious men's room into a ladies' restroom for female faculty, even playfully offering the suggestion of putting flowers in the porcelain fixtures that had served as urinals. Nor was the issue of women's bathrooms unique to law schools or the judicial branch of the government. In 1933, when Hattie Caraway became the first woman elected to the United States Senate, the restroom just off the Senate chamber was for males only. Caraway served in the Senate until 1945 and was followed by several other women serving full terms. She may or may not have been surprised to learn that female senators finally did get a restroom of their own—in 1993, half a century later.

Women Judges. The group presented the justices with two T-shirts, one for Justice O'Connor that read "I'm Sandra, Not Ruth" and the other for Justice Ginsburg stating "I'm Ruth, Not Sandra."

RBG has said publicly that she enjoyed serving with Justice O'Connor because it showed that even though they were so different in many ways—appearance, background, ideology—they showed that women had varying opinions about many different issues. Neither female Justice could be said to represent *all* women.

RIGHT AND TIGHT

Beginning from her early days on the Court, Justice Ginsburg and her staff settled into a productive routine. Her law clerks have said that under RBG's guidance and example, they were obliged to make sure their research was impeccably accurate. They also needed to keep it as free of legal jargon and lengthy, confusing verbiage as possible so that average people could understand it. The mandate was to "get it right and keep it tight."

They were also obliged to practice courtesy. According to Kanefield (2016), Justice Ginsburg once had a clerk who was arrogant and rude to a secretary. Annoyed at such behavior, RBG allegedly told her clerks,

"If push came to shove, I could do your work—but I can't do without my secretaries" (237).

Justices, clerks, and secretaries are all part of the Supreme Court process, although most of it happens without fanfare or headlines. Any case that makes it all the way to the Supreme Court is tremendously important to the participants involved in the suit. However, apart from setting precedent, many of those cases do not generate headlines or substantially alter the course of American life. The cases RBG heard during her first term as a Supreme Court justice concerned a broad spectrum of jurisprudence even though they are not the a cases for which she became famous. Whether or not they were of special interest to her is unknown. Still, she had to formulate a legal opinion on all of them.

On October 12, 1993, about a week after she settled in at the Court, the case of *Albright v. Oliver* was heard. It involved a warrant by Illinois police to arrest an individual who was allegedly seen selling a substance that look liked an illegal drug. After various legal twists based on probable cause, the question was whether a citizen prosecuted without probable cause could obtain relief for the deprivation of due process rights. In a 7–2 decision, with RBG joining the majority, the Court said No.

A JUSTICE'S FIRST YEAR

As RBG's first year on the Court wore on throughout the 1993–1994 term, she and the other justices heard cases like *Barclay's Bank, PLC v. Franchise Tax Bd. of California* (whether multinational corporations must provide a disproportionately large amount of financial information to calculate taxes, thereby violate the anti-discrimination requirement), *Davis v. United States* (regarding whether a police interrogator must stop questioning until the suspect is provided with counsel after the suspect makes an ambiguous reference to having an attorney), and *West Lynn Creamery, Inc. v. Healy* (whether a Massachusetts pricing order was a breach of the Commerce Clause).

All of those cases, like the others in RBG's early years on the Court, were important to those who were involved. Whether or not they were of special interest to the justices, including Justice Ginsburg, is unknown. However, a few cases from RBG's first year may well have been.

J.E.B. v. Alabama ex rel T.B. determined whether the use of peremptory challenges to exclude jurors solely because of their gender was a violation of the Equal Protection Clause of the Fourteenth Amendment. The Supreme Court's 6–3 decision, including RBG, ruled that it was a violation.

National Organization for Women, Inc. v. Scheidler was argued by invoking the Racketeer Influenced and Corrupt Organizations (RICO) act as to whether RICO requires an organization to have an economic motive to be defined as a racketeering enterprise. The allegation was that anti-abortion protesters constituted a conspiracy to obstruct women's access to abortion clinics through the threat of violence. In a unanimous decision, the Supreme Court held that even those organizations without economic motives can "affect interstate or foreign commerce" and could be defined as a racketeering enterprise under RICO.

Madsen v. Women's Health Center asked if limiting protestors at an abortion clinic to a 36-foot buffer zone and imposing noise limitations were an infringement of the First Amendment right to free speech. In a 6–3 vote, including RBG, the Supreme Court held that protestors could indeed be restricted so as not to interfere with staff and patients, and that limitations on noise were needed to insure the well-being of patients as the noise could not be ignored.

By the end of her first term on the Supreme Court in 1993–1994, RBG had successfully navigated the demands of the job. During the next term, there would be a new justice on the Court, Stephen Breyer, who was the second and final Supreme Court jurist appointed by Bill Clinton. Breyer replaced Justice Blackmun in time for the 1994–1995 high court session.

Midway through the 1995–1996 session, a case was argued at the Court that held echoes of RBG's past and repercussions for the future. It was the first of the cases for which Justice Ginsburg's opinions have made her well known, but it would not be the last.

UNITED STATES V. VIRGINIA (1996)

On January 17, 1996, the Court heard oral arguments in the case of *United States v. Virginia*. The Virginia Military Institute (VMI) was the only exclusively male public undergraduate institution of higher learning in the state of Virginia. It was also funded by public monies. A suit was filed against Virginia and VMI based on the accusation that the male-only admissions policy violated the Fourteenth Amendment's Equal Protection Clause, making it unconstitutional.

After previous court decisions against VMI, the state proposed to create the Virginia Women's Institute for Leadership. VMI, founded in 1839, stated it was unique because of its "adversative method" of education that involved harsh and demeaning treatment that was said to bond its cadets through extreme adversity.

Critics claimed that the Women's Institute for Leadership would not provide its students with the same high degree of military training, nor comparable courses, facilities, or faculty. In addition, it was said that VMI held the kind of status for its alumni that provided them with enhanced career and financial opportunities throughout the rest of their lives.

On June 26, 1996, the high court released a 7-to-1 decision. Justice Antonin Scalia was in the minority, with Justice Clarence Thomas abstaining. The majority held that the male-only policy at VMI was unconstitutional.

The majority opinion was authored and read aloud in the courtroom by Ruth Bader Ginsburg. The opinion stated that the male-only VMI violated the Equal Protection Clause of the Fourteenth Amendment, and VMI could not use gender to deny admission to women.

According to the *Oyez* legal website, "Justice Ginsburg's announcement of the Court's opinion may be considered an address to the American public. It is a plain-spoken and forceful summary of the majority position."

The *Justia* legal website states that VMI considered circumventing the ruling by going private, and thus no longer remaining a state-supported institution. However, the VMI board decided in an 8–7 vote to admit women, which according to *Justia* ended the existence of all-male American public universities.

BUSH V. GORE (2000)

The *Bush v. Gore* matter was the next major case that drew public attention to Justice Ginsburg. In it, the Supreme Court involved itself in the presidential election of 2000 between George W. Bush and Al Gore. The results in the key state of Florida were in dispute. A Florida court ordered that thousands of contested ballots from Miami-Dade County be counted by hand, along with contested votes in other Florida counties because it was alleged that there were enough questionable ballots to cast doubt on the outcome of the election.

The question before the U.S. Supreme Court was whether the Florida court violated the Constitution by creating new election law, which some said was after the fact. Also in question was whether manual recounts—or excluding recounts—violate the Constitution's Equal Protection and Due Process clauses.

The U.S. Supreme Court ordered the recount to be stopped, not hearing oral argument until two days later. Ultimately, the 7–2 decision was issued in favor of George W. Bush, who became president and served from 2001 to 2009. During that time, he appointed two Supreme Court justices. Dissenting were Justices Ginsburg and John Paul Stevens, claiming that the Constitution requires every vote to be counted. RBG also argued that the matter should have been left to the state of Florida's judicial body, and not brought to the Supreme Court. In a later case, *Shelby County v. Holder* (2013), the 5–4 majority stated that *Shelby* was a States Rights issue in which the Court could not meddle, a complete reversal of their action in *Bush v. Gore*. RBG noticed, and said so. (The text of RBG's dissent can be seen in the PRIMARY SOURCE DOCUMENTS in this book.)

LEDBETTER V. GOODYEAR TIRE & RUBBER (2007)

Lilly Ledbetter was a long-time employee and one of the few female supervisors at Goodyear Tire & Rubber. Her life changed in an instant one day when she went to her mailbox. An anonymous person had left a torn piece of paper that turned out to be an internal document listing the salaries of the males who held the same position as Ledbetter at work. The males performed the same job as she did with one notable exception: they were all paid about $15,000 a year more than she was. Ledbetter had faced sexual harassment at the workplace as well as improper advances by superiors, all of which the bosses could simply have denied. But having solid evidence of wage discrimination based on gender, Ledbetter sought justice.

In *Ledbetter v. Goodyear Tire & Rubber*, the Supreme Court voted 5–4 in favor of Goodyear, who claimed that Ledbetter had not filed her discrimination complaint in time. Justice Ginsburg's strong dissent pointed out that Ledbetter could not have filed her complaint sooner for the simple reason that she did not know she was being discriminated against. This is not unusual as many companies have strict rules about employees discussing salaries, in some cases explicitly making it a firing offense. Justice Ginsburg pointed out that pay information "is often hidden from the employee's view" therefore the employee has no way of knowing the facts. She also pointed out that Ledbetter's salary gap did not only pertain to the difference in what she earned while employed, but the cumulative effect of having retirement benefits like Social Security pegged to a person's salary. RBG read her dissent from the bench, making her objection public.

Two years later, on January 29, 2009, President Barack Obama enacted the first piece of legislation of his administration. With Lilly Ledbetter in attendance, he signed the Lilly Ledbetter Fair Pay Act, paving the way more effectively for employees to win claims of pay discrimination. Justice Ginsburg was widely credited with having inspired that law.

SAFFORD UNITED SCHOOL DISTRICT V. REDDING (2009)

Savana Redding was an eighth grader at Arizona's Safford Middle School where administrators said they received an uncorroborated accusation from another student that Savana might have violated school policy by being in possession of ibuprofen. Ibuprofen, sold over the counter under trade names like Advil and Motrin, is used for treating pain in such conditions as migraine headaches or painful menstrual periods. The 13-year-old girl was ordered to strip down to her bra and underpants, then "shaking out" those undergarments so that female officials could search for drugs.

The ACLU represented Savana's mother, April Redding, in *Safford United School District v. Redding*. The suit alleged a violation of her minor child's Fourth Amendment right against unreasonable search and seizure. When lower courts found that the strip search was not justified and the intrusion was not reasonably related to the circumstances, the school district appealed that decision. In an 8–1 vote with Clarence Thomas in the minority, the U.S. Supreme Court held that the girl's rights were violated when school officials unreasonably searched her underwear for the nonprescription painkillers. Some of the male high court justices found the situation humorous, making jokes about items in underwear. This was the case in which RBG's argument contained the fact that none of her male colleagues could fully appreciate the effect of a strip search on the child because none of them had ever been a 13-year-old girl.

CITIZENS UNITED V. FEDERAL ELECTION COMMISSION (2010)

Citizens United is a conservative organization founded in 1988. It brought the *Citizens United v. Federal Election Commission* lawsuit to the Supreme Court in 2010. The high court's ruling found that federal law prohibiting corporations and other organizations from making unlimited political contributions was unconstitutional.

On January 21, 2010, the 5–4 judgment was announced. Observers claimed it was along ideological lines, holding that political spending is a form of free speech protected under the First Amendment. Therefore, the majority said, corporations or other organizations cannot be restricted from giving money to denounce or support political candidates through such means as deprecating movies, advertisements, etc. Justices Ginsburg, Breyer, Sotomayor, and Stevens dissented. RBG warned of money's corrupting influence in the politics of a democracy, later stating publicly, "If there was one decision I'd overrule, it would be *Citizens United*."

NOT A JOT LESS

At the Supreme Court, the Spring term of 2010 brought other cases that were not always as far-reaching as *Citizens United*. Still, they were highly important to the people involved in bringing the suit, and were treated as such not only for the plaintiffs but also for future citation as precedent. Out of more than 10,000 cases submitted annually, the Supreme Court only selects about 75 to be heard each year.

Some of those considered by RBG and the other justices during the Spring 2010 session included *Carachuri-Rosendo v. Holder*, regarding whether a minor drug offense is automatic grounds for deportation of a legal immigrant. *Dolan v. U.S.* concerned a federal statute providing defendants to make restitution to their victims within 90 days after sentencing. *Monsanto Company v. Geertson Seed Farms* involved genetically engineered alfalfa seeds.

On June 24, 2010, as the Court was ending its term for the year, the justices issued their opinion on *Doe v. Reed*, regarding whether disclosing the identity of persons who sign petitions for ballot referenda violates the First Amendment if it could expose the signers to harm.

During the past few months, Ruth and Martin Ginsburg also had concerns at home. Marty had been carrying on with his characteristic good cheer, although he was increasingly experiencing severe back pain. He continued his endeavors as a gourmet cook even though he was in more and more pain standing up in the kitchen. Finally, doctors were able to diagnose the problem as a tumor growing near his spine.

Doctors eventually declared it was metastatic cancer. It was spreading, and there was nothing more to be done. Near the time of their 56th wedding anniversary on June 23, Marty was brought home from the hospital so he could at least enjoy the peaceful surroundings.

The day he was released from the hospital was June 25, the day Ruth's mother, Celia, had died. At age 78, Marty died at home on Sunday, June 27, 2010. The next morning, Monday, June 28, Justice Ginsburg was on the bench to read the majority opinion on the final day of the Court's term. She has said publicly that she and the family believed that is how Marty would have wanted it.

Although said to be pale and subdued, RBG read the majority opinion in *Christian Legal Society Chapter of University of California, Hastings College of Law v. Martinez* in which the justices found that a public college does not abridge the First Amendment by declining to acknowledge a student group that refuses to permit all students to join.

The session had opened that day with Chief Justice John Roberts reading a statement about the death of Martin Ginsburg. According to the *New York Times*, Marty was praised for being "an accomplished lawyer and law professor known for his sharp wit and gourmet cooking" (n.p.). As the Chief Justice read his statement, Justice Antonin Scalia, a close friend of the couple and RBG's occasional nemesis, "seemed to wipe away a tear" (n.p.).

In a private ceremony, Martin David Ginsburg was buried at Arlington National Cemetery. His gravestone reads, "Caring citizen, advocate, teacher, and family man."

It was also on that same day, June 28, 2010, that Elena Kagan, the first female dean of Harvard Law School, began confirmation hearings as the country's fourth woman to serve on the Supreme Court.

SHELBY COUNTY V. HOLDER (2013)

A few years later, another monumental case came before the Supreme Court. It would affect both jurisprudence and the trajectory of Ruth's life. In *Shelby County v. Holder*, the question before the Court was grounded in the Voting Rights Act, which Congress had enacted in 1965. The basis for the suit goes back to the years following the Civil War as well as the civil rights era a century later. The Constitution's Fourteenth Amendment (1868) was intended to protect every citizen's right to due process of law. The Fifteenth Amendment (1870) granted African American men the right to vote by stating that the right of citizens to vote "shall not be denied or abridged by the United States or by any state on account of race, color, or previous condition of servitude."

During the Jim Crow era, those rights and protections were severely limited for African Americans. Therefore, the Voting Rights Act of 1965 was enacted to prohibit districts from making changes to their election laws that could curtail the right to vote without gaining authorization from the federal government. Shelby County, Alabama, filed suit.

The question before the Supreme Court was whether the pertinent section of the Voting Rights Act that involved making those changes violated the Constitution. In a 5–4 decision, the high court found for Shelby County, claiming that the requirement was based on old data that was no longer valid 50 years later.

Justices Breyer, Kagan, and Sotomayor joined Justice Ginsburg in disagreeing. Since that time, RBG has been widely quoted in her famous dissent as stating that throwing out the relevant provision of the Voting Rights Act when it was working to stop discriminatory actions "is like throwing away your umbrella in a rainstorm because you are not getting wet."

After the Supreme Court's *Shelby* ruling, several states subsequently passed laws to make voting more difficult for many. News sources including the *New York Times* and *USA Today* reported that within a few years after *Shelby*, hundreds of polling places, many in predominantly African American and Hispanic areas, were shut down. The Leadership Conference on Civil and Human Rights reported that 1,688 polling places were closed by 2018. A report by the Pew Charitable Trusts noted that there were also moves in some states to block early voting for college students.

BURWELL V. HOBBY LOBBY STORES (2014)

Hobby Lobby, an arts and crafts chain, has more than 500 stores nationwide, employing about 13,000 people. Because of religious beliefs claimed by the owners, they refused to offer healthcare benefits that included contraception. The Supreme Court ruled 5–4 in favor of Hobby Lobby's religious exemption.

RBG dissented, stating that the decision affected not only Hobby Lobby but any employer from then on who does not wish to provide insurance coverage for birth control or other health-related areas if it is said to conflict with the employer's religious beliefs. In her dissent, Justice Ginsburg argued that the ruling prevented women from obtaining contraceptive care, jeopardizing the health and well-being of female employees. In the high court's ruling that a for-profit business can claim an exemption on religious grounds, she said, "The Court, I fear, has ventured into a minefield."

HONORABLE MENTION

The cases outlined above were some of the most noteworthy in which RBG has been involved, either for her spot with the majority or for her minority opinion. There are also some others that legal sources consider worthy of mention during her career on the high court bench. Details of each can be found at the *Oyez.org* website.

In 1997, for example, Justice Ginsburg issued the Court's opinion for the 6–3 ruling in *United States v. O'Hagan*. This case concerned the issue of a security trader who fails to disclose personal profits gained from exclusive information.

In Justice Ginsburg's majority opinion, the Court found that the trader knowingly abused his fiduciary duty. The Supreme Court held that in *O'Hagan*, the U.S. Securities and Exchange Commission has the authority to take actions reasonably designed to prevent fraudulent acts. It may have been a flashback to the unpleasant federal court interview RBG had experienced years before with the disapproving panel of Wall Street lawyers. Here, she spoke for the majority in decrying some Wall Street practices.

The question in *Friends of the Earth v. Laidlaw Environmental Services* during the high court's 2000 session was whether a civil suit by an environmental group under the Clean Water Act becomes moot when the defendant comes into compliance after the start of the litigation. The Supreme

Court's answer in a 7–2 opinion delivered by Justice Ginsburg was No. The majority held that a claim for civil penalties need not be dismissed when the defendant comes into compliance after litigation begins. Writing for the Court's majority, Justice Ginsburg stated that civil penalties in cases involving the Clean Water Act not only promote compliance but also deter future violations.

Eldred v. Ashcroft (2003) asked whether extending existing copyrights under the 1998 Copyright Term Extension Act's exceed the power of Congress. It also asked if the extension of existing and future copyrights violate the First Amendment. In RBG's 7–2 majority opinion statement for the Court, the answers were No and No. The Court ruled that Congress acted within its authority. Nor did it breach its constitutional limitations regarding future copyrights. The Court also found that extending existing and future copyrights does not violate the First Amendment. Only Justices Stevens and Breyer dissented. In this decision, Justices Ginsburg and Scalia, who were often seen as adversaries, were on the same side.

SCALIA/GINSBURG

On June 26, 2013, the Supreme Court handed down its 5-4 ruling on a difficult case, *United States v. Windsor*, concerning same-sex marriages. The Court found in favor of same-sex couples, with the majority consisting of Justices Ginsburg, Breyer, Kagan, Kennedy, and Sotomayor. Opposing the decision were Justices Scalia, Alito, Roberts, and Thomas. Although the ruling itself concerned a controversial issue, one thing remained constant: close friends Ruth Bader Ginsburg and Antonin Scalia (1936–2016) were, as was so often the case, on opposite sides of the fence. The very next day, on June 27, 2013, composer Derrick Wang entertained the Supreme Court by premiering scenes from his new opera, *Scalia/Ginsburg*, subtitled *An American Comic Opera in One Act Inspired by the Opinions of U.S. Supreme Court Justices Ruth Bader Ginsburg and Antonin Scalia*. After its launch at that auspicious venue, *Scalia/Ginsburg* has been presented to sold-out crowds around the country, garnering rave reviews. Opera-loving justices Ginsburg and Scalia wrote prefaces to the libretto, which has been published in the *Columbia Journal of Law and the Arts*. As noted on the website http://www.derrickwang.com/scalia-ginsburg, a number of performances of *Scalia/Ginsburg* were scheduled for election year 2020, including in Florida, site of the contentious Supreme Court decision concerning the outcome of 2000 presidential election. The *Los Angeles Times* review of the opera offered a suggestion: "Could we please make it a constitutional requirement that no one can be sworn into office in the White House or Congress without having first seen *Scalia/Ginsburg*?" It is not known if such a prerequisite will be enacted, but if the legislative branch follows the judicial, members of Congress might have to get ready for their close-up.

In 2009's *Ricci v. DeStefano*, Justices Ginsburg and Scalia were back on familiar ground: opposite sides of the fence. In the case, whites who were candidates for promotion in the fire department of New Haven, Connecticut, sued when the city's Civil Service Board did not certify certain exams that were required for the plaintiffs to be promoted. They argued that the tests were not certified because the results would have promoted a "disproportionate" number of white candidates in comparison to minorities. They felt this violated their rights under the Civil Rights Act of 1964 and the Equal Protection Clause of the Constitution's Fourteenth Amendment. The question was whether a municipality can reject results from an otherwise valid civil service exam when the results may unintentionally prevent the promotion of minority candidates. The Supreme Court's majority, including Justice Scalia, found that the city of New Haven violated the Civil Rights Act by discarding the exams. Joined by Justices Breyer, Souter, and Stevens, RBG dissented on the grounds that New Haven had cause to believe it would be vulnerable to a lawsuit if the exams were certified.

DISSENT AND LONELINESS

When Justice Sandra Day O'Connor retired to care for her ailing husband in 2006, RBG was left as the only woman on the Supreme Court. She would remain in that lone position for three years. During that time President George W. Bush appointed John Roberts and Samuel Alito to the high court bench.

Before other female justices arrived, it was a time that Justice Ginsburg has said publicly was "lonely." But in 2009, President Barack Obama nominated Sonia Sotomayor to the Supreme Court. RBG would finally be joined on the Court by another woman, a like-minded colleague whose birthday was June 25, the anniversary of Celia Bader's death.

It was around this time when decisions by the 5–4 conservative majority on the Court led RBG to authoring dissenting opinions more and more often.

Dissents are meant to be responses to decisions of the Court when the opinion is something other than unanimous. They show the thinking of other justices. Dissents matter because they offer opposing opinions in cases that have sometimes had repercussions of historical magnitude. Sometimes, the dissenters were found by future generations to have been right all along.

Soon after Justice Sandra Day O'Connor's departure, Justice Ginsburg read her dissents more frequently from the bench. To some observers, doing so signaled her increasingly intense disagreement with what the majority had ruled, especially in the 5–4 votes that many felt were simply along ideological lines.

GOING PUBLIC

Ruth Bader Ginsburg is said to be a modest person who is not primarily driven to garner attention. She is described as someone who would prefer to be part of a unified, collegial decision rather than being an outlier. However, when Justice John Paul Stevens retired in 2010, RBG inherited the role of being the senior member of what is sometimes referred to as the "liberal wing" of the Court. Because of her seniority, she can assign dissents to other justices who take issue with the decision of the majority, or she can write them herself.

Dissents are generally prepared in written form, to be part of the Court's official record. Usually, they are not necessarily read aloud. Court observers began to note that when RBG *did* read dissents aloud, it seemed to be a signal of extreme disagreement with the conservative majority. Justice Ginsburg's dissents appeared to indicate her belief that the majority had made decisions she thought were very wrong on legal and/or moral lines, and wished to make her views known to the public.

"I DISSENT"

In *Bush v. Gore* (2000) for example, results in Florida for the presidential election of 2000 between George W. Bush and Al Gore were in question. A Florida court ordered a recount of the votes but while the hand tabulation was in progress, the Supreme Court ruled 5–4 to stop the recount. The Court then decided the votes could not be counted because they would not be within the timeline laid out in the U.S. Code. That decision effectively handed the presidency to Bush. To use a sports metaphor, Justice Ginsburg and other observers noted that the five men of the Court's conservative majority let the clock run down before then deciding it was too late. In her dissent, Justice Ginsburg said that while the Florida state court and its election officials had performed their duties quickly, the five men of the Supreme Court instigated a self-fulfilling prophecy that the recount could not be done in time—after they themselves had stopped it. In RBG's words, the "conclusion that a constitutionally adequate recount is impractical is a prophecy the Court's own judgment will not allow to be tested. Such an untested prophecy should not decide the Presidency of the United States. I dissent." This was the RBG opinion that observers noted did not, as was customary, include the word "respectfully" in the phrase "I dissent." (See Primary Source Documents.)

CATCH 22

People who did not normally follow the pronouncements of the Supreme Court began scanning online legal sites for Justice Ginsburg's dissents.

One that caught the eye of many people was the 5–4 decision on *Lilly M. Ledbetter v. Goodyear Tire & Rubber* in 2007. Justice Ginsburg wrote the dissent herself. Justices Breyer, Souter, Stevens joined her in arguing against the majority's opinion the Lilly Ledbetter had waited too long to file suit on wage discrimination based on gender. The men of the majority ignored the fact that employees were forbidden to discuss salaries, so Ledbetter had no way of knowing her situation until she received an anonymous document, solid evidence showing the males in identical jobs received $15,000 a year more than she. It was a classic "Catch 22" situation.

When the five men of the majority ruled Ledbetter had waited too long, despite the fact that she had no way of knowing, Justice Ginsburg's dissent argued that each discriminatory paycheck had furthered the injustice. She added that the discrimination against Ledbetter was not all that long ago. "Goodyear continued to treat Ledbetter differently because of sex each pay period, with mounting harm." RBG added, "The realities of the workplace reveal why the discrimination with respect to compensation that Ledbetter suffered does not fit within the category of singular discrete acts 'easy to identify.' A worker knows immediately if she is denied a promotion or transfer, if she is fired or refused employment. And promotions, transfers, hirings, and firings are generally public events, known to co-workers." In those situations, "an employee can immediately seek out an explanation and evaluate it for pretext."

However, in her *Ledbetter* dissent, RBG continues, "Compensation disparities, in contrast, are often hidden from sight. It is not unusual, decisions in point illustrate, for management to decline to publish employee pay levels, or for employees to keep private their own salaries." With employees forbidden to discuss the paychecks, "Goodyear kept salaries confidential; employees had only limited access to information regarding their colleagues' earnings."

It was not just a matter of tens of thousands of dollars in wages while Ledbetter was employed; future Social Security and other retirement benefits are based on earnings. When President Barack Obama signed the Lilly Ledbetter Fair Pay Act of 2009, meant to address such injustice, it was said that Justice Ginsburg's dissent was a deciding factor.

SHAKESPEAREAN PROPORTIONS

Shelby County v. Holder (2013) was the 5–4 decision that involved eliminating certain protections under the Voting Rights Act of 1965. That legislation was intended to end discrimination that was said to be suffered by would-be voters in the South who were African American. Impediments included measures like complicated rules for registration, literacy tests, poll taxes, property requirements, and "white primaries" created by internal political party rulings that only white voters were permitted to participate.

Shelby was the opinion that generated RBG's famed "Umbrella Dissent," that throwing out civil rights protection when it was working was like throwing away your umbrella in a rainstorm because you are not getting wet. But she had a few other thoughts as well. She felt that the majority's opinion was based on the "States Rights" rationale that the federal government should not intervene in electoral policies of individual states, even historically discriminatory ones. Some observers felt intervention into the policies of an individual state was exactly what the majority had done in *Bush v. Gore*, but were now saying they could *not* do.

RBG called the Court's damage to the Voting Rights Act in *Shelby* an act of "hubris," a term used in Greek tragedy to indicate arrogance. She said that when the U.S. Congress prepared the Voting Rights Act prior to its passage, they had approached its elements "with great care and seriousness. The same cannot be said of the Court's opinion today. . . . In my judgment, the Court errs egregiously by overriding Congress' decision."

She did not stop with metaphors from Greek tragedy in her dissent of the majority's ruling in *Shelby*, offering other literary allusions to future repercussions regarding civil rights. RBG stated that the Court ignored the maxim, "What's past is prologue," which she quotes from Shakespeare's *The Tempest*. She also added philosopher George Santayana's pronouncement, "Those who cannot remember the past are condemned to repeat it." (RBG's dissent can be found in the PRIMARY SOURCE DOCUMENTS.)

In another nod to coincidence Shakespeare might have appreciated, the Court's *Shelby* decision was announced on June 25, 2013. RBG's highly publicized response to *Shelby* rocketed her to an unprecedented iconic status. As with the case of *Reed v. Reed* in 1971, RBG's first important case before the Supreme Court, the landmark announcement of *Shelby* came on June 25, the anniversary of her mother Celia Bader's death.

THE MINEFIELD

In 2014, *Burwell v. Hobby Lobby Stores* resulted in a 5–4 decision exempting Hobby Lobby from providing full health insurance benefits to its female employees in light of what the owners said were their religious beliefs. Joining minority Justices Breyer, Kagan, and Sotomayor in her opinion, the 35-page dissent by Ruth Bader Ginsburg swept the internet. "In a decision of startling breadth," she wrote, "the Court holds that commercial enterprises, including corporations . . . can opt out of any law (saving only tax laws) they judge incompatible with their sincerely held religious beliefs."

Many observers interpreted this as an indictment of the Supreme Court conservative majority's decision that essentially authorized businesses with an excuse for not complying with equal protection under the law, in this case affecting women. RBG wrote that such an alternative will always be available to "an enterprise claiming a religion-based exemption." Through its ruling, "[the] Court, however, sees nothing to worry about."

Citing legal precedent and constitutional law, she states that there is an overriding interest in keeping the courts "out of the business of evaluating the relative merits of differing religious claims . . . or the sincerity with which an asserted religious belief is held." She adds that "approving some religious claims while deeming others unworthy of accommodation could be perceived as favoring one religion over another," which the Constitution was designed to avoid. Her ultimate thought on the Hobby Lobby ruling was this: "The Court, I fear, has ventured into a minefield."

Throughout the years that followed, RBG continued to traverse that minefield. She was widely becoming known as "The Great Dissenter." It was a title she shared with Justice John Marshall Harlan who had issued the lone dissenting vote against *Plessy v. Ferguson* in 1896. Harlan had objected to the Court's approval of the "separate but equal" doctrine in matters of race, a ruling that is often cited as one of the Supreme Court's worst decisions.

Justice Ruth Bader Ginsburg earned widespread notice for her legal opinions, especially her dissents. By the time she was in her 80s, RBG also had an intriguing new development in her life. It was one she had never sought but was thrust upon her: stardom.

SOURCES

Carmon, Irin, and Shana Knizhnik. *Notorious RBG: The Life and Times of Ruth Bader Ginsburg.* New York: Dey Street Books, 2015.

"Democracy Diverted: Polling Place Closures and the Right to Vote," *The Leadership Conference on Civil and Human Rights.* https://civilrights.org/democracy-diverted/.

Hirshman, Linda. *Sisters in Law: How Sandra Day O'Connor and Ruth Bader Ginsburg Went to the Supreme Court and Changed the World.* New York: Harper Perennial, 2016.

Kalb, Deborah. "Ruth Bader Ginsburg Takes Oath as First Jewish Justice since 1969," *Daily News Bulletin*, Jewish Telegraphic Agency, August 11, 1993, Vol. 71, No. 150, p. 3. https://www.jta.org/1993/08/11/archive/ruth-bader-ginsburg-takes-oath-as-first-jewish-justice-since-1969.

Kanefield, Teri. *Free to Be Ruth Bader Ginsburg: The Story of Women and Law.* San Francisco, CA: Armon Books, 2016.

Liptak, Adam. "Justices Bid Farewells on Last Day," *New York Times*, June 28, 2010. https://www.nytimes.com/2010/06/29/us/29lastday.html.

Oyez.org. https://www.oyez.org/.

"Supreme Court, The: Home to America's Highest Court, 2010 Edition," *C-SPAN*, December 20, 2010. https://www.c-span.org/video/?297213-1/the-supreme-court-home-americas-highest-court-2010-edition.

Toobin, Jeffrey. *The Nine: Inside the Secret World of the Supreme Court.* New York: Anchor, 2008.

Trachtman, Michael. *The Supremes' Greatest Hits: The 44 Supreme Court Cases That Most Directly Affect Your Life.* New York: Sterling, 2016.

Vasilogambros, Matt. "Polling Places Remain a Target Ahead of November Elections," *The Pew Charitable Trusts*, September 4, 2018. https://www.pewtrusts.org/en/research-and-analysis/blogs/stateline/2018/09/04/polling-places-remain-a-target-ahead-of-november-elections.

Woodward, Bob, and Scott Armstrong. *The Brethren: Inside the Supreme Court.* New York: Simon & Schuster, 2005.

8

Meme Supreme: The Icon

In 2012, Trayvon Martin, an unarmed African American high school student, was shot and killed in Florida while visiting relatives in a gated community. George Zimmerman, who said he was a participant in the neighborhood watch, was charged with murder but acquitted in a highly publicized trial in 2013 after claiming self-defense. The incident ignited a heated national debate about the kind of racial issues that many people felt still simmered just below the surface of life in America.

A year later came the death of an unarmed black man in New York City whose last words to the police who held him down were "I can't breathe," repeated eleven times. Then there would be a week of riots in Ferguson, Missouri, following the shooting of a black teen by a white policeman. After that came riots in Baltimore, Maryland, that were spurred by the death of a young black man while in police custody.

The racially tinged events in New York, Missouri, and Baltimore were still to come when a Supreme Court decision two weeks before the Zimmerman trial caught the attention of Court watchers. On June 25, 2013, the Supreme Court announced its 5–4 ruling in the case of *Shelby County v. Holder*, which rolled back provisions of the Civil Rights Act of 1965.

The Court's announcement certainly caught the attention of civil rights leader John Lewis. Carmon and Knizhnik (2015) state that his skull had been shattered by Alabama state troopers in early 1965 during a peaceful march in Selma, Alabama, about 60 miles from Shelby County (3). The protest group was attacked when they stopped to pray. As chairman of the

Student Nonviolent Coordinating Committee, Lewis, who later became a member of the U.S. Congress, was present at the signing of the Civil Rights Act of 1965.

As seen in video footage of news interviews the day of the 2013 *Shelby* ruling, Lewis said, "What the Supreme Court did was to put a dagger in the heart of the Voting Rights Act of 1965."

According to the website *Politico.com*, Lewis also "drew attention to the fact that none of the justices ever experienced the discrimination that the Voting Rights Act protects against." This was a direct reference to Justice Ginsburg's statement four years earlier in *Safford United School District v. Redding* (2009) in which she pointed out that none of the male justices had ever undergone a strip search as a 13-year-old girl.

COMFORTING PICTURE

Carmon and Knizhnik (2015) state that the 5–4 conservative majority's decision, read by Chief Justice John Roberts, seemed to provide the "comforting picture" that racism "was pretty much over now, and everyone could just move on" (3).

Justice Ruth Bader Ginsburg disagreed. The day before, she had read two dissents aloud, one involving the Court's decision on affirmative action and the other on workplace discrimination. After the *Shelby* ruling the following day, again she read her dissent from the bench. Justice Samuel Alito, part of the conservative majority, was said by sources including the online *ABA Journal* to appear to have shown disrespect by rolling his eyes while she spoke. In any case, Justice Ginsburg continued presenting her historic "Umbrella Dissent."

People who by this time had started seeking out RBG's legal opinions, not only took notice but also took to the internet. After *Shelby*, online postings mushroomed. One group of digital artists created an image of RBG with a crown drawn over her head alongside the slogan, "No Truth without Ruth." Not only did it hit Instagram, but the creators turned it into stickers that they posted around Washington, D.C.

In Cambridge, Massachusetts, a law student drew a comic strip that first showed RBG patiently trying to have a courteous discussion about issues with large men in robes who voiced their support for making life easier "for racist, sexist employers." In the next panel, they claim that "trying to fix racism is racist." In the last panel, with a reference to *Shelby*, they claim that "racism is fixed!" Losing patience after being unsuccessful in responding to them in a civil manner, the "RBG" character finally shouts, "NO." The comic strip went viral on the internet.

T-SHIRTS, MUGS, AND MINTS

Along with generating an audience of millions on the internet, other RBG-related images and slogans started appearing on T-shirts, mugs, pins, posters, and tote bags. There were even mints advertised on Amazon.com with RBG's image on the tin. Called JudgMints, the product came with the tagline, "Don't lose your appeal."

T-shirts became especially popular. They included those printed with "You Can't Spell Truth without Ruth" and the slogan, "Fear the Frill." The latter referred to RBG's "dissent jabot" which had taken on a life of its own as her preferred neckline accessory on days she read aloud her disagreement with the five-man majority.

Another image of RBG on T-shirts modified her hairstyle to mimic that of Princess Leia from the *Star Wars* movies, adding a quote from that series, "You're Our Only Hope." Other *Star Wars* T-shirt variations included, "Help Us RBG" and "The Resistance Never Dies," both with the RBG-as-Princess-Leia graphic.

Yet another T-shirt superimposes RBG's face into the famed "Rosie the Riveter" image. The World War II–era "Rosie" poster had shown a determined-looking woman along with the phrase "We Can Do It!"

The front of one T-shirt shows a judicial gavel into which is carved the initials "RBG," while printed on the back of the shirt are the words in boldface block typography, "Hero/Icon/Dissenter."

One T-shirt emblazoned her picture above the word "dissent." Another showed her portrait alongside the quote, "Women Belong in All Places Where Decisions Are Being Made." Still another shows an RBG portrait with the phrase, "Never Underestimate the Power of a Girl with a Book." Another T-shirt asks the question, "You Down with RBG?" while yet another references her rigorous physical fitness regime, stating "I Workout like RBG."

A T-shirt with a popular culture reference pertains to the fictional universe of Harry Potter with the statement "RBG is my Patronus," which refers to a powerful charm in the Potter world of wizardry. Another T-shirt needs no verbiage, just a stark graphic design of a woman in glasses wearing a black robe and white collar. Yet another T-shirt comes emblazoned with its own pre-printed jabot around the neckline.

NOTABLE QUOTABLES

Some of the T-shirts and posters contained notable quotes pertaining to RBG in which it is helpful to understand the context. A poster-size print has her silhouette serving as the background for the phrase, "Fight for the things you care about, but do it in a way that will lead others to join you." In a 2015 speech at Harvard's Radcliffe Institute for Advanced Study, that sentence was RBG's response when asked what advice she would give to the young women present that day.

Another shows RBG's face with the succinct statement, "LIBERTY AND JUSTICE FOR ALL." While some people believe that phrase comes from the Constitution or Declaration of Independence, it is contained in what is officially called *The Pledge of Allegiance* that was formally adopted in 1945, but was composed for schoolchildren in 1892. It reads: "I pledge allegiance to the Flag of the United States of America, and to the Republic for which it stands, one Nation under God, indivisible, with *liberty and justice for all.*"

A poster shows RBG's photograph with the tagline, "All Them Fives Need to Listen When a Ten Is Talking." Grammatical construction notwithstanding, it makes reference to the five Supreme Court justices who prevailed as the majority in such 5–4 decisions as *Burwell v. Hobby Lobby, Ledbetter v. Goodyear Tire & Rubber,* and *Shelby County v. Holder.* A "ten," as popularized in the 1979 movie *10,* is based on a scale of 1–10 in ranking people, with 10 being virtually perfect.

FORGET PRINCESS

Some of the T-shirts, posters, mugs, and so on include RBG's colleagues as well as herself. One refers to a popular singing group from the 1960s with the tagline "The Supremes." Instead of the vocalists, there are bold black cutout images of RBG with Sandra Day O'Connor, Elena Kagan, and Sonia Sotomayor, the first four women on the Supreme Court. Some omit the graphic and contain only the words "Sandra & Ruth & Elena & Sonia," while others opt for "O'Connor & Ginsburg & Sotomayor & Kagan."

Yet others include a likeness of the four women with the tagline, "FORGET PRINCESS, CALL ME YOUR HONOR."

At Halloween, some trick-or-treaters shun typical princess costumes in favor of Supreme Court robes, jabots, and large glasses.

As might be expected, some T-shirts and posters stretch the boundaries of taste, including one with an image of RBG raising her third fingers in a two-handed gesture. As might also be expected, there are anti-RBG items with crude messages scrawled across the image of her face. If Justice Ginsburg is aware of them, it is likely she has treated them with the same indifference as the death threat that greeted her on her first day at the Court.

Along with her place in history, one reason her image is so distinctive on the RBG-related items is that her appearance is very recognizable and easily caricatured. A search of the internet does not reveal such a cornucopia of items with images of the male Supreme Court justices.

NOTORIOUS

In the cascade of RBG-related items, probably the most iconic was created in 2013 by a New York University law student, Shana Knizhnik. According to Carmon and Knizhnik (2015), she was "aghast at the gutting of voting rights" (6) through the majority's ruling in *Shelby County v. Holder*. Justice Ginsburg's dissent was applauded by many, but it did not alleviate Knizhnik's ire.

Justice Ginsburg has frequently quoted her mother Celia Bader's belief about the futility of wasting your own time by being angry. Celia considered anger to be a useless emotion that takes up time and energy which could be better utilized elsewhere. After being inspired by a classmate, law student Knizhnik put that maxim to work on the internet's Tumblr site with the creation of the "Notorious RBG."

The "notorious" tagline for Justice Ginsburg is a play on her initials "RBG" combined with the "Notorious B.I.G." stage name of rapper Christopher George Latore Wallace (1972–97). A practitioner of "gangsta rap," he was 6'3" tall, weighed 395 pounds at the time of his death at age 25, and was known professionally as Biggie Smalls as well as The Notorious B.I.G. According to the Merriam Webster dictionary, the word "notorious" means something well known and widely discussed, generally unfavorably as in the case of a notorious outlaw.

After Knizhnik noticed her classmate jokingly referring to Justice Ginsburg in the context of the rapper as the "Notorious RBG," that nickname struck a chord. It became part of Knizhnik's internet blog the day of the decision, praising Justice Ginsburg's dissent on *Shelby*. On that day, "The Notorious RBG" meme was born. The date was June 25, 2013. As with other significant points in Justice Ginsburg's life, it was the anniversary of Celia Bader's death.

GOING VIRAL

With rap star Notorious B.I.G. as a basis, "The Notorious RBG" was a juxtaposition of Ginsburg's similar initials, her tiny height of barely five feet tall, and her trailblazing stature as a jurist who is an upholder of human rights against all opposition. Both the blog and the nickname went viral not only on the internet but also out on the street with mugs, tote bags, and T-shirts bearing the Notorious RBG image.

> **WAIT FOR 2058**
>
> Just as Carmon and Knizhnik (2015) refer to the *Shelby* decision as the Supreme Court's majority fictionally declaring "Racism is fixed!" (46), there are those who feel that the efforts expended over a lifetime by Ruth Bader Ginsburg "fixed" the problem of gender equality. In fact, there remains work to be done. In 2019, numerous sources claim that women earn an average of 80 cents for every dollar earned by men. Each year, Equal Pay Day is the date dedicated to raising awareness of the gender pay gap in the United States, with its date symbolizing how far into the year an average woman must work to earn what men earned in the previous calendar year. In 2019, that date was April 2; in 2020, Equal Pay Day is March 31. The good news is that the pay gap recently closed from 78 cents on the dollar to 80 cents. The bad news, making the point that women do not get a discount on what they buy equivalent to their lost earnings, the website https://www.pay-equity.org/day.html features a tongue-in-cheek "coupon" offering "All goods and services 23 percent off for any female bearer." In a 2015 episode of *The Daily Show with Jon Stewart*, a report called "The Future of Gender Wage Equality" cited a study by the Institute for Women's Policy Research which claims that, at its current rate of growth, the time when American women will be paid as much as men for the same work is likely to take place in the year 2058. Stewart says that the 2058 date is "right around the time scientists predict the earth will be covered in water . . . Hope your precious money floats, ladies."

In 2015, Knizhnik partnered with journalist Irin Carmon to publish the book *Notorious RBG: The Life and Times of Ruth Bader Ginsburg*. Its RBG-worthy dedication reads, "To the women on whose shoulders we stand." The book became a best-seller.

Justice Ginsburg is said not to mind the "Notorious" nickname in the least; quite the contrary. She has told interviewers that since she and the Notorious B.I.G. both came from Brooklyn, New York, it was entirely natural. She has also admitted keeping a supply of Notorious RBG T-shirts on hand, some of which she gives as gifts.

Just as the rap music performed by the Notorious B.I.G. alarms some people, RBG's quest for equality against the entrenched hierarchy is also alarming to some. To the opposition, RBG's continuing fight for the equality of all Americans makes her truly notorious.

OPERATIC PROPORTIONS

When the U.S. Supreme Court handed down its 5–4 ruling on *United States v. Windsor* in 2013, concerning same-sex marriages, Supreme Court

Justices Ruth Bader Ginsburg and Antonin Scalia were, as was often the case, on opposite sides of the decision. The next day, composer Derrick Wang brought scenes from his new opera, *Scalia/Ginsburg*, to the Supreme Court. Inspired by the opinions of Justices Ginsburg and Scalia, it may have been a special treat for the two opera-loving justices. They both contributed prefaces to the libretto.

As a recent law school graduate, Wang wanted to double-check the legalities. He wrote to both Justice Ginsburg and Justice Scalia asking permission to use their words, even though Supreme Court decisions and dissents are considered public information. Both justices replied that he did not require their permission.

Along with becoming icons in the *Scalia/Ginsburg* opera about them, Justices Ginsburg and Scalia often attended the opera together after Martin Ginsburg's passing in 2010. Justices Ginsburg and Scalia also appeared onstage portraying non-singing roles in operas like *Ariadne auf Naxos* and *Die Fledermaus* at the Washington National Opera. In a 2016 Kennedy Center opening night production of *The Daughter of the Regiment*, RBG even had lines, which she penned herself. She portrayed the role of the Duchess of Krakenthorp, a character played in the past by performers including Bea Arthur of *The Golden Girls*.

Generally Supreme Court justices and other government officials are not immortalized as opera characters as Justices Ginsburg and Scalia have been. One of the few operas that did so premiered in 1947, *The Mother of Us All*, by Virgil Thomson with a libretto by Gertrude Stein, portrayed Susan B. Anthony's struggle for women's right to vote. Public figures who appear in that opera include John Quincy Adams and Ulysses S. Grant.

Another, *Nixon in China*, by composer John C. Adams and his librettist Alice Goodman, premiered in 1987 and features President Richard Nixon, First Lady Pat Nixon, and presidential advisor Henry Kissinger as characters.

LIVE FROM NEW YORK

For those like Justice Ginsburg who love opera, being immortalized in an operatic context may be a rare treat. However, even at its most popular, opera rarely attracts millions of audience members on a single night.

Although being immortalized operatically is a rare distinction, becoming an icon of popular culture, as Ruth Bader Ginsburg has done, is arguably more so. Beyond that, it is an unlikely path for a Supreme Court justice.

On television's popular satiric program *Saturday Night Live* (*SNL*), comedian Kate McKinnon has presented Justice Ginsburg as a tough-talking rabble rouser in a caricature whose demeanor has little to do with the actual woman. But the underlying truth is that Justice Ginsburg is unafraid to speak truth to power in the cause of human rights. McKinnon's parody even spawned a catchphrase for gaining the upper hand: "Ya just got Gins-burned!"

To many, being featured on *SNL* is the pinnacle of pop culture iconography. No other Supreme Court justices have become recurring characters on *SNL*.

In August 2019, some saw signs of pop culture nirvana when Kate McKinnon came face to face with Justice Ginsburg herself. In a coincidental encounter, both McKinnon and RBG separately attended a production of *Fiddler on the Roof* in New York City. McKinnon introduced herself, and the smiling pair posed for innumerable photos as the audience was said by online sources to have "gone crazy" for RBG.

To paraphrase *SNL*'s tagline, "Live from New York, it's Saturday Night!" many people were thrilled to see RBG "live" in New York amid the constantly swirling rumors of her health.

SUPERPOWERS

Ruth Bader Ginsburg has suffered health issues that would have sent many other people into a downward spiral. Instead, with what seemed to many to be the powers of a superhero, she bounced back, not missing a day in court.

To highlight a few, in 1999, at age 66, RBG was diagnosed with colon cancer that required surgery, chemotherapy, and radiation therapy. Through it all, she did not miss one day at the high court bench.

Instead of slowing down when her body became physically weakened by the cancer treatment in 1999, she stepped it up. At her husband Marty's urging, RBG began working with a personal trainer. Bryant Johnson is a 30-year Army veteran, former paratrooper, and Army reservist attached to Special Forces Airborne. He and Justice Ginsburg have trained together twice a week since 1999, with her fitness improving to the point that in a well-publicized event, she completed 20 push-ups just prior to her 80th birthday.

With Justice Ginsburg's permission, Bryant Johnson published a book in 2017 called *The RBG Workout: How She Stays Strong . . . and You Can Too!* The fitness book is illustrated with drawings of RBG herself. The book became a best seller, and the workout it described became fodder for late-night talk show hosts like Stephen Colbert who challenged themselves to completing the routine and failed.

RBG's physical strength would be needed at the years rolled by. In 2009, at age 76, she was diagnosed with pancreatic cancer, one of the most deadly conditions. She underwent surgery and returned to work when the high court went back into session ten days later. About six months after that, she was again hospitalized for lightheadedness after a treatment for iron deficiency.

In 2014, at age 81, she had a stent placed in an artery leading to the heart after experiencing chest pain during her workout with Bryant Johnson. Then, in 2018, at age 85, she fell in her office at the Supreme Court, fracturing three ribs. Falls and fractures are often devastating to older people. She was taken to the hospital but was back at work the next day.

Cancerous nodules in her lungs were discovered during an examination of her ribs following the fall. In December 2018, she underwent surgery to remove the cancerous nodules. For the first time in a quarter century at the Supreme Court, the 85-year-old Ginsburg missed oral argument in January 2019 in order to recuperate. By mid-February, she was back.

RESIGNED TO IT

To many people, it sometimes seems as though both opponents and supporters of RBG clamor periodically for her to resign due to her age and

---

SEEMS LIKE OLD TIMES

RBG has regularly declined to step down when some people suggest she resign due to her age. They may not realize she has precedent on her side. Justice Oliver Wendell Holmes (1841–1935) took his seat on the Supreme Court at age 60, like RBG. Holmes retired in 1932 at age 90. Justice John Paul Stevens (1920–2019) retired in 2010, also at age 90. Roger B. Taney (1777–1864) sat on the Supreme Court until 1864 when he reached the age of 87. Justice Harry Blackmun (1908–1999) stepped down in 1994 at age 86. Hugo Black (1886–1971) was the first of nine justices nominated by President Franklin Roosevelt and outlasted almost all of them, retiring in 1971 during the Nixon administration at age 85. It is not only Supreme Court justices who show remarkable longevity. At age 96, comedian George Burns (1896–1996) signed a lifetime contract with Caesar's Palace in Las Vegas to perform stand-up comedy there, with the lucrative contract negotiated by Burns's 85-year-old business manager. Singer Tony Bennett (1926–) continued his recording career and onstage performances into his 90s. Bennett became the oldest living artist to hit the charts of the Billboard Hot 100 and kicked off a tour with Lady Gaga when he was 88. Comedian Bob Newhart (1929–) had a recurring role on TV's *The Big Bang Theory* in his late 80s. At age 97, fashion icon Iris Apfel (1921–) signed a modeling contract with global agency IMG. Following Apfel's example, modeling might be a new career opportunity for the always impeccably attired Ruth Bader Ginsburg whenever she might decide—on her own terms—to leave the Supreme Court.

past health issues. During the presidential administration of Barack Obama, some people who styled themselves as progressives called upon Justice Ginsburg to retire so that Obama would be able to appoint a successor who held similar values. They noted that if a Republican was elected president in 2016, that person might not nominate a choice who leaned toward liberalism.

RBG has deflected those calls for her resignation, stating publicly that she planned to remain on the high court bench as long as her memory is sharp and she can perform the job well. What may not have been clear to those who called on her to resign is that much of the operation of the Supreme Court relies exclusively on seniority. At the time of this writing, she is the most senior of the justices in the Court's "liberal" wing and the second most senior justice overall.

In declining to leave the Court, RBG points to her former colleague, Justice John Paul Stevens, who had been nominated in 1975 by President Gerald Ford. After 35 years of service at the Supreme Court, he retired in 2010 at age 90.

HALL OF FAMER

The honors and recognitions that have steadily come to Justice Ginsburg have not been a recent development. Even before going to the Supreme Court, she was already receiving recognitions. When she was a circuit court judge, honorary degrees came her way from institutions including American University, Amherst College, Brooklyn Law School, Georgetown University Law Center, Hebrew Union College, Lewis and Clark College, Rutgers University, and Vermont Law School.

After RBG took her place at the Supreme Court in 1993, the awards and recognitions have become virtually too numerous to name. One of the most significant was her induction into the National Women's Hall of Fame in 2002. The people of Seneca Falls, New York, created the Hall of Fame in 1969 with their website's stated belief that "the contributions of American women deserved a permanent home in the town where the fight for women's rights began." The Seneca Falls Convention was held there in 1848, launching what historians cite as the official start of the women's suffrage movement.

According to the National Women's Hall of Fame in Seneca Falls, it is the nation's oldest membership organization dedicated to recognizing and celebrating the achievements of great American women. When RBG was inducted, she joined other distinguished honorees as Abigail Adams, Maya Angelou, Amelia Earhart, Coretta Scott King, Rosa Parks, Eleanor Roosevelt, and Harriet Tubman.

As a Supreme Court justice, more honorary Doctor of Law degrees followed those RBG had received as a federal judge, including degrees bestowed on her by Willamette University in 2009, Princeton University in 2010, and Harvard University in 2011.

In 1997, the elite Smith College awarded RBG the first Sophia Smith Award. The award was presented to honor the 200th birthday of the college's founder. According to Smith College, the award recognizes "individuals like Sophia Smith who, by virtue of their intelligence, energy, vision and courage, have made significant and lasting contributions to the education of women."

Rivaling Sophia Smith, an award was later created in the name of RBG herself. The Ruth Bader Ginsburg Prize, established at Columbia Law School in 2011, is awarded annually to law students who have earned the highest academic honors all three years.

THE POWER AND THE GLORY

Time magazine listed her as an "Icon" in the *Time 100* issue published in 2015. The latter recognition may have held a special place in RBG's heart. In the *Time 100* issue, the tribute to her was written by her close friend and occasional adversary, Justice Antonin Scalia. In praising her work, Scalia called her "the Thurgood Marshall" of women's rights, a reference to the legendary civil rights leader. Scalia noted that he "had the good fortune to serve" with RBG on both the D.C. Circuit and the Supreme Court, with her opinions always being thoroughly considered, carefully crafted, "and almost always correct (which is to say we sometimes disagree)." He added that her suggestions "improve the opinions the rest of us write, and she is a source of collegiality and good judgment in all our work."

In 2013, a pictorial tribute at the Smithsonian's National Portrait Gallery in Washington, D.C., came in the form of a portrait featuring Justices Ginsburg, Kagan, O'Connor, and Sotomayor, the first four female justices to have served on the Supreme Court in its 250-year history.

All of the tributes in these examples, as well as the many others RBG received throughout her long career, were no doubt gratifying. One more came in late September 2019 when she received the Meredith College "Women of Achievement Award," in Raleigh, North Carolina. According to Meredith, a private women's liberal arts college, the award honors inspirational role models. News sources quoted a student as saying, "I get to see this woman, I get to see this trailblazer. Maybe I could do something like that. Maybe I could make a difference." That may be the highest tribute the iconic RBG might hope for.

> **BY THE NUMBERS**
>
> Perhaps moved by RBG's inspiration, the number of women enrolled in law schools across the nation has increased dramatically during her lifetime. The American Bar Association (ABA) website https://abaforlawstudents.com tracks gender representation in law schools. They note that in 2016, the number of women enrolled in ABA-approved law schools slightly exceeded 50 percent for the first time in American history, marking that point at which there were more women enrolled in law school than men. In 2017, that number of females was 51.3 percent, and in 2018, the data showed that women made up 52.39 percent of law students. It is not known if male law students, by that time in the minority, were told by their dean to justify taking the place of a female student. On the other side of the coin, the National Association of Women Lawyers tracks women's representation in the legal field, specifically in leadership positions. There, the numbers of women in top spots remained low. According to a 2018 report from the ABA, published at https://www.law.com/americanlawyer/2018/10/10/new-report-finds-female-path-to-law-firm-partnership-a-sluggish-crawl, women made up only 22.7 percent of partners in private law firms. The percentage of women serving as general counsel for Fortune 500 companies was 26.4 percent. Females accounted for 27.1 percent of federal and state-level judges. Only 32.4 percent of law school deans were women. In 2019, according to the Center for American Women in Politics (CAWP) at Rutgers University, where RBG used to teach, women comprised 23.4 percent of the U.S. House of Representatives, and 25 percent in the Senate. As of the 2010 U.S. Census, women comprise 50.8 percent of the total U.S. population, or slightly over half. At this writing, with three female justices—Ginsburg, Kagan, and Sotomayor—serving among the nine members of the nation's highest judicial bench, women currently comprise a third of the Supreme Court. Contrasted to the 110 male justices who served over the four centuries of Supreme Court history, however, women comprised just 0.036 percent of America's highest court.

A-LIST GREETINGS

Along with academic and institutional honors, in contemporary life, there is also the ever-present iconography of popular culture. Even there, RBG reigns supreme. For example, in June 2019, Supreme Court Justice Ruth Bader Ginsburg was named "Best Real-Life Hero" at the annual MTV awards. Justice Ginsburg beat out fellow contenders including barrier-breaking comedian Hannah Gadsby, rock climber Alex Honnold, who was the only person to free solo Yosemite's El Capitan, and tennis star Serena Williams, who has won more Grand Slam singles titles than any other player during the open era, male or female.

Other pop culture accolades include the 2018 season of Zooey Deschanel's situation comedy *New Girl* on television in which the two lead characters name their daughter Ruth Bader Schmidt in honor of RBG.

In the 2018 film *Deadpool 2*, RBG's photo is shown as the character Deadpool considers her for his X-Force, a team of superheroes. In the film, based on Marvel Comics characters, the final selections for the X-Force squad of deadly mercenaries include those named Bedlam, Domino, and Zeitgeist, which would have been interesting company for Ginsburg.

In 2019's *Lego Movie 2*, a Lego mini-figure of Justice Ginsburg is shown. She gave her blessing to the cameo appearance, as well as permission to have the figurine produced as part of Lego toy sets.

Justice Ginsburg has also been immortalized by the world of science. In 2016, researchers at the Cleveland Museum of Natural History named a species of praying mantis *Ilomantis ginsburgae* after RBG. The name was bestowed because the neck plate of the mantis bears somewhat of a resemblance to a jabot, Justice Ginsburg's decorative collar. According to the website *Politico.com*, the name honored RBG's "commitment to women's rights and gender equality" as well as popularizing iconic accessories resembling the insect's neck plate.

SUPREME MEME

It is not often that members of the U.S. Supreme Court become such cultural touchstones, especially when they are past 80 years of age. Many Americans who could not name any other members of the Supreme Court know the name Ruth Bader Ginsburg, or simply "RBG."

Much of the recognition factor stems from the 2015 best-selling book *Notorious RBG: The Life and Times of Ruth Bader Ginsburg*. The year 2018 saw not one but two major films: the documentary *RBG* spanning Justice Ginsburg's life, plus *On the Basis of Sex*, a feature film based on her early career. It is not typical for anyone of any age to earn that much adulation, especially a Supreme Court justice.

It is also unusual for a person over 80 years of age to become what is known in the internet age as a "meme." Memes are defined as cultural elements that are rapidly passed along to others, usually millions of them. Such memes might be humorous images, portions of text, or videos that are spread virally by being forwarded over the internet.

Some of the better-known memes inspired by Justice Ginsburg include the slogan, "No Truth without Ruth" alongside a picture of RBG with a stylized crown on her head, similar to the "Notorious RBG" crown-bedecked meme. There are also RBG-inspired Halloween costumes of tiny judicial robes for little girls as well as those for masquerading adults. With great respect for the other Supreme Court justices, Halloween costumes in *their* likenesses are not often seen.

Nor are there internet-based tribute songs for most other public officials, at least, not positive ones. The online "*Song for RBG—Hang on Ruthie*" is performed to the tune of *Hang on Sloopy*, which was a hit tune from 1965. The updated song parody expresses admiration for Justice Ginsburg in her early life when everybody "tried to keep our Ruthie down" and encourages her to continue fighting for the rights of all people, with the repetitive coda, "Hang on, hang on."

It might seem to some that at this point in time, RBG has become an outsized cultural hero. Her achievements, longevity, and tenacity are awe-inspiring. If it sometimes seems as though RBG has lived an iconic life beyond that of the normal person, it may be that she has indeed lived as if she were living for two people. Perhaps her accomplishments reflect well both on herself and on her late mother, Celia. Perhaps Celia's spirit, even though long dead, has reinforced Ruth Bader Ginsburg's determination to become what she said in her Supreme Court nomination speech, to be all that Celia would have been "had she lived in an age when women could aspire and achieve, and daughters are cherished as much as sons."

Perhaps inspiring others as Celia inspired her is the ultimate meme that Ruth Bader Ginsburg might have wished.

After the death of RBG on September 18, 2020, the tributes that poured in from around the world from people of all ages and backgrounds clearly showed that she succeeded.

SOURCES

Carmon, Irin, and Shana Knizhnik. *Notorious RBG: The Life and Times of Ruth Bader Ginsburg.* New York: Dey Street Books, 2015.

Elliott, Rebecca. "Lewis: SCOTUS Ruling 'a Dagger,'" *Politico*, June 25, 2013. https://www.politico.com/story/2013/06/john-lewis-voting-rights-act-supreme-court-ruling-093339.

Nelson, Louis. "Researchers Name New Praying Mantis Species after Ruth Bader Ginsburg," *Politico*, June 1, 2016. https://www.politico.com/story/2016/06/insect-ruth-bader-ginsburg-223791.

Scalia, Antonin. "Ruth Bader Ginsburg," *Time*, April 15, 2015. https://time.com/3823889/ruth-bader-ginsburg-2015-time-100/.

"Song for RBG—Hang On, Ruthie." https://m.youtube.com/watch?feature=youtu.be&v=bQ8JQGpsi4A.

Timeline

1930s

March 15, 1933 — Joan Ruth Bader is born to furrier Nathan Bader and homemaker Celia Amster Bader in Brooklyn, New York; soon nicknamed "Kiki" by older sister Marilyn.

1934 — Eight-year-old Marilyn Bader dies of meningitis.

1938 — Joan Ruth Bader begins elementary school at Public School 238 in Brooklyn; becomes known by her middle name of "Ruth."

September 1, 1939 — World War II breaks out in Europe.

1940s

December 8, 1941 — America enters World War II, which runs until 1945.

September 1946 — Ruth Bader enters Brooklyn's James Madison High School.

Summer 1948 — At Camp Che-Na-Wah in upstate New York, which she attends each summer, Ruth Bader serves as camp rabbi, a position traditionally held by males.

1950s

June 25, 1950 — Official beginning of Korean War; conflict runs until 1953.

June 25, 1950 — Celia Amster Bader dies of cancer at age 47.

June 27, 1950 — James Madison High School celebrates graduation day but honor student Ruth Bader is unable to attend following death of her mother.

Fall 1950	Ruth Bader enrolls at Cornell University in Ithaca, New York; soon meets sophomore Martin David "Marty" Ginsburg on a blind date.
Fall 1950	Harvard Law School begins to admit women.
November 4, 1952	Dwight D. Eisenhower wins the first of two terms as U.S. president.
1953	After several years of friendship, Ruth Bader becomes romantically involved with Martin Ginsburg during her junior year at Cornell.
May 17, 1954	In landmark *Brown v. Board of Education* decision, U.S. Supreme Court unanimously declares racial concept of "separate but equal" in public schools to be unconstitutional.
June 14, 1954	Ruth Bader graduates at top of her class at Cornell with a bachelor's degree in government, Phi Beta Kappa, Phi Kappa Phi, College of Arts and Sciences Class Marshal, high honors in government, distinction in all subjects.
June 23, 1954	Ruth Bader marries Martin Ginsburg at his parents' home in Rockville Centre, Long Island, New York.
1954	Martin and Ruth Bader Ginsburg (now styled RBG) are stationed at Fort Sill, Oklahoma, through 1956 for Marty's military service; RBG works in clerical positions at nearby Lawton, Oklahoma.
July 21, 1955	RBG and Marty's daughter Jane Carol Ginsburg is born at Freeport, Long Island, New York.
November 1, 1955	According to the Department of Defense, official beginning of American involvement in Vietnam War; conflict runs until 1975.
December 1, 1955	Rosa Parks of Montgomery, Alabama, is jailed for not giving up her seat on a city bus to a white man as required by local law, triggering civil rights protests.
Fall 1956	RBG enrolls as one of nine women out of 552 in class at Harvard University Law School; later becomes first female member of *Harvard Law Review*.
September 4, 1957	Nine black students attempt to desegregate Central High School in Little Rock, Arkansas, facing angry white mobs.

October 4, 1957	*Sputnik*, the first artificial space satellite to orbit the Earth, is launched by the Soviet Union, marking the start of the "Space Race."
1957	Martin Ginsburg is diagnosed with cancer while he and RBG are at Harvard Law School but is able to recover after experimental treatment.
Spring 1958	Martin Ginsburg graduates from Harvard Law School.
1958	Martin Ginsburg joins law firm of Weil, Gotshal and Manges in New York City.
1958	RBG transfers to New York's Columbia University Law School as one of 12 female students in a class of about 500; earns seat on *Columbia Law Review*.
May 1959	RBG graduates from Columbia Law School; ties for first in her class.
1959	After no private law firm will hire a woman, RBG becomes legal clerk for U.S. District Court Judge Edmund Palmieri, Southern District of New York; serves through 1961.

1960s

May 11, 1960	U.S. Food and Drug Administration announces approval of oral contraceptive tablet for birth control, later simply abbreviated as "The Pill."
November 8, 1960	John F. Kennedy is elected U.S. president.
Spring 1962	As part of Columbia Law School Project on International Procedure, RBG studies legal system in Sweden after quickly learning the Swedish language.
February 19, 1963	*The Feminine Mystique* by Betty Friedan is published, appraising the status of women in American society.
August 28, 1963	Martin Luther King Jr. delivers "I Have a Dream" speech at Lincoln Memorial in Washington, D.C.
Fall semester 1963	RBG becomes second woman to teach full-time at Rutgers University Law School.
November 22, 1963	President John F. Kennedy is assassinated at Dallas, Texas.
July 2, 1964	U.S. Congress passes Civil Rights Act of 1964 outlawing discrimination on basis of race, color, religion, sex or national origin.

1965	RBG publishes book *Civil Procedure in Sweden*.
August 6, 1965	U.S. Congress passes Voting Rights Act to end discrimination at the polls.
September 8, 1965	RBG and Marty's son James Steven Ginsburg is born.
June 30, 1966	National Organization for Women (NOW) is founded to "achieve and protect the equal rights of all women and girls in all aspects of social, political, and economic life."
August 30, 1967	Civil rights attorney Thurgood Marshall is confirmed as first African American justice on U.S. Supreme Court.
April 4, 1968	Martin Luther King Jr. assassinated in Memphis, Tennessee.
June 20, 1968	RBG's father Nathan Bader dies at age 71.
1969	RBG earns tenure at Rutgers.
June 28, 1969	Stonewall riots in New York City spark gay rights movement.
July 20, 1969	American astronauts land on the moon.

1970s

Spring 1970	RBG teaches Rutgers University's first class on women and the law.
November 1971	U.S. Supreme Court rules in RBG's favor on *Reed v. Reed*, first major case addressing discrimination based on gender and first brief RBG helped prepare for Supreme Court.
January 1972	RBG becomes first tenured female professor at Columbia Law School.
Spring 1972	Women's Rights Project at American Civil Liberties Union (ACLU) is co-founded by RBG.
June 17, 1972	Watergate scandal begins with break-in at Democratic National Committee office, ultimately leading to Richard Nixon's resignation as President of the United States in 1974.
June 23, 1972	President Richard Nixon signs Title IX, banning gender-based discrimination in education.
November 22, 1972	10th Circuit Court of Appeals rules on *Moritz v. Commissioner of Internal Revenue*, first gender

	discrimination suit successfully argued in court by RBG.
January 17, 1973	RBG successfully presents *Frontiero v. Richardson*, her first oral argument as a litigator before the U.S. Supreme Court, regarding gender discrimination pertaining to military spousal dependency.
February 25, 1974	RBG unsuccessfully argues *Kahn v. Shevin* before the U.S. Supreme Court regarding property tax exemption for widows without similar exemption for widowers.
October 16, 1974	RBG argues *Edwards v. Healy* before the U.S. Supreme Court regarding jury exclusion for women in Louisiana; case becomes moot pursuant to change in Louisiana law.
1974	RBG's book *Text, Cases, and Materials on Sex-Based Discrimination* (with Kenneth Davidson and Herma Hill Kay), America's first casebook on gender discrimination, is published.
January 20, 1975	RBG successfully argues *Weinberger v. Wiesenfeld* before the U.S. Supreme Court regarding discrimination by the Social Security Act on the basis of gender.
October 5, 1976	RBG successfully argues *Califano v. Goldfarb* before the U.S. Supreme Court regarding survivor's benefits under the Social Security Act.
November 1, 1978	RBG successfully argues *Duren v. Missouri* before the U.S. Supreme Court regarding women being disproportionally excluded from jury service.
1980s	
June 15, 1980	U.S. president Jimmy Carter nominates RBG to U.S. Court of Appeals for the District of Columbia, usually called the "D.C. Circuit," where she serves as a federal judge until 1993.
1980	RBG and Martin Ginsburg leave New York City for Washington, D.C., where they move to an apartment in the Watergate complex.
August 19, 1981	U.S. president Ronald Reagan nominates Sandra Day O'Connor as first woman in history on the U.S. Supreme Court where she serves until 2006.
October 6, 1986	Martin's father Morris Ginsburg dies at age 79.

1990s

June 14, 1993	U.S. president Bill Clinton nominates RBG as the second woman to join the U.S. Supreme Court.
August 10, 1993	As Marty holds the Bible, RBG takes the oath of office as the 107th justice of the U.S. Supreme Court.
September 12, 1994	RBG's mother-in-law, Evelyn Bayer Ginsburg, dies at age 86.
July 15, 1996	RBG writes for the Supreme Court's majority in landmark *United States v. Virginia* decision ordering Virginia Military Institute to admit female cadets.
1999	RBG is diagnosed with colon cancer; despite surgery, chemotherapy, and radiation, does not miss any days at the Court.

2000s

December 12, 2000	With her famous "I dissent" statement, RBG objects to Supreme Court majority's decision regarding *Bush v. Gore* case that favored Bush in the presidential election.
September 11, 2001	Terrorists attack the United States by crashing airplanes into New York's World Trade Center, the Pentagon in Washington, and rural Shanksville, Pennsylvania, killing thousands.
2002	RBG is inducted into National Women's Hall of Fame.
January 31, 2006	Supreme Court Justice Sandra Day O'Connor retires, leaving RBG as the only serving female justice until 2009.
May 29, 2007	RBG dissents from the bench on Supreme Court's gender discrimination ruling in *Ledbetter v. Goodyear Tire & Rubber*.
November 4, 2008	Barack Obama is elected the nation's first African American President of the United States.
January 29, 2009	First bill signed into law by President Barack Obama is Lilly Ledbetter Fair Pay Act, said to be inspired by RBG.
February 5, 2009	RBG has surgery to remove cancerous tumor but does not miss any days at the Court.

May 26, 2009	President Barack Obama nominates Sonia Sotomayor as third woman in history to serve on U.S. Supreme Court.
June 25, 2009	RBG successfully argues for the majority in *Safford United School District v. Redding* Supreme Court ruling regarding strip search of an eighth-grade girl.

2010s

January 21, 2010	Supreme Court ruling on *Citizens United v. Federal Election Commission* regarding corporate political donations prompts strong RBG dissent, saying later "If there was one decision I'd overrule, it would be *Citizens United*."
May 10, 2010	President Barack Obama nominates Elena Kagan as fourth woman in history to serve on U.S. Supreme Court.
June 27, 2010	RBG's husband, Martin Ginsburg, dies of cancer at age 78.
June 25, 2013	Supreme Court rules on *Shelby County v. Holder* regarding voting rights; RBG issues famed "Umbrella Dissent" saying that the ruling is "like throwing away your umbrella in a rainstorm because you are not getting wet."
June 25, 2013	"Notorious RBG" meme goes viral on the internet.
June 27, 2013	Opera *Scalia/Ginsburg* premiers with special performance at U.S. Supreme Court.
June 30, 2014	Supreme Court rules on *Burwell v. Hobby Lobby Stores* regarding religious exemption from laws; RBG dissents saying, "The Court, I fear, has ventured into a minefield."
November 26, 2014	RBG has heart stent implanted; works from the hospital after surgery.
October 27, 2015	*Notorious RBG* book is published, becomes a *New York Times* bestseller.
February 25, 2018	Kate McKinnon's RBG character begins appearances in recurring role on TV's *Saturday Night Live* complete with tagline, "Ya just got Gins-burned!"
May 4, 2018	*RBG* documentary in general release after highly publicized premier and guest appearance by Ginsburg in January at Sundance Film Festival.

December 25, 2018	*On the Basis of Sex*, hit feature film starring Felicity Jones about RBG's early career, is released.
December 25, 2018	RBG leaves hospital after breaking ribs in a fall at her office; also has cancerous nodules removed from her lung but quickly returns to Supreme Court bench.
August 2019	RBG undergoes three-week radiation treatment for cancerous tumor.
October 7, 2019	RBG begins 26th year as a justice on Supreme Court bench.
September 18, 2020	At age 87, RBG dies at her home in Washington, D.C. of complications from cancer of the pancreas.

Appendix A
An Evening with Ruth Bader Ginsburg

On September 3, 2019, Supreme Court Justice Ruth Bader Ginsburg spoke to a sold-out crowd of 15,000 people in Little Rock, Arkansas. The following first-hand account by the author presents excerpts of what it was like to be in the audience.

The event was sponsored by the Clinton Foundation and the Clinton School of Public Service at the University of Arkansas at Little Rock. After being moved to progressively larger locations around town due to the demand for tickets, it was held at Little Rock's 15,000-seat Verizon Arena, a venue for major concerts. All 15,000 seats for RBG's program were quickly taken, with news media reporting that there was a waiting list of an additional 30,000 people wanting tickets.

Outside Verizon Arena, hundreds of people began arriving at 10:00 a.m., some with tents to camp out under in the late-summer sun in order to claim good seats for the program that was scheduled to start at 6:30 p.m. Inside the arena, when a voice came over the loudspeakers around 6:30 p.m. announcing that the program was about to begin, it was drowned out by the cheers of 15,000 people before the presentation even began. The cheers continued regularly throughout the evening and will not be specified here other than at exceptional moments.

Accompanied by cheering, a video came over the arena's big screen. It was the 1993 swearing-in ceremony of Ruth Bader Ginsburg as a Supreme Court Justice with Chief Justice William Rehnquist delivering the oath. Then-president Bill Clinton and RBG's husband, Martin Ginsburg, stood at her side. The cheers from the crowd at Verizon Arena drowned out much of her oath of office.

The announcer then introduced the 42nd President of the United States as Bill Clinton came to the stage.

In his remarks, former President Clinton said he had not met RBG until he interviewed her at the White House for a possible Supreme Court nomination. He relayed the particulars of her life for the crowd, from her childhood in Brooklyn through her federal judgeship. Clinton encouraged audience members to see the movie *On the Basis of Sex* and the documentary *RBG* for a fuller picture of her life. Adding that although Justice Ginsburg was one of only nine women out of a class of more than 500 at Harvard Law School, Clinton said, "Today, most law school students are women."

He relayed his 1993 White House interview with RBG as a possible nominee for the nation's highest court, saying, "At that Sunday meeting, I forgot it was an interview for the Supreme Court. I was just a guy talking to someone I really liked." He said there were reasons he liked her: "First, I knew she was one of our best judges. Second, she had a lifetime of pioneering work for women. Third, she had the ability to build common ground, for the court to be an instrument of unity. She proved herself to be a healer."

Clinton concluded his introduction by saying, "She has far exceeded even my expectations. [However], I did not see her ascendancy into pop culture icon. She reminds me of why I still believe in America." [MASSIVE CHEERS]

As Clinton prepared to leave the stage, the initials RBG began flashing repeatedly on the big screen as the crowd chanted "RBG! RBG!" Justice Ginsburg came onstage, helped up the steps by National Public Radio's Nina Totenberg who would serve as interviewer. RBG wore a gray checked jacket over black top and slacks, with the added touch of black lace gloves through which her wedding ring could be seen. An assistant carried a black tote bag imprinted with "I Dissent," which RBG kept by her chair. As the chanting and standing ovation continued, RBG smiled as she settled into her seat. She seemed appreciative but did not appear overwhelmed by the crowd's intensity; after several moments, she simply said, "Thank you. Thank you. Please be seated."

Justice Ginsburg spoke in a clear, articulate, New York–inflected voice that was peppered with the pauses for which she is well known, allowing her to think about what she was going to say.

She acknowledged President Clinton and how he had put her at ease during the fateful Sunday morning interview before the official Supreme Court nomination. That morning, she had to go directly from the airport to the White House in her traveling clothes, having been in Vermont for a wedding. Despite assurances from White House aides that he would be dressed casually, Clinton arrived for the meeting in his "Sunday best."

However, she said, "It was very easy to talk to the President. We talked about constitutional law since he had been a constitutional law professor. We talked about family, we talked about many things," adding that Clinton seemed comfortable conversing with her as a woman.

In Clinton's late-night call to her that same Sunday, he stated he would nominate her to the Supreme Court. She said "I was on Cloud 9. He said there would be a ceremony the next day in the Rose Garden [at the White House] and I would be asked to make some remarks. So I had to come down from the cloud."

Because there was only a short time between his phone call to her late Sunday night and the announcement the next morning, she had to stay up late composing her statement "at my little writing table. I liked my remarks. It was the only time in that entire episode when the White House handlers didn't have time to go over what I had to say. It was in my own words, unedited."

Totenberg asked about a situation that was evident as soon as Justice Ginsburg arrived at the Supreme Court. "Justice [Sandra Day] O'Connor was the lone only woman on the Court for 12 years," said Ginsburg. "In our robing room, there was a bathroom that said 'Men.' Justice O'Connor, when the need arose, had to go all the way back to her chambers. When I came on board, they rushed a renovation. They created a women's bathroom equal in size to the men's."

RBG said that in oral arguments at the Supreme Court, attorneys often referred to her as Justice O'Connor. "The lawyers had learned there was a woman on the court and her name was Justice O'Connor, so when they heard a woman's voice, [they thought] it had to be Justice O'Connor." RBG said that the National Association of Women Judges gave O'Connor a T-shirt saying, "I'm Sandra, not Ruth," and gave Ginsburg a shirt saying, "I'm Ruth, not Sandra."

Justice Ginsburg said, "There was a lot of attention paid to the two of us and how we interacted. One day, I think in *USA Today*, there was a headline that said, 'Rude Ruth Interrupts Sandra.' Justice O'Connor had asked in question in argument, I thought she was finished, and she said, 'Just a minute. I have follow-up questions.' I apologized to her and she said, 'Ruth, don't give it another thought. The guys do it all the time.'"

From 2006, when O'Connor retired, until 2009, Ginsburg was the lone woman on the court. "It was a lonely position," she said. "Viewing the Court, there was something wrong with the picture. The public would see these eight rather well-fed men coming on the bench [PROLONGED LAUGHTER] and then there was this rather small woman."

Justice Ginsburg said she faced a situation that was—and is—familiar to many women. In her days as the sole woman on the court after Justice O'Connor retired, "That happened at conference more than once. I would make a comment. No reaction. Then one of my male colleagues would say basically the same thing and people would react: 'That's a good idea; let's discuss it.' It's a habit that developed. You don't expect very much from a woman, so you kind of tune out when she speaks, but you listen when a male speaks. Now I can tell you that that experience—which I had as a member of the law faculty, as a member of the Court of Appeals—now that I have two 'sisters in law,' it doesn't happen," drawing applause with her reference to current Supreme Court justices Sonia Sotomayor and Elena Kagan.

Totenberg asked how RBG was feeling since she had recently undergone three weeks of radiation treatment for a tumor. Appearing to be at a loss for words, Totenberg blurted out, "*Why* are we here?!"

Justice Ginsburg said, "August 23 was the last radiation session. But I had promised the Clinton Library that I would be here and I just was not going to . . . [INTERRUPTED BY MASSIVE CHEERS AND PROLONGED STANDING OVATION] . . . Thank you, thank you. And I am pleased to say I am feeling very good tonight." [PROLONGED OVATION]

RBG said, "I think my work is what saved me. Because instead of dwelling on physical discomforts, if I have an opinion to write or I have a brief to read, I know that I've just got to get it done and so I have to get over it. This is another instance when I got very good advice from Justice O'Connor. She told me in my first cancer bout to schedule chemotherapy for a Friday, then get over it on Saturday and Sunday, then be back at court on Monday."

Totenberg asked RBG about her late husband's illness when they were in law school, with RBG caring for him and their small daughter as well as going to Harvard Law School and serving on *Law Review*. "We took it day by day," said RBG. "We always believed that we would prevail, that we would beat the cancer. It was not an easy time. . . . I was getting along on two hours of sleep a night for weeks on end. We always had a positive attitude, that we would live."

Regarding similar life challenges as female attorneys that were faced both by herself and Sandra Day O'Connor, such as being unable to get a job even after graduating top of the class in law school, RBG recalled, "That's an example of how something that may seem dreadful, very bad luck, turns out to be the most fortunate thing that ever happened to you. Justice O'Connor put it this way: suppose we'd graduated from law school when there was no discrimination, when women were welcome at the bar, we would be retired partners from some large law firm. But that route wasn't open to us. So we had to find another path, [one] that led us to becoming Supreme Court justices."

Totenberg stated that as a legal affairs reporter, she had noted how Ginsburg's arguments before becoming a Supreme Court justice were presented so that different groups of justices saw the cases in different ways.

Asked about her Supreme Court victory arguing the 1975 *Wiesenfeld* case, Justice Ginsburg said that the case came to her attention after Mr. Wiesenfeld wrote a letter to the editor of his local newspaper describing what he felt was discrimination against him, even though, as he said, "Women's Lib" was getting all the attention. His wife had died of an embolism in childbirth and she was the principal breadwinner in the family. He wanted to claim the Social Security benefits she had paid into the system but he was denied because he was told the benefits were only for women who had lost their husbands.

RBG said, "It was obvious to me that although the plaintiff was a man, the discrimination was against a woman as the wage-earner. She paid the same Social Security taxes that a man would pay but her contributions did not net for her family the same protections. So I think it was the dominant view of the Court that this was discrimination against the woman as wage-earner." In addition, she stated that "some of the justices thought it was discrimination against a male as a parent while one justice said it was arbitrary from the point of view of the baby, that an infant would get parental care only if it was from the mother. So it was an example of how discrimination hurts everyone: men, women, and children."

RBG spoke about a complicated case regarding a female Air Force officer who was discharged from the Air Force in 1972 due to pregnancy but was later reinstated, although she was still denied the chance to take flight training, Ginsburg said, "We both knew that back then it was still an impossible dream to win that case. The difference between then and now is one of the reasons I am optimistic about the future. Today it would be unthinkable to deny flight training to women."

Totenberg then asked a question regarding RBG's view of the Constitution, a document that was written in the late 1700s. Justice Ginsburg replied, "Our Constitution begins with the words, 'We the People of the United States in order to form a more perfect union.' So think how things were in 1787. Who were 'We the People'? Certainly not people who were held in human bondage. The original Constitution preserved slavery. And certainly not women, whatever their color. And not even men who owned no property. So it was a rather elite group, 'We the People.' But I think the genius of our Constitution is what Justice Thurgood Marshall said, that he doesn't celebrate the original Constitution but he does celebrate what the Constitution has become in well over two centuries. The concept of 'We the People' has become ever more inclusive. People who were left out at the beginning—slaves, women, men without property, Native Americans—are now a part of 'We the People.' The once left-out people are part of our political constituency. And we are certainly a more perfect union as a result of that. The original Constitution preserved the slave trade until 1808. One of the provisions that's an embarrassment is the Fugitive Slave clause that said if someone held as a slave escapes to a free state and the master asks to get the slave back, the slave must be returned to the master. The Fugitive Slave clause is in Article 4 of the Constitution. You can see it today but there will be a star next to it that says it was changed by the 14th Amendment."

Justice Ginsburg was asked about her long-term friendship with conservative Supreme Court Justice Antonin Scalia. The two families often socialized, spending New Year's Eve together annually. RBG related the "Elephant Story," in which once, when they were serving together on the Supreme Court, Justices Ginsburg and Scalia attended an international conference in India. On a free day, they took a ride on an "elegantly painted elephant." A photographer caught the moment, with Scalia riding in front and Ginsburg in back. She said, "When my feminist friends saw the picture, they were appalled that I was sitting in the back. I told them it was a matter of weight distribution."

Justice Ginsburg was then asked to comment on the opera *Scalia/Ginsburg*, which she said tries to portray the differences between them. Asked why Justice Scalia's name is first in the opera's title, RBG said, "At the Supreme Court, seniority is everything. He was appointed before I was."

She said the Scalia/Ginsburg opera is roughly based on *The Magic Flute* by Mozart and treated the crowd to a few lines. "Scalia's opening area is a 'Rage' aria and it goes like this: *'The Justices are blind / how can they possibly spout this / the Constitution says / absolutely nothing/about this.'* And then I answer, *'Dear Justice Scalia, you are searching for solutions to problems that don't have easy answers. The great thing about our Constitution is that like our society, it can evolve.'* Then there's like a jazz riff, and *'Let It Grow, Let It Grow.'* "

Toward the end of the opera, she said, the RBG character descends from a glass ceiling to help the Scalia character escape from the dark room in which he is held prisoner "for excessive dissenting." Asked by another character why she is helping her enemy, the RBG character replies, "'*He's not my enemy, he's my dear friend.*' And then we sing a wonderful duet. It's titled '*We Are Different / We Are One.*' Different in our approach to reading a legal text, but one in our reverence for the Constitution and for the institution we serve."

When the hour-long program came to an end, Justice Ginsburg was helped to go offstage by former President Clinton before disappearing behind the black stage drapes.

The cheers from the crowd continued unabated.

Appendix B
Pioneering Women Lawyers

Ruth Bader Ginsburg has always acknowledged the pioneering women in the legal field who preceded her. She has stated that she became interested in the law during college when she saw attorneys helping people who were targeted by McCarthyism, including some she knew personally. It is important for people today to recognize that while female attorneys are currently not unusual, that has not always been the case. Many, not too long ago, had to struggle to join that field. We will never know the names of women who tried but did not succeed against the odds. Below is a timeline showing the progress of trailblazing women in the law, followed by brief biographies of major figures considered to be pioneering females in the legal field.

TIMELINE OF WOMEN'S MILESTONES IN THE LAW

1648
Margaret Brent of Maryland is first documented woman lawyer in the American colonies.

1869
Lemma Barkaloo is admitted to law school at Washington University in St. Louis; although she does not stay due to male harassment, she is often cited as the first American woman to attend law school.

1869
Arabella Mansfield of Iowa becomes first American woman admitted to the practice of law.

1870

Ada Kepley of Illinois is first American woman to graduate from law school when she earns degree from Union College of Law in Chicago, currently Northwestern University.

1870

Esther McQuigg Morris is named Justice of the Peace in South Pass City, Wyoming, becoming first woman judge appointed in the United States.

1872

Charlotte E. Ray of Washington D.C. becomes first African American woman admitted to the bar.

1872

Boston University and the University of Michigan admit women to their law schools.

1879

Belva Lockwood of New York becomes first woman admitted to practice before the U.S. Supreme Court.

1888

New York University admits women to its law classes; in 1893, one of its graduates, Stanleyetta Titus, becomes first female lawyer admitted to the New York State Bar.

1899

"Women Lawyers Club" is established in New York City by 18 women who were denied admission to other bar associations; later becomes known as the National Association of Women Lawyers.

1906

Belva Lockwood is the first woman to argue a case before the U.S. Supreme Court.

1910

Lyda Burton Conley of Kansas becomes the first Native American woman admitted to the bar.

1918

Mary Grossman of Cleveland and Mary Florence Lathrop of Denver are first women admitted to the American Bar Association.

1918

Fordham University and Yale University admit women to their law schools.

1919
Columbia University School of Law admits women.

1919
At the University of California at Berkeley, Barbara Armstrong is appointed to be the nation's first female full-time law professor.

1920
Women gain the right to vote in the United States with the ratification of the Nineteenth Amendment to the Constitution.

1922
Florence Ellinwood Allen of Ohio is first woman elected to a state Supreme Court.

1933
Marguerite Rawalt becomes first woman president of the Federal Bar Association.

1934
Florence Ellinwood Allen becomes first female federal court judge.

1944
Lucile Lomen becomes first woman to serve as a clerk at the U.S. Supreme Court.

1947
Soia Mentschikoff becomes first woman to teach at Harvard Law School.

1950
Harvard Law School admits women.

1951
Miriam Theresa Rooney of New Jersey's Seton Hall University is first woman appointed to serve as dean of an accredited American law school.

1951

Sybil Jones Dedmond of North Carolina Central University is first African American woman to become a full-time professor at an accredited law school.

1962
Constance Baker Motley of New York City is first African American woman to argue before the U.S. Supreme Court.

1966
Constance Baker Motley becomes first African American woman appointed to the federal bench, serving on the U.S. District Court for the Southern District of New York.

1979
The National Association of Women Judges is established.

1981
Sandra Day O'Connor becomes first woman appointed to serve as a justice of the U.S. Supreme Court.

1991
Minnesota Supreme Court becomes the first state with a majority of women on its highest bench.

1993
Janet Reno is named first woman to serve as U.S. Attorney General.

1993
Ruth Bader Ginsburg becomes first Jewish woman appointed to the U.S. Supreme Court.

1995
Roberta Cooper Ramo is first female president of the American Bar Association.

2008
Elena Kagan becomes first woman to be named U.S. Solicitor General.

2009
Sonya Sotomayor becomes first woman of Hispanic descent named to the U.S. Supreme Court.

2010
Elena Kagan is appointed to the U.S. Supreme Court.

2015
Loretta Lynch becomes first African American woman to serve as U.S. Attorney General.

BIOGRAPHICAL SKETCHES OF PIONEERING WOMEN IN THE LAW

Florence Ellinwood Allen (1884–1966) was the first female federal appellate court judge in the country, having been appointed to the U. S. Court of Appeals by President Franklin Roosevelt in 1934. She graduated from New York University Law School in 1913, cum laude. In 1919, she was appointed Assistant Prosecutor for Cuyahoga County, Ohio, the first American woman named to such a position. Barely two years after women won the right to vote in the United States, she defeated both the Democratic and the Republican candidates in a 1922 election for the Ohio Supreme Court, becoming the first woman to sit on a state supreme court. After winning re-election, she received FDR's nomination for the federal court's Sixth Circuit, a position she held for 25 years before her retirement at age 75.

Lemma Barkaloo (1840–1870) has been called the first woman in America to attend law school. She first applied for admission to New York's Columbia University School of Law in 1868. Her application was denied. Two other women applied around the same time and were also rejected. New York attorney George Templeton Strong, who had attended Columbia and paid a substitute to fight in his place during the Civil War, wrote in his often-quoted journal that three "infatuated young women" had applied to Columbia, adding, "No woman shall degrade herself by practicing law in New York especially if I can save [sic] her." He called 'Women's Rights Women' "uncommonly loud and offensive . . . I loathe the lot." Fortunately for Barkaloo, she was accepted to the law school at Washington University in St. Louis, Missouri, in 1869. Unfortunately, she was forced to endure near-constant harassment from male classmates and left school after a year. Despite not graduating, Barkaloo passed the Missouri bar exam in 1870 to become the state's first documented female attorney. That year, she became the first woman to try a case in an American court. However, she died a few months later, a victim of the typhoid epidemic of 1870.

Myra Colby Bradwell (1831–1894) of Chicago is sometimes misidentified as the first woman to practice law in the United States. Bradwell launched the *Chicago Legal News* in 1868, a law journal that gained immediate success. It was the first known legal publication in the United States to be edited by a woman. She passed the Illinois bar exam in 1869, two months after Belle Mansfield had been accepted by the Iowa state bar. However, Bradwell was turned away from admittance to the bar and the practice of law by the Illinois Supreme Court on the grounds that as a married woman, she would not be bound by contracts. In 1873, Bradwell appealed to the U.S. Supreme Court in what is often believed to be the America's first sexual discrimination case. In *Bradwell v. Illinois*, she argued she was qualified to practice law because she was a U.S. citizen, citing the Fourteenth Amendment. The all-male Supreme Court rejected her argument, deciding that states could deny women the right to practice law. In 1875, Bradwell attained widespread fame when she helped her friend Mary Todd Lincoln from being held against her will in a mental asylum. Bradwell published stories of how Mrs. Lincoln had been committed by her only living son, businessman Robert Lincoln. Bradwell brought reporters to visit Mrs. Lincoln at the asylum; in their stories, they claimed that Mrs. Lincoln seemed entirely sane. Publicly embarrassed, Robert Lincoln eventually allowed his mother to be released. Bradwell continued fighting for women's rights including the right of married women to keep their own earnings, and for married women to have equal guardianship of their children. The Illinois Supreme Court granted Bradwell a law license in Illinois in 1890. In 1892, she was granted permission to argue before the U.S. Supreme Court. However, she never did, dying of cancer two years later.

Margaret Brent (1601–1671), popularly known as the first recorded woman to practice law in what became the United States of America, arrived in the colonies from England during 1638. Due to her influential family, she received a large tract of land in Maryland. She herself became a person of some influence in colonial America, earning a place as a trusted counselor to Maryland Governor Leonard Calvert, the first proprietary governor of the Province of Maryland and son of George Calvert, first Lord Baltimore. Leonard Calvert died in 1647, but before doing so, he wrote a will naming Margaret Brent executor of his estate. She declared herself Calvert's attorney without facing opposition, representing the estate's interests in what was called the court of common law. However, the political turmoil of the English Civil War reached the colonies, and Margaret found her family on the side that was out of favor, fleeing to Virginia. Few other records of her life exist because the Brent family estates were burned by British raiders in the American Revolution and the War of 1812, and during the American Civil War, Union troops vandalized the Brent family graveyard. Today, Margaret Brent is considered a "Founding Mother" of Maryland, alongside its "Founding Fathers." After Margaret Brent died, there is virtually no record of another female attorney in America for more than two hundred years. The Margaret Brent Women Lawyers of Achievement Award was established in 1991 by the American Bar Association's Commission on Women in the Profession.

Lyda Burton Conley (1869–1946), a member of the Wyandot tribe, is known as the nation's first Native American female attorney. She was admitted to the Missouri State Bar in 1902. Her motivation in becoming a lawyer was not based in establishing a legal practice as a career. She taught herself the law in order to protect a Native American cemetery that was the burial ground for many Wyandots. Although the preservation of the cemetery had been guaranteed by the U.S. government in an 1855 treaty, starting in 1890, repeated attempts were made by the federal government to remove the bodies and sell the land for commercial development. Congress approved the sale of the land in 1906, whereupon Lyda Conley filed an injunction to halt the sale. She lost that case, seeking relief from the U.S. Supreme Court, who first refused to hear it and later determined Congress had the right to sell the land. However, Conley's efforts aroused public support. There were no buyers for the land. The Indian Affairs Committee of the U.S. House of Representatives banned the desecration of the cemetery in 1912. In her suit, Lyda Conley's argument became known as the first time a plaintiff contended that the federal government had the duty to protect the burial grounds of Native American people. It is said that throughout the continued rebuffs in the courts and until her death, Lyda Conley and her sisters stood as armed guards over the cemetery. In 1971, it was added to the National Register of Historic Places.

Clara Shortridge Foltz (1849–1934), the first known female attorney on America's West Coast, is credited with pioneering the concept of the public defender in 1893, arguing for such an office to provide an equal opportunity for justice regardless of financial means. Married at age 15, her husband abandoned the family in San Jose, California, around 1876. In order to feed her five children, Clara Foltz began studying law with her father. Clara Foltz supported her family by giving public lectures on women's rights, especially the right to vote. She wanted to take the California bar examination but state law allowed only white males to become members of the bar. With the help of a state senator and the publisher of a small newspaper, Foltz authored legislation known as the "Woman Lawyer Bill," intended to replace the words "white male" in the statute with "person." It passed in 1878, after which Foltz passed the exam to become the first woman admitted to the California bar, and the first known female attorney on the West Coast. However, she had little formal education, and wished to study at law school to improve her skills. She applied to California's Hastings College of Law but was denied admission because of her gender. Using the Woman Lawyer Bill as precedent, she argued that if women could serve as lawyers they must be allowed to attend law school. She ultimately won, but her efforts, along with having few legal clients, left her impoverished. In 1910, she was named to the Los Angeles District Attorney's Office, becoming America's first female Deputy District Attorney. As a single mother, she was admired for raising all five of her children. When she died at age 85, her pallbearers included California's governor along with prominent federal and state judges. In 2002, the Los Angeles Criminal Courts Building was renamed the Clara Shortridge Foltz Criminal Justice Center.

Barbara Jordan (1936–1996) of Houston, Texas, faced segregation in the 1950s, and was therefore unable to attend the University of Texas at Austin. Instead she chose Texas Southern University in Houston, a historically black institution, where she majored in history and political science. Before graduating magna cum laude in 1956, Jordan distinguished herself at Texas Southern for being a national champion debater. She won victories over opponents from Ivy League schools like Yale and Brown Universities, and tied a match against Harvard. Jordan went on to attend Boston University School of Law, graduating in 1959. Returning to Texas, she was the first African American elected to the Texas Senate since Reconstruction and the first black woman to serve in that legislative body when she took office in 1966. Attorney Jordan was elected to the U.S. House of Representatives in 1972, the first woman elected in her own right to represent Texas there, and also the first Southern black woman elected to the House. With the assistance of then-former president Lyndon Johnson, she secured a position on the powerful House Judiciary Committee. An eloquent speaker, in 1976 attorney Jordan became the first woman and the first African American to deliver a keynote address at a Democratic National Convention. At the time, she was mentioned as a possible running mate for Jimmy Carter. Jordan began to suffer from multiple sclerosis in 1973, retiring from politics in 1979. She then taught ethics at the University of Texas at Austin. In 1992, she was again a keynote speaker at the Democratic National Convention. President Bill Clinton is quoted as saying he had wanted to nominate Jordan for the U.S. Supreme Court, but could not do so due to Jordan's health problems, which later also included leukemia. In 1996, Jordan died at age 59. She was the first African American woman to be honored with a burial among other distinguished Texans in the Texas State Cemetery, often called the "Arlington of Texas."

Elena Kagan (1960–) of New York received her law degree, magna cum laude, from Harvard Law School in 1986. At Harvard, she was supervisory editor of the *Law Review*. In 1987, Kagan became a law clerk for a colleague of RBG's at the U.S. Court of Appeals for the District of Columbia Circuit. Kagan then clerked for Justice Thurgood Marshall of the U.S. Supreme Court starting in 1988. Justice Marshall said he hired Kagan to help him put the "spark" back into his opinions. In 1999, President Bill Clinton named Kagan to the U.S. Court of Appeals for the District of Columbia Circuit, RBG's home before leaving for the Supreme Court. Kagan attained a landmark achievement in 2003 by being named the first female Dean of

RBG's alma mater, Harvard Law School, where Kagan served until 2009. That year, Kagan was confirmed as the first woman named to the position of America's Solicitor General after being nominated by President Barack Obama. The Solicitor General is one of the top four highest-ranking officials in the U.S. Department of Justice, representing cases involving the federal government before the Supreme Court. Kagan served as Solicitor General from March 2009 to May 2010, when President Obama nominated her to fill an unexpected seat on the Supreme Court. After Senate confirmation, she took the bench at the nation's highest court in 2010, earning a place in history as the fourth woman to sit on the Supreme Court since its inception in 1787. After more than 200 years, Kagan's arrival marked the first time that the Court had three sitting justices who were women: Justices Ginsburg, Kagan, and Sotomayor.

Ada Harriet Miser Kepley (1847–1925) of Illinois was the first American woman to graduate from law school, which she did in 1870 from what is today Chicago's Northwestern University School of Law. At that time, she was prohibited from legal practice by state law that denied women a license to what was called the "learned professions." Her husband, Illinois attorney Henry B. Kepley, was similar to Martin Ginsburg in his support of his wife's legal career. It was at Henry's urging that Ada Kepley attended law school. When Illinois law denied her admission to the state bar because she was a woman, Henry Kepley drafted a bill banning sex discrimination in professional occupations that became state law in 1872. By that time, Ada was more interested in social reform than legal practice, but when she finally applied for admission to the Illinois state bar in 1881, she easily earned admission. While Ada Kepley appeared a few times in court, she was more involved with women's suffrage and the antialcohol temperance movement. After her husband's death in 1906, she tried farming and writing books to earn a living. In 1925, she died in poverty, considered by local townspeople to be an eccentric charity case.

Belva Ann Bennett Lockwood (1830–1917) was the first female member of the U.S. Supreme Court Bar, having been admitted in 1879 after successfully petitioning Congress to do so. She thus became the first woman attorney to earn that privilege, which she did in the *Kaiser v. Stickney* case during 1880 but more significantly in *United States v. Cherokee Nation* later that year when she successfully argued for the United States to uphold a judgment to the Cherokee people for money owed to them for ceded lands. As a young woman, despite local opposition, Lockwood attended New York's Genesee College. There, she became attracted to the law, but the school had no law department. A local legal professor offered private classes, and agreed to accept her as one of his students. She graduated from

Genesee College with honors in 1857 and found a job as school headmistress at several New York schools. Soon she discovered that she was paid half of what the males were making, either for teaching or serving as an administrator. Lockwood became an advocate for equal pay in education for both men and women. In addition, she was a strong advocate for women's right to vote. Although Victoria Woodhull proclaimed herself to be running for President of United States in 1872, Lockwood was the first woman to have her name printed on official ballots, ultimately receiving several thousand votes in the elections of 1884 and 1888 as the National Equal Rights Party candidate. In both, Lockwood alleged that ballots supporting her were torn up or simply thrown away. In 1880, Lockwood sponsored Samuel R. Lowery to the Supreme Court bar, after which he became the first African American to argue a case before the Supreme Court.

Arabella Mansfield (1846–1911), born in Iowa as Belle Aurelia Babb, became the first woman admitted to a state bar in the United States when, at age 23, she was admitted to the Iowa bar in 1869. She had graduated as valedictorian from Iowa Wesleyan College, after which she joined her brother's law firm in Mount Pleasant, serving an apprenticeship. An Iowa state law at the time restricted the bar examination to males. However, she was permitted to take the test, which she passed with high scores. After she challenged the licensing statute in court, the Iowa legislature removed the restrictive language in 1870, opening the legal profession to women and minorities. Iowa was the first state to accept women into its bar. However, Mansfield never practiced law. She became a faculty member and administrator at Iowa Wesleyan College and at Indiana's DePauw University. Mansfield toured the lecture circuit as an active supporter of the movement for women's right to vote. She chaired the Iowa Women's Suffrage Convention in 1870, working with Susan B. Anthony. Mansfield died in 1911 before being able to see the passage of the Nineteenth Amendment to the U.S. Constitution that became effective in 1920, giving women the right to vote.

Sandra Day O'Connor (1930–) holds the distinction of being the first woman to serve on the U.S. Supreme Court. She sat on the bench of the nation's highest court from 1981 to 2006 after being appointed by President Ronald Reagan who was keeping a campaign promise to nominate a woman justice. O'Connor's interview before the Senate Judiciary Committee in 1981 was the first televised confirmation hearing for a Supreme Court Justice. O'Connor was confirmed unanimously by the Senate. During her tenure on the Court, O'Connor was the lone woman from 1981 until Ruth Bader Ginsburg was appointed in 1993. As a law student at California's Stanford Law School, O'Connor served on the *Stanford Law*

Review. After earning her law degree from Stanford in 1952, she served two terms in the Arizona State Senate, becoming the first female majority leader of a state senate. She won election to the Arizona Court of Appeals, serving there from 1979 until President Reagan appointed her to the Supreme Court. In 2005, two senior Supreme Court justices were absent during an oral argument, making O'Connor the first female senior presiding justice. After retiring from the Supreme Court in 2006, O'Connor moved to Phoenix, Arizona, where she became involved in raising awareness of Alzheimer's disease. In 2013, during her retirement, O'Connor made pop culture history by appearing via video on the television show *Jeopardy* where she offered clues pertaining to the Supreme Court.

Charlotte E. Ray (1850–1911) is often cited as the first African American woman in the legal field when she is said to have applied for the District of Columbia bar under the name "C. E. Ray" and being admitted under the assumption that she was a male. That story is debated, along with the account that in 1872 she was admitted to the Howard School of Law in the District of Columbia because she also applied under the name "C. E. Ray." Her use of initials has not been documented, especially since at the time, Howard University had a policy of accepting both women and African Americans. In any case, Charlotte Ray was one of the first women to graduate from a university law school as opposed to reading the law or serving an apprenticeship with an established attorney. There is documentation that she was the first woman to argue in the District of Columbia's Superior Court, where she pleaded a domestic abuse case in 1875, representing an uneducated woman petitioning for divorce. Although Ray advertised her legal services in the field of corporate law in civil rights leader Frederick Douglass's weekly newspaper, *The New National Era and Citizen*, her practice was not sufficient to sustain her practice as an attorney. In 1879, she became a teacher in Brooklyn, New York, before her death 20 years later.

Janet Reno (1938–2016) of Florida was the first female Attorney General of the United States, a position she held from 1993 to 2001. After serving for both presidential terms of Bill Clinton, who had nominated her, she became one of the longest-serving Attorneys General in U.S. history, with her eight years making her second only to William Wirt who served 12 years in the early 1800s. Reno bore some similarities to Ruth and Martin Ginsburg, majoring in chemistry at Cornell as Marty had initially done. In 1960, she enrolled at Harvard Law School, where there were 16 women in a class of 500 students, or seven more than in RBG's time. In early 1978, Reno was appointed the State Attorney for Dade County (today's Miami-Dade County), making her the first woman to serve as a state attorney in Florida. After winning an election for the position in late 1978, voters elected her to five terms in the post where she served until 1993. After Reno's term as U.S. Attorney General ended in 2001, she ran for governor of Florida in 2002, losing in the Democratic primary by the small margin of 0.4 percent. Allegations of voting irregularities arose in the election, as they had in the Bush/Gore presidential election of 2000. Reno then became a founding member of the board of directors for the Innocence Project, assisting prisoners seeking exoneration through DNA testing. In 2016, Reno died from Parkinson's disease.

Sonya Sotomayor (1954–) of New York was appointed by President Barack Obama in 2009 to be the first Supreme Court justice of Hispanic descent. She was the child of Puerto Rican-born parents in New York City. The family struggled after her father died when she was nine years old, but she went on to graduate summa cum laude from Princeton University. Sotomayor went to Yale Law School, serving as an editor at the *Yale Law Journal*. President George H. W. Bush nominated her to the U.S. District Court for the Southern District of New York where she began serving in 1992. At age 38, she was the youngest judge in the Southern District as well as being the first Hispanic federal judge in New York State and the first Puerto Rican woman to serve as a judge in a U.S. federal court. She became nationally known with her ruling that ended the 1994 baseball strike, endearing her to fans of the game. Sotomayor was nominated by President Bill Clinton in 1997 to the U.S. Court of Appeals for the Second Circuit, preceding her 2009 appointment to the U.S. Supreme Court. In, 2013, Sotomayor administered the oath of office for the second term of Vice President Joe Biden, making her the first Hispanic to administer the oath to a president or vice president of the United States.

Mabel Walker Willebrandt (1889–1963) was the first female to serve an extended term as U.S. Assistant Attorney General after being appointed in 1921 by President Warren Harding, making her the highest-ranking woman in the federal government at the time. Willebrandt taught elementary school in Los Angeles while studying law at night. In 1916, she earned a law degree from the University of Southern California. She became the city's first female public defender, working pro bono and taking only women's cases. Willebrandt was brought to Harding's attention for Assistant AG through an endorsement from judges in southern California, where she had argued thousands of cases. Holding the U.S. Assistant Attorney General position until 1929, Willebrandt was primarily tasked with handling cases concerning violations of the nation's Volstead Act, or Prohibition, becoming a nationally-known figure. After she openly campaigned for Herbert Hoover in the 1928 election, Hoover did not nominate her for Attorney General. She resigned as Assistant AG in 1929, returning to private practice in Los Angeles where she pioneered the fields of aviation law and radio law. Willebrandt represented major movie stars and companies like Metro-Goldwyn-Mayer. After becoming interested in aviation and befriending Amelia Earhart, Willebrandt became the first woman to chair a committee for the American Bar Association as head of its committee on aeronautical law. She died of cancer at age 73 in 1963. Her longtime friend Judge John J. Sirica, who presided over the Watergate case, is quoted as saying that if it had not been for her gender, Willebrandt could have been president.

SOURCES

Morello, Karen. *The Invisible Bar: The Woman Lawyer in America 1638 to Present*. New York: Random House, 1986.

Norgren, Jill. *Rebels at the Bar: The Fascinating, Forgotten Stories of America's First Women Lawyers*. New York: New York University Press, 2013.

Norgren, Jill. *Stories from Trailblazing Women Lawyers: Lives in the Law*. New York: New York University Press, 2018.

Smith, J. Clay, Jr., editor. *Rebels in Law: Voices in History of Black Women Lawyers*. Ann Arbor: University of Michigan, 1998.

"13 Pioneering Women in American Law," *ABA Journal*. http://www.abajournal.com/gallery/historical_women/766.

PRIMARY SOURCE DOCUMENTS

The Fourteenth Amendment of the Constitution, 1868

In many of the cases in which RBG has been involved, the matter centered around interpretation of the Fourteenth Amendment of the United States Constitution, particularly the Equal Protection Clause in Section 1 (in italics by the author, below). That clause, which took effect in 1868 after the Civil War, says that no state will deny to any person equal protection of the law. Often, in cases of race or gender, the argument involved the definition—at that particular point in time—of a "person." What follows is the text of the Fourteenth Amendment.

Section 1. All persons born or naturalized in the United States, and subject to the jurisdiction thereof, are citizens of the United States and of the State wherein they reside. No State shall make or enforce any law which shall abridge the privileges or immunities of citizens of the United States; nor shall any State deprive any person of life, liberty, or property, without due process of law; *nor deny to any person* within its jurisdiction the equal protection of the laws.

Section 2. Representatives shall be apportioned among the several States according to their respective numbers, counting the whole number of persons in each State, excluding Indians not taxed. But when the right to vote at any election for the choice of electors for President and Vice President of the United States, Representatives in Congress, the Executive and Judicial officers of a State, or the members of the Legislature thereof, is denied to any of the male inhabitants of such State, being twenty-one years of age, and citizens of the United States, or in any way abridged, except for participation in rebellion, or other crime, the basis of representation therein shall be reduced in the proportion which the number of such male citizens shall bear to the whole number of male citizens twenty-one years of age in such State.

Section 3. No person shall be a Senator or Representative in Congress, or elector of President and Vice President, or hold any office, civil or military, under the United States, or under any State, who, having previously taken an oath, as a member of Congress, or as an officer of the United States, or as a member of any State legislature, or as an executive or judicial officer of any State, to support the Constitution of the United States, shall have engaged in insurrection or rebellion against the same, or given aid or comfort to the enemies thereof. But Congress may, by a vote of two-thirds of each House, remove such disability.

Section 4. The validity of the public debt of the United States, authorized by law, including debts incurred for payment of pensions and bounties for services in suppressing insurrection or rebellion, shall not be questioned. But neither the United States nor any State shall assume or pay any debt or obligation incurred in aid of insurrection or rebellion against the United States, or any claim for the loss or emancipation of any slave; but all such debts, obligations and claims shall be held illegal and void.

Section 5. The Congress shall have power to enforce, by appropriate legislation, the provisions of this article.

> **Source:** The House Joint Resolution proposing the 14th amendment to the Constitution, June 16, 1866; Enrolled Acts and Resolutions of Congress, 1789–1999; General Records of the United States Government; Record Group 11; National Archives.

Acceptance Address by Ruth Bader Ginsburg on the Occasion of Her Nomination by President Bill Clinton as a U.S. Supreme Court Justice, 1993

During her nomination acceptance ceremony, held in the White House Rose Garden in Washington, D.C. on June 14, 1993, RBG wore her late mother, Celia's, circle pin. During a public appearance in 2019, at which the author was present, Justice Ginsburg said that after President Clinton's late-night phone call to her saying he planned to nominate her to the Supreme Court, she was "on Cloud 9." Because there was only a short time between his call Sunday night and the announcement the next morning, she had to stay up late composing her statement, which follows below.

Mr. President,

I am grateful beyond measure for the confidence you have placed in me; and I will strive with all that I have to live up to your expectations in making this appointment.

I appreciate, too, the special caring of Senator Daniel Patrick Moynihan, the more so because I do not actually know the Senator. I was born and brought up in New York, the state Senator Moynihan represents, and he was the very first person to call with good wishes when President Carter nominated me in 1980 to serve on the U.S. Court of Appeals for the District of Columbia Circuit. Senator Moynihan has offered the same encouragement on this occasion.

May I introduce at this happy moment three people very special to me: my husband, Martin B. Ginsburg, my son-in-law, George T. Spera, Jr., and my son, James Steven Ginsburg.

The announcement the President just made is significant, I believe, because it contributes to the end of the days when women, at least half the talent pool in our society, appear in high places only as one-at-a-time performers. Recall that when President Carter took office in 1976, no woman ever served on the Supreme Court, and only one woman, Shirley Hufstedler of California, then served at the next Federal court level, the United States courts of appeals.

Today, Justice Sandra Day O'Connor graces the Supreme Court bench, and close to 25 women serve at the Federal Court of Appeals level, two as Chief Judges. I am confident that more will soon join them. That seems to me inevitable, given the change in law school enrollment.

My law school class in the late 1950's numbered over 500. That class included less than 10 women. As the President said, not a law firm in the entire city of New York bid for my employment as a lawyer when I earned my degree. Today few law schools have female enrollment under 40 percent, and several have reached or passed the 50 percent mark. And thanks to Title VII, no entry doors are barred.

My daughter, Jane, reminded me a few hours ago in a good-luck call from Australia of a sign of the change we have had the good fortune to experience. In her high school yearbook on her graduation in 1973, the listing for Jane Ginsburg under "ambition" was "to see her mother appointed to the Supreme Court." The next line read, "If necessary, Jane will appoint her." Jane is so pleased, Mr. President, that you did it instead, and her brother, James, is, too.

I expect to be asked in some detail about my views of the work of a good judge on a High Court bench. This afternoon is not the moment for extended remarks on that subject, but I might state a few prime guides.

Chief Justice Rehnquist offered one I keep in the front of my mind: A judge is bound to decide each case fairly in a court with the relevant facts and the applicable law even when the decision is not—as he put it—what the home crowd wants.

Next, I know no better summary than the one Justice O'Connor recently provided drawn from a paper by New York University Law School Professor Burt Neuborne. The remarks concern the enduring influence of Justice Oliver Wendell Holmes. They read: When a modern constitutional judge is confronted with a hard case, Holmes is at her side with three gentle reminders: first, intellectual honesty about the available policy choices; second, disciplined self-restraint in respecting the majority's policy choice; and third, principled commitment to defense of individual autonomy even in the face of majority action. To that I can only say, Amen.

I am indebted to so many for this extraordinary chance and challenge: to a revived women's movement in the 1970s that opened doors for people like me, to the civil rights movement of the 1960s from which the women's movement drew inspiration, to my teaching colleagues at Rutgers and Columbia and for 13 years my D.C. Circuit colleagues who shaped and heightened my appreciation of the value of collegiality.

Most closely, I have been aided by my life partner, Martin D. Ginsburg, who has been, since our teenage years, my best friend and biggest booster; by my mother-in-law, Evelyn Ginsburg, the most supportive parent a person could have; and by a daughter and son with the tastes to appreciate that Daddy cooks ever so much better than Mommy and so phased me out of the kitchen at a relatively early age.

Finally, I know Hillary Rodham Clinton has encouraged and supported the President's decision to utilize the skills and talents of all the people of the United States. I did not, until today, know Mrs. Clinton, but I hasten to add that I am not the first member of my family to stand close to her. There is another I love dearly to whom the First Lady is already an old friend. My wonderful granddaughter, Clara, witnessed this super, unposed photograph taken last October when Mrs. Clinton visited the nursery school in New York and led the little ones in "The Toothbrush Song." The small person right in front is Clara.

I have a last thank you. It is to my mother, Celia Amster Bader, the bravest and strongest person I have known, who was taken from me much too soon. I pray that I may be all that she would have been had she lived in an age when women could aspire and achieve, and daughters are cherished as much as sons.

I look forward to stimulating weeks this summer and, if I am confirmed, to working at a neighboring court to the best of my ability for the advancement of the law in the service of society.

Thank you.

Source: The William J. Clinton Presidential Library & Museum. https://www.youtube.com/watch?v=MHwoosXsybQ.

Congressional Hearing on the Nomination of Ruth Bader Ginsburg to Be an Associate Justice of the Supreme Court of the United States, 1993

What follows is an excerpted account of the lengthy hearings that were held before the United States Senate's Committee on the Judiciary on July 20, 21, 22, and 23, 1993. In her opening statement, Judge Ginsburg acknowledges a number of people, especially her parents, stating that she is a first-generation American on her father's side, barely second-generation on her mother's. She notes that they taught her to love learning, care about people, and work hard. Judge Ginsburg recognizes her unlikely journey to that point, stating, "What has become of me could happen only in America."

Committee on the Judiciary:
Joseph R. Biden, Jr., Delaware, Chairman
Edward M. Kennedy, Massachusetts
Howard M. Metzenbaum, Ohio
Dennis Deconcini, Arizona
Patrick J. Leahy, Vermont
Howell Heflin, Alabama
Paul Simon, Illinois
Herbert Kohl, Wisconsin
Dianne Feinstein, California
Carol Moseley-Braun, Illinois
Orrin G. Hatch, Utah
Strom Thurmond, South Carolina
Alan K. Simpson, Wyoming
Charles E. Grassley, Iowa
Arlen Specter, Pennsylvania
Hank Brown, Colorado
William S. Cohen, Maine
Larry Pressler, South Dakota

PREPARED STATEMENT OF CHAIRMAN BIDEN Today, the Judiciary Committee welcomes Judge Ruth Bader Ginsburg, the President's nominee to be Associate Justice of the United States Supreme Court. This is a familiar setting for us—since I became chairman of the committee seven years ago, we have now convened hearings on five nominees to the Supreme Court.

Our task today—as in all Supreme Court confirmation hearings—is to consider the character, the qualities and the judicial philosophy of Ruth Bader Ginsburg. Judge Ginsburg, you come before the committee with your place in history already secure. In the 1970s you argued a series of landmark cases that changed the way our laws could distinguish between men and women. You have already helped to change the meaning of equality in our nation. Now, as you face a new opportunity to help shape the future of America, we welcome you and we invite you to share with us and the American people your vision of the shape of that future. . . .

Judge, the floor is now yours. Again, welcome.

Judge GINSBURG. Thank you, Mr. Chairman, Senator Hatch, and other members of the committee. May I say first how much I appreciate the time committee members took to greet me in the weeks immediately following the President's nomination. It was a particularly busy time for you, and I thank you all the more for your courtesy. To Senator Moynihan, who has been at my side every step of the way, a thousand thanks could not begin to convey my appreciation. Despite the heavy demands on his time, during trying days of budget reconciliation, he accompanied me on visits to Senate members, he gave over his own desk for my use, he buoyed up my spirits whenever a lift was needed. In all, he served as the kindest, wisest counselor a nominee could have. Senator D'Amato, from my great home State of New York, volunteered to join Senator Moynihan in introducing and sponsoring me, and I am so grateful to him. I have had many enlightening conversations in Senate Chambers since June 14, but my visit with Senator D'Amato was sheer fun.

The CHAIRMAN. It always is. [Laughter.]

Judge GINSBURG. My children decided at an early age that mother's sense of humor needed improvement. They tried to supply that improvement, and kept a book to record their successes. The book was called "Mommy Laughed." My visit with Senator D'Amato would have supplied at least three entries for the "Mommy Laughed" book. Representative Norton has been my professional colleague and friend since days when we were still young. As an advocate of human rights and fair chances for all people, Eleanor Holmes Norton has been as brave and as vigilant as she is brilliant. I am so pleased that she was among my introducers, and so proud to be one of Eleanor's constituents. Most of all, the President's confidence in my capacity to serve as a Supreme Court Justice is responsible for the proceedings about to begin. There are no words to tell him what is in my heart.

I can say simply this: If confirmed, I will try in every way to justify his faith in me. I am, as you know from my responses to your questionnaire, a Brooklynite, born and bred—a first-generation American on my father's side, barely second-generation on my mother's. Neither of my parents had the means to attend college, but both taught me to love learning, to care about people, and to work hard for whatever I wanted or believed in. Their parents had the foresight to leave the old country, when Jewish ancestry and faith meant exposure to pogroms and denigration of one's human worth. What has become of me could happen only in America. Like so many others, I owe so much to the entry this Nation afforded to people yearning to breathe free.

I have had the great fortune to share life with a partner truly extraordinary for his generation, a man who believed at age 18 when we met, and who believes today, that a woman's work, whether at home or on the job, is as important as a man's. I attended law school in days when women were not wanted by most members of the legal profession. I became a lawyer because Marty and his parents supported that choice unreservedly.

I have been deeply moved by the outpouring of good wishes received in recent weeks from family, neighbors, camp mates, classmates, students at Rutgers and Columbia, law-teaching colleagues, lawyers with whom I have worked, judges across the country, and many women and men who do not know me. That huge, spirit-lifting collection shows that for many of our people, an individual's sex is no longer remarkable or even unusual with regard to his or her qualifications to serve on the Supreme Court.

Indeed, in my lifetime, I expect to see three, four, perhaps even more women on the High Court Bench, women not shaped from the same mold, but of different complexions. Yes, there are miles in front, but what a distance we have traveled from the day President Thomas Jefferson told his Secretary of State: "The appointment of women to [public] office is an innovation for which the public is not prepared." "Nor," Jefferson added, "am I."

The increasingly full use of the talent of all of this Nation's people holds large promise for the future, but we could not have come to this point—and I surely would not be in this room today—without the determined efforts of men and women who kept dreams of equal citizenship alive in days when few would listen. People like Susan B. Anthony, Elizabeth Cady Stanton, and Harriet Tubman come to mind. I stand on the shoulders of those brave people. Supreme Court Justices are guardians of the great charter that has served as our Nation's fundamental instrument of government for over 200 years. It is the oldest written constitution still in force in the world.

But the Justices do not guard constitutional rights alone. Courts share that profound responsibility with Congress, the President, the States, and the people. Constant realization of a more perfect Union, the Constitution's aspiration, requires the widest, broadest, deepest participation on matters of government and government policy. One of the world's greatest jurists, Judge Learned Hand, said, as Senator Moseley-Braun reminded us, that the spirit of liberty that imbues our Constitution must lie first and foremost in the hearts of the men and women who compose this great Nation. Judge Hand defined that spirit, in a way I fully embrace, as one which is not too sure that it is right, and so seeks to understand the minds of other men and women and to weigh the interests of others alongside its own without bias. The spirit Judge Learned Hand described strives for a community where the least shall be heard and considered side by side with the greatest. I will keep that wisdom in the front of my mind as long as I am capable of judicial service. Some of you asked me during recent visits why I want to be on the Supreme Court. It is an opportunity beyond any other for one of my training to serve society.

The controversies that come to the Supreme Court, as the last judicial resort, touch and concern the health and well-being of our Nation and its people. They affect the preservation of liberty to ourselves and our posterity. Serving on this Court is the highest honor, the most awesome trust, that can be placed in a judge. It means working at my craft—working with and for the law—as a way to keep our society both ordered and free. Let me try to state in a nutshell how I view the work of judging. My approach, I believe, is neither liberal nor conservative. Rather, it is rooted in the place of the judiciary, of judges, in our democratic society.

The Constitution's preamble speaks first of "We, the People," and then of their elected representatives. The judiciary is third in line and it is placed apart from the political fray so that its members can judge fairly, impartially, in accordance with the law, and without fear about the animosity of any pressure group. In Alexander Hamilton's words, the mission of judges is "to secure a steady, upright, and impartial administration of the laws." I would add that the judge should carry out that function without fanfare, but with due care. She should decide the case before her without reaching out to cover cases not yet seen. She should be ever mindful, as Judge and then Justice Benjamin Nathan Cardozo said, "Justice is not to be taken by storm. She is to be wooed by slow advances."

We—this committee and I—are about to embark on many hours of conversation. You have arranged this hearing to aid you in the performance of a vital task, to prepare your Senate colleagues for consideration of my nomination. The record of the Constitutional Convention shows that the delegates had initially entrusted the power to appoint Federal judges, most prominently Supreme Court Justices, not to the President, but to you and your colleagues, to the Senate acting alone. Only in the waning days of the Convention did the Framers settle on a nomination role for the President and an advice and consent role for the Senate. The text of the Constitution, as finally formulated, makes no distinction between the appointment process for Supreme Court Justices and the process for other offices of the United States, for example, Cabinet officers.

But as history bears out, you and Senators past have sensibly considered appointments in relation to the appointee's task. Federal judges may long outlast the President who appoints them. They may serve as long as they can do the job. As the Constitution says, they may remain in office "during good Behaviour." Supreme Court Justices, most notably, participate in shaping a lasting body of constitutional decisions. They continuously confront matters on which the Framers left things unsaid, unsettled, or uncertain. For that reason, when the Senate considers a Supreme Court nomination, the Senators are properly concerned about the nominee's capacity to serve the Nation, not just for the here and now, but over the long term.

You have been supplied, in the 5 weeks since the President announced my nomination, with hundreds of pages about me and thousands of pages I have penned—my writings as a law teacher, mainly about procedure; 10 years of briefs filed when I was a courtroom advocate of the equal stature of men and women before the law; numerous speeches and articles on that same theme; 13 years of opinions—counting the unpublished together with the published opinions, well over 700 of them—all decisions I made as a member of the U.S. Court of Appeals for the District of Columbia Circuit; several comments on the roles of judge and lawyers in our legal system. That body of material, I know, has been examined by the committee with care. It is the most tangible, reliable indicator of my attitude, outlook, approach, and style. I hope you will judge my qualifications principally on that written record, a record spanning 34 years, and that you will find in that written record assurance that I am prepared to do the hard work and to exercise the informed, independent judgment that Supreme Court decision-making entails.

I think of these proceedings much as I do of the division between the written record and briefs, on the one hand, and oral argument on the other hand, in appellate tribunals. The written record is by far the more important component in an appellate court's decision-making, but the oral argument often elicits helpful clarifications and concentrates the judges' minds on the character of the decision they are called upon to make.

There is, of course, this critical difference. You are well aware that I come to this proceeding to be judged as a judge, not as an advocate. Because I am and hope to continue to be a judge, it would be wrong for me to say or to preview in this legislative chamber how I would cast my vote on questions the Supreme Court may be called upon to decide. Were I to rehearse here what I would say and how I would reason on such questions, I would act injudiciously. Judges in our system are bound to decide concrete cases, not abstract issues. Each case comes to court based on particular facts and its decision should turn on those facts and the governing law, stated and explained in light of the particular arguments the parties or their representatives present.

A judge sworn to decide impartially can offer no forecasts, no hints, for that would show not only disregard for the specifics of the particular case, it would display disdain for the entire judicial process. Similarly, because you are considering my capacity for independent judging, my personal views on how I would vote on a publicly debated issue were I in your shoes—were I a legislator—are not what you will be closely examining.

As Justice Oliver Wendell Holmes counseled, "[O]ne of the most sacred duties of a judge is not to read [her] convictions into [the Constitution]." I have tried and I will continue to try to follow the model Justice Holmes set in holding that duty sacred. I see this hearing, as I know you do, as a grand opportunity once again to reaffirm that civility, courtesy and mutual respect properly keynote our exchanges. Judges, I am mindful, owe the elected branches—the Congress and the President—respectful consideration of how court opinions affect their responsibilities.

And I am heartened by legislative branch reciprocal sensitivity. As one of you said 2 months ago at a meeting of the Federal Judges Association, "We in Congress must be more thoughtful and more deliberate in order to enable judges to do their job more effectively." As for my own deportment or, in the Constitution's words, "good Behaviour," I prize advice received on this nomination from a dear friend, Frank Griffin, a recently retired Justice of the Supreme Court of Ireland. Justice Griffin wrote: "Courtesy to and consideration for one's colleagues, the legal profession, and the public are among the greatest attributes a judge can have."

It is fitting, as I conclude this opening statement, to express my deep respect for, and abiding appreciation to Justice Byron R. White for his 31 years and more of fine service on the Supreme Court. In acknowledging his colleagues' good wishes on the occasion of his retirement, Justice White wrote that he expects to sit on U.S. courts of appeals from time to time, and so to be a consumer of, instead of a participant in, Supreme Court opinions. He expressed a hope shared by all lower court judges. He hoped "the Supreme Court's mandates will be clear and crisp, leaving as little room as possible for disagreement about their meaning."

If confirmed, I will take that counsel to heart and strive to write opinions that both "get it right" and "keep it tight."

Thank you for your patience.

Source: Hearings before the Committee On the Judiciary, United States Senate, One Hundred Third Congress, First Session on the Nomination of Ruth Bader Ginsburg, to be Associate Justice of the Supreme Court of the United States, July 20, 21, 22, and 23, 1993. Washington, D.C.: U.S. Government Printing Office, 1994.

Dissent: *Bush v. Gore*, 2000

In Bush v. Gore, *the United States Supreme Court settled a dispute regarding a recount of ballots in Florida during the presidential election of 2000 between George W. Bush and Al Gore. The Court's ruling halted the Florida recount that was in progress. The Chief Justice referred to in this document is William Rehnquist who joined the majority opinion halting the recount. Justice Ginsburg's opinion arguing against the Court's decision was noted for concluding with the statement "I dissent," not "I respectfully dissent." Some believed including the word "respectfully" was standard operating procedure for the Court in general, but a closer look at*

Supreme Court records indicates that is not so. However, RBG's famed "I dissent" in this case made headlines along with T-shirts, tote bags, and coffee mugs.

Dissent

SUPREME COURT OF THE UNITED STATES

No. 00—949

GEORGE W. BUSH, et al., PETITIONERS v. ALBERT GORE, Jr., et al. ON WRIT OF CERTIORARI TO THE FLORIDA SUPREME COURT

December 12, 2000

Justice Ginsburg, with whom Justice Stevens joins, and with whom Justice Souter and Justice Breyer join as to Part I, dissenting.

I. The Chief Justice acknowledges that provisions of Florida's Election Code "may well admit of more than one interpretation." But instead of respecting the state high court's province to say what the State's Election Code means, the Chief Justice maintains that Florida's Supreme Court has veered so far from the ordinary practice of judicial review that what it did cannot properly be called judging. My colleagues have offered a reasonable construction of Florida's law. . . .

I might join the Chief Justice were it my commission to interpret Florida law. But disagreement with the Florida court's interpretation of its own State's law does not warrant the conclusion that the justices of that court have legislated. There is no cause here to believe that the members of Florida's high court have done less than "their mortal best to discharge their oath of office," and no cause to upset their reasoned interpretation of Florida law.

This Court more than occasionally affirms statutory, and even constitutional, interpretations with which it disagrees. For example, when reviewing challenges to administrative agencies' interpretations of laws they implement, we defer to the agencies unless their interpretation violates "the unambiguously expressed intent of Congress." We do so in the face of the declaration in Article I of the United States Constitution that "All legislative Powers herein granted shall be vested in a Congress of the United States." Surely the Constitution does not call upon us to pay more respect to a federal administrative agency's construction of federal law than to a state high court's interpretation of its own state's law. And not uncommonly, we let stand state-court interpretations of federal law with which we might disagree.

Notably, in the habeas context, the Court adheres to the view that "there is 'no intrinsic reason why the fact that a man is a federal judge should make him more competent, or conscientious, or learned with respect to [federal law] than his neighbor in the state courthouse.'"

. . .

No doubt there are cases in which the proper application of federal law may hinge on interpretations of state law. Unavoidably, this Court must sometimes examine state law in order to protect federal rights. But we have dealt with such cases ever mindful of the full measure of respect we owe to interpretations of state law by a State's highest court. In the Contract Clause case, General Motors Corp. v. Romein, 503 U.S. 181 (1992), for example, we said that although "ultimately we are bound to decide for ourselves whether a contract was made," the Court "accord[s] respectful consideration and great weight to the views of the State's highest court."

And in Central Union Telephone Co. v. Edwardsville, 269 U.S. 190 (1925), we upheld the Illinois Supreme Court's interpretation of a state waiver rule, even though that interpretation resulted in the forfeiture of federal constitutional rights. Refusing to supplant Illinois law with a federal definition of waiver, we explained that the state court's declaration "should bind us unless so unfair or unreasonable in its application to those asserting a federal right as to obstruct it."

In deferring to state courts on matters of state law, we appropriately recognize that this Court acts as an "'outside[r]' lacking the common exposure to local law which comes from sitting in the jurisdiction."

That recognition has sometimes prompted us to resolve doubts about the meaning of state law by certifying issues to a State's highest court, even when federal rights are at stake. Cf. Arizonans for Official English v. Arizona, 520 U.S. 43, 79 (1997) ("Warnings against premature adjudication of constitutional questions bear heightened attention when a federal court is asked to invalidate a State's law, for the federal tribunal risks friction-generating error when it endeavors to construe a novel state Act not yet reviewed by the State's highest court.").

Notwithstanding our authority to decide issues of state law underlying federal claims, we have used the certification devise to afford state high courts an opportunity to inform us on matters of their own State's law because such restraint "helps build a cooperative judicial federalism." Lehman Brothers, 416 U.S.

Just last Term, in Fiore v. White, 528 U.S. 23 (1999), we took advantage of Pennsylvania's certification procedure. In that case, a state prisoner brought a federal habeas action claiming that the State had failed to prove an essential element of his charged offense in violation of the Due Process Clause. Instead of resolving the state-law question on which the federal claim depended, we certified the question to the Pennsylvania Supreme Court for that court to "help determine the proper state-law predicate for our determination of the federal constitutional questions raised" (asking the Pennsylvania Supreme Court whether its recent interpretation of the statute under which Fiore was convicted "was always the statute's meaning, even at the time of Fiore's trial").

The Chief Justice's willingness to reverse the Florida Supreme Court's interpretation of Florida law in this case is at least in tension with our reluctance in Fiore even to interpret Pennsylvania law before seeking instruction from the Pennsylvania Supreme Court. I would have thought the "cautious approach" we counsel when federal courts address matters of state law, Arizonans, 520 U.S., at 77, and our commitment to "build[ing] cooperative judicial federalism," Lehman Brothers, 416 U.S., at 391, demanded greater restraint.

Rarely has this Court rejected outright an interpretation of state law by a state high court. Fairfax's Devisee v. Hunter's Lessee, 7 Cranch 603 (1813), NAACP v. Alabama ex rel. Patterson, 357 U.S. 449 (1958), and Bouie v. City of Columbia, 378 U.S. 347 (1964), cited by The Chief Justice, are three such rare instances.

But those cases are embedded in historical contexts hardly comparable to the situation here. Fairfax's Devisee, which held that the Virginia Court of Appeals had misconstrued its own forfeiture laws to deprive a British subject of lands secured to him by federal treaties, occurred amidst vociferous States' rights attacks on the Marshall Court. G. Gunther & K. Sullivan, Constitutional Law 61—62 (13th ed. 1997). The Virginia court refused to obey this Court's Fairfax's Devisee mandate to enter judgment for the British subject's successor in interest. That refusal led to the Court's pathmarking decision in Martin v. Hunter's Lessee, 1 Wheat. 304 (1816).

Patterson, a case decided three months after Cooper v. Aaron, 358 U.S. 1 (1958), in the face of Southern resistance to the civil rights movement, held that the Alabama Supreme Court had irregularly applied its own procedural rules to deny review of a contempt order against the NAACP arising from its refusal to disclose membership lists. We said that "our jurisdiction is not defeated if the nonfederal ground relied on by the state court is without any fair or substantial support." 357 U.S., at 455.

Bouie, stemming from a lunch counter "sit-in" at the height of the civil rights movement, held that the South Carolina Supreme Court's construction of its trespass laws–criminalizing conduct not covered by the text of an otherwise clear statute–was "unforeseeable" and thus violated due process when applied retroactively to the petitioners. 378 U.S., at 350, 354.

The Chief Justice's casual citation of these cases might lead one to believe they are part of a larger collection of cases in which we said that the Constitution impelled us to train a skeptical eye on a state court's portrayal of state law. But one would be hard pressed, I think, to find additional cases that fit the mold.

As Justice Breyer convincingly explains, . . . (dissenting opinion), this case involves nothing close to the kind of recalcitrance by a state high court that warrants extraordinary action by this Court. The Florida Supreme Court concluded that counting every legal vote was the overriding concern of the Florida Legislature when it enacted the State's Election Code. The court surely should not be bracketed with state high courts of the Jim Crow South.

The Chief Justice says that Article II, by providing that state legislatures shall direct the manner of appointing electors, authorizes federal superintendence over the relationship between state courts and state legislatures, and licenses a departure from the usual deference we give to state court interpretations of state law. Ante, at 5 ("To attach definitive weight to the pronouncement of a state court, when the very question at issue is whether the court has actually departed from the statutory meaning, would be to abdicate our responsibility to enforce the explicit requirements of Article II.")

The Framers of our Constitution, however, understood that in a republican government, the judiciary would construe the legislature's enactments. See U.S. Const., Art. III; The Federalist No. 78 (A. Hamilton). In light of the constitutional guarantee to States of a "Republican Form of Government," U.S. Const., Art. IV, §4, Article II can hardly be read to invite this Court to disrupt a State's republican regime.

Yet the Chief Justice today would reach out to do just that. By holding that Article II requires our revision of a state court's construction of state laws in order to protect one organ of the State from another, The Chief Justice contradicts the basic principle that a State may organize itself as it sees fit. See, e.g., Gregory v. Ashcroft, 501 U.S. 452, 460 (1991) ("Through the structure of its government, and the character of those who exercise government authority, a State defines itself as a sovereign."); Highland Farms Dairy, Inc. v. Agnew, 300 U.S. 608, 612 (1937) ("How power shall be distributed by a state among its governmental organs is commonly, if not always, a question for the state itself."). Article II does not call for the scrutiny undertaken by this Court.

The extraordinary setting of this case has obscured the ordinary principle that dictates its proper resolution: Federal courts defer to state high courts' interpretations of their state's own law. This principle reflects the core of federalism, on which all agree. "The Framers split the atom of sovereignty. It was the genius of their idea that our citizens would have two political capacities, one state and one federal, each protected from incursion by the other." Saenz v. Roe, 526 U.S. 489, 504, n. 17 (1999) (citing U.S.

Term Limits, Inc. v. Thornton, 514 U.S. 779, 838 (1995), Kennedy, J., concurring).

The Chief Justice's solicitude for the Florida Legislature comes at the expense of the more fundamental solicitude we owe to the legislature's sovereign. U.S. Const., Art. II, §1, cl. 2 ("Each State shall appoint, in such Manner as the Legislature thereof may direct," the electors for President and Vice President) (emphasis added); ante, at 1—2 (Stevens, J., dissenting). Were the other members of this Court as mindful as they generally are of our system of dual sovereignty, they would affirm the judgment of the Florida Supreme Court.

II. I agree with Justice Stevens that petitioners have not presented a substantial equal protection claim. Ideally, perfection would be the appropriate standard for judging the recount. But we live in an imperfect world, one in which thousands of votes have not been counted. I cannot agree that the recount adopted by the Florida court, flawed as it may be, would yield a result any less fair or precise than the certification that preceded that recount. See, e.g., McDonald v. Board of Election Comm'rs of Chicago, 394 U.S. 802, 807 (1969) (even in the context of the right to vote, the state is permitted to reform "'one step at a time'") (quoting Williamson v. Lee Optical of Oklahoma, Inc., 348 U.S. 483, 489 (1955).

Even if there were an equal protection violation, I would agree with Justice Stevens, Justice Souter, and Justice Breyer that the Court's concern about "the December 12 deadline," ante, at 12, is misplaced. Time is short in part because of the Court's entry of a stay on December 9, several hours after an able circuit judge in Leon County had begun to superintend the recount process. More fundamentally, the Court's reluctance to let the recount go forward–despite its suggestion that "[t]he search for intent can be confined by specific rules designed to ensure uniform treatment," ante, at 8–ultimately turns on its own judgment about the practical realities of implementing a recount, not the judgment of those much closer to the process.

Equally important, as Justice Breyer explains, post, at 12 (dissenting opinion), the December 12 "deadline" for bringing Florida's electoral votes into 3 U.S.C. § 5's safe harbor lacks the significance the Court assigns it. Were that date to pass, Florida would still be entitled to deliver electoral votes Congress must count unless both Houses find that the votes "ha[d] not been ... regularly given." 3 U.S.C. § 15. The statute identifies other significant dates. See, e.g., §7 (specifying December 18 as the date electors "shall meet and give their votes"); §12 (specifying "the fourth Wednesday in December"—this year, December 27—as the date on which Congress, if it has not received a State's electoral votes, shall request the state secretary of state to send a certified return immediately). But none of these dates has ultimate significance in light of Congress' detailed provisions for determining, on "the sixth day of January," the validity of electoral votes.

The Court assumes that time will not permit "orderly judicial review of any disputed matters that might arise." But no one has doubted the good faith and diligence with which Florida election officials, attorneys for all sides of this controversy, and the courts of law have performed their duties. Notably, the Florida Supreme Court has produced two substantial opinions within 29 hours of oral argument.

In sum, the Court's conclusion that a constitutionally adequate recount is impractical is a prophecy the Court's own judgment will not allow to be tested. Such an untested prophecy should not decide the Presidency of the United States.

I dissent.

Source: *Bush v. Gore*, 531 U.S. 98 (2000).

Dissent: *Shelby County v. Holder*, 2013

This is one of RBG's most famous dissents, containing her often-repeated quote, that throwing out civil rights protection when it was working "is like throwing away your umbrella in a rainstorm because you are not getting wet." The Voting Rights Act (VRA) of 1965 was intended to ensure that state and local governments do not deny citizens the equal right to vote based on race. In 2010, Shelby County, Alabama, sought to eliminate the practice of federal preclearance before implementing changes to their voting laws. In 2013, the Supreme Court heard Shelby County v. Holder, *with the 5–4 majority deciding that because the information on which it was based was more than 40 years old, it no longer reflected current needs. Along with Justices Breyer, Kagan and Sotomayor, Justice Ginsburg dissented, or disagreed with the Court's decision. These are excerpts from her dissenting opinion:*

Dissent

SUPREME COURT OF THE UNITED STATES

No. 12–96

SHELBY COUNTY, ALABAMA, PETITIONER v. ERIC H. HOLDER, Jr., ATTORNEY GENERAL, et al. on writ of certiorari to the United States court of Appeals for the District of Columbia Circuit

June 25, 2013

Justice Ginsburg, with whom Justice Breyer, Justice Sotomayor, and Justice Kagan join, dissenting.

I. In the Court's view, the very success of §(Section) 5 of the Voting Rights Act demands its dormancy. Congress was of another mind. Recognizing that large progress has been made, Congress determined, based on a voluminous record, that the scourge of discrimination was not yet extirpated. The question this case presents is who decides whether, as currently operative, §5 remains justifiable, this Court, or a Congress charged with the obligation to enforce the post-Civil War Amendments "by appropriate legislation."

With overwhelming support in both Houses, Congress concluded that, for two prime reasons, §5 should continue in force, unabated. First, continuance would facilitate completion of the impressive gains thus far made; and second, continuance would guard against backsliding. Those assessments were well within Congress' province to make and should elicit this Court's unstinting approbation....

A century after the Fourteenth and Fifteenth Amendments guaranteed citizens the right to vote free of discrimination on the basis of race, the "blight of racial discrimination in voting" continued to "infec[t] the electoral process in parts of our country." South Carolina v. Katzenbach, 383 U. S. 301, 308 (1966).

Early attempts to cope with this vile infection resembled battling the Hydra. Whenever one form of voting discrimination was identified and prohibited, others sprang up in its place. This Court repeatedly encountered the remarkable "variety and persistence" of laws disenfranchising minority citizens. Id., at 311. To take just one example, the Court, in 1927, held unconstitutional a Texas law barring black voters from participating in primary elections, Nixon v. Herndon, 273 U. S. 536, 541; in 1944, the Court struck down a "reenacted" and slightly altered version of the same law, Smith v. Allwright, 321 U. S. 649, 658; and in 1953, the Court once again confronted an attempt by Texas to "circumven[t]" the Fifteenth Amendment by adopting yet another variant of the all-white primary, Terry v. Adams, 345 U. S. 461, 469.

During this era, the Court recognized that discrimination against minority voters was a quintessentially political problem requiring a political solution. As Justice Holmes explained: If "the great mass of the white population intends to keep the blacks from voting," "relief from [that] great political wrong, if done, as alleged, by the people of a State and the State itself, must be given by them or by the legislative and political department of the government of the United States." Giles v. Harris, 189 U. S. 475, 488 (1903).

Congress learned from experience that laws targeting particular electoral practices or enabling case-by-case litigation were inadequate to the task. In the Civil Rights Acts of 1957, 1960, and 1964, Congress authorized and then expanded the power of "the Attorney General to seek injunctions against public and private interference with the right to vote on racial grounds." Katzenbach, 383 U. S., at 313. . . .

Patently, a new approach was needed. Answering that need, the Voting Rights Act became one of the most consequential, efficacious, and amply justified exercises of federal legislative power in our Nation's his-tory. Requiring federal preclearance of changes in voting laws in the covered jurisdictions—those States and localities where opposition to the Constitution's commands were most virulent—the VRA provided a fit solution for minority voters as well as for States. Under the preclearance regime established by §5 of the VRA, covered jurisdictions must submit proposed changes in voting laws or procedures to the Department of Justice (DOJ), which has 60 days to respond to the changes. 79Stat. 439, codified at 42 U. S. C. §1973c(a).

A change will be approved unless DOJ finds it has "the purpose [or] . . . the effect of denying or abridging the right to vote on account of race or color." Ibid. In the alternative, the covered jurisdiction may seek approval by a three-judge District Court in the District of Columbia.

After a century's failure to fulfill the promise of the Fourteenth and Fifteenth Amendments, passage of the VRA finally led to signal improvement on this front. "The Justice Department estimated that in the five years after [the VRA's] passage, almost as many blacks registered [to vote] in Alabama, Mississippi, Georgia, Louisiana, North Carolina, and South Carolina as in the entire century before 1965." Davidson, The Voting Rights Act: A Brief History, in Controversies in Minority Voting 7, 21 (B. Grofman & C. Davidson eds. 1992). And in assessing the overall effects of the VRA in 2006, Congress found that "[s]ignificant progress has been made in eliminating first generation barriers experienced by minority voters, including increased numbers of registered minority voters, minority voter turnout, and minority representation in Congress, State legislatures, and local elected offices. This progress is the direct result of the Voting Rights Act of 1965." Fannie Lou Hamer, Rosa Parks, and Coretta Scott King Voting Rights Act Reauthorization and Amendments Act of 2006 (hereinafter 2006 Reauthorization), §2(b)(1), 120Stat. 577. On that matter of cause and effects there can be no genuine doubt. . . .

Congress did not take this task lightly. Quite the opposite. . . .

After considering the full legislative record, Congress made the following findings: The VRA has directly caused significant progress in eliminating first-generation barriers to ballot access, leading to a marked increase in minority voter registration and turnout and the number of minority elected officials. 2006 Reauthorization §2(b)(1). But despite this progress, "second generation barriers constructed to prevent minority voters from fully participating in the electoral process" continued to exist, as well as racially polarized voting in the covered jurisdictions, which increased the political vulnerability of racial and language minorities in those jurisdictions. §§2(b)(2)–(3), 120Stat. 577. Extensive "[e]vidence of continued discrimination," Congress concluded, "clearly show[ed] the continued need for Federal oversight" in covered jurisdictions. §§2(b)(4)–(5), id., at 577–578. The overall record demonstrated to the federal lawmakers that, "without the continuation of the Voting Rights Act of 1965 protections, racial and language minority citizens will be deprived of the opportunity to exercise their right to vote, or will have their votes diluted, undermining the significant gains made by minorities in the last 40 years." §2(b)(9), id., at 578.

Based on these findings, Congress reauthorized preclearance for another 25 years, while also undertaking to reconsider the extension after 15 years to ensure that the provision was still necessary and effective. 42 U. S. C. §1973b(a)(7), (8) (2006 ed., Supp. V). The question before the Court is whether Congress had the authority under the Constitution to act as it did.

II. In answering this question, the Court does not write on a clean slate. It is well established that Congress' judgment regarding exercise of its power to enforce the Fourteenth and Fifteenth Amendments warrants substantial deference. The VRA addresses the combination of race discrimination and the right to vote, which is "preservative of all rights." Yick Wo v. Hopkins, 118 U. S. 356, 370 (1886). When confronting the most constitutionally invidious form of discrimination, and the most fundamental right in our democratic system, Congress' power to act is at its height.

The basis for this deference is firmly rooted in both constitutional text and precedent. The Fifteenth Amendment, which targets precisely and only racial discrimination in voting rights, states that, in this domain, "Congress shall have power to enforce this article by appropriate legislation."[2] In choosing this language, the Amendment's framers invoked Chief Justice Marshall's formulation of the scope of Congress' powers under the Necessary and Proper Clause: "Let the end be legitimate, let it be within the scope of the constitution, and all means which are appropriate, which are plainly adapted to that end, which are not prohibited, but consist with the letter and spirit of the constitution, are constitutional." McCulloch v. Maryland, 4 Wheat. 316, 421 (1819). . . .

III. The 2006 reauthorization of the Voting Rights Act fully satisfies the standard stated in McCulloch, 4 Wheat., at 421: Congress may choose any means "appropriate" and "plainly adapted to" a legitimate constitutional end. As we shall see, it is implausible to suggest otherwise. . . .

A. I begin with the evidence on which Congress based its decision to continue the preclearance remedy. The surest way to evaluate whether that remedy remains in order is to see if preclearance is still effectively preventing discriminatory changes to voting laws. See City of Rome, 446 U. S., at

181 (identifying "information on the number and types of submissions made by covered jurisdictions and the number and nature of objections interposed by the Attorney General" as a primary basis for upholding the 1975 reauthorization). On that score, the record before Congress was huge. In fact, Congress found there were more DOJ objections between 1982 and 2004 (626) than there were between 1965 and the 1982 reauthorization (490). 1 Voting Rights Act: Evidence of Continued Need, Hearing before the Subcommittee on the Constitution of the House Committee on the Judiciary, 109th Cong., 2d Sess., p. 172 (2006) (hereinafter Evidence of Continued Need).

All told, between 1982 and 2006, DOJ objections blocked over 700 voting changes based on a determination that the changes were discriminatory. H. R. Rep. No. 109–478. Congress found that the majority of DOJ objections included findings of discriminatory intent, see 679 F. 3d, and that the changes blocked by preclearance were "calculated decisions to keep minority voters from fully participating in the political process." H. R. Rep. 109–478. On top of that, over the same time period the DOJ and private plaintiffs succeeded in more than 100 actions to enforce the §5 preclearance requirements. 1 Evidence of Continued Need 186, 250.

[*Author's note: Justice Ginsburg gives numerous examples of how minority groups, particularly African Americans, were impeded in seeking to vote before being assisted by preclearance, including these:*]

In 2004, Waller County, Texas, threatened to prosecute two black students after they announced their intention to run for office. The county then attempted to reduce the availability of early voting in that election at polling places near a historically black university. 679 F. 3d.

In 1990, Dallas County, Alabama, whose county seat is the City of Selma, sought to purge its voter rolls of many black voters. DOJ rejected the purge as discriminatory, noting that it would have disqualified many citizens from voting "simply because they failed to pick up or return a voter update form, when there was no valid requirement that they do so."

These examples, and scores more like them, fill the pages of the legislative record. The evidence was indeed sufficient to support Congress' conclusion that "racial discrimination in voting in covered jurisdictions [remained] serious and pervasive." 679 F. 3d.

B. I turn next to the evidence on which Congress based its decision to reauthorize the coverage formula in §4(b). Because Congress did not alter the coverage formula, the same jurisdictions previously subject to preclearance continue to be covered by this remedy. The evidence just described, of preclearance's continuing efficacy in blocking constitutional violations in the covered jurisdictions, itself grounded Congress' conclusion that the remedy should be retained for those jurisdictions.

There is no question, moreover, that the covered jurisdictions have a unique history of problems with racial discrimination in voting. Ante, at 12–13. Consideration of this long history, still in living memory, was altogether appropriate. The Court criticizes Congress for failing to recognize that "history did not end in 1965."

But the Court ignores that "what's past is prologue." —W. Shakespeare, *The Tempest*, act 2, sc. 1.

And "[t]hose who cannot remember the past are condemned to repeat it." - G. Santayana, *The Life of Reason* 284 (1905). Congress was especially mindful of the need to reinforce the gains already made and to prevent backsliding. 2006 Reauthorization §2(b)(9).

Of particular importance, even after 40 years and thousands of discriminatory changes blocked by preclearance, conditions in the covered jurisdictions demonstrated that the formula was still justified by "current needs." Northwest Austin, 557 U. S., at 203. . . .

IV. Congress approached the 2006 reauthorization of the VRA with great care and seriousness. The same cannot be said of the Court's opinion today. The Court makes no genuine attempt to engage with the massive legislative record that Congress assembled. Instead, it relies on increases in voter registration and turnout as if that were the whole story. See supra, at 18–19. Without even identifying a standard of review, the Court dismissively brushes off arguments based on "data from the record," and declines to enter the "debat[e about] what [the] record shows." Ante, at 20–21. One would expect more from an opinion striking at the heart of the Nation's signal piece of civil-rights legislation.

I note the most disturbing lapses. First, by what right, given its usual restraint, does the Court even address Shelby County's facial challenge to the VRA? Second, the Court veers away from controlling precedent regarding the "equal sovereignty" doctrine without even acknowledging that it is doing so. Third, hardly showing the respect ordinarily paid when Congress acts to implement the Civil War Amendments, and as just stressed, the Court does not even deign to grapple with the legislative record.

A. Shelby County launched a purely facial challenge to the VRA's 2006 reauthorization. "A facial challenge to a legislative Act," the Court has other times said, "is, of course, the most difficult challenge to mount successfully, since the challenger must establish that no set of circumstances exists under which the Act would be valid." United States v. Salerno, 481 U. S. 739, 745 (1987). . . .

Alabama is home to Selma, site of the "Bloody Sunday" beatings of civil-rights demonstrators that served as the catalyst for the VRA's enactment. Following those events, Martin Luther King, Jr., led a march from Selma to

Montgomery, Alabama's capital, where he called for passage of the VRA. If the Act passed, he foresaw, progress could be made even in Alabama, but there had to be a steadfast national commitment to see the task through to completion. In King's words, "the arc of the moral universe is long, but it bends toward justice." G. May, *Bending Toward Justice: The Voting Rights Act and the Transformation of American Democracy 144* (2013).

History has proved King right. Although circumstances in Alabama have changed, serious concerns remain. . . .

[*Author's note: Justice Ginsburg gives numerous examples of voting rights and other abuses that persist in Alabama, including these:*]

In 2008, for example, the city of Calera, located in Shelby County, requested preclearance of a redistricting plan that "would have eliminated the city's sole majority-black district, which had been created pursuant to the consent decree" . . .

A recent FBI investigation provides a further window into the persistence of racial discrimination in state politics. . . . Recording devices worn by state legislators cooperating with the FBI's investigation captured conversations between members of the state legislature and their political allies. The recorded conversations are shocking. Members of the state Senate derisively refer to African-Americans as "Aborigines" and talk openly of their aim to quash a particular gambling-related referendum because the referendum, if placed on the ballot, might increase African-American voter turnout. . . . The District Judge presiding over the criminal trial at which the recorded conversations were introduced commented that the "recordings represent compelling evidence that political exclusion through racism remains a real and enduring problem" in Alabama. Id., at 1347. Racist sentiments, the judge observed, "remain regrettably entrenched in the high echelons of state government." . . .

Leaping to resolve Shelby County's facial challenge without considering whether application of the VRA to Shelby County is constitutional, or even addressing the VRA's severability provision, the Court's opinion can hardly be described as an exemplar of restrained and moderate decision making. Quite the opposite. Hubris is a fit word for today's demolition of the VRA.

B. The Court stops any application of §5 by holding that §4(b)'s coverage formula is unconstitutional. It pins this result, in large measure, to "the fundamental principle of equal sovereignty.". . .

In the Court's conception, it appears, defenders of the VRA could not prevail upon showing what the record overwhelmingly bears out, i.e., that there is a need for continuing the preclearance regime in covered States. . . . I am aware of no precedent for imposing such a double burden on defenders of legislation.

C. The Court has time and again declined to upset legislation of this genre unless there was no or almost no evidence of unconstitutional action by States. See, e.g., City of Boerne v. Flores, 521 U. S. 507, 530 (1997) (legislative record "mention[ed] no episodes [of the kind the legislation aimed to check] occurring in the past 40 years") . . .

Volumes of evidence supported Congress' de-termination that the prospect of retrogression was real. *Throwing out preclearance when it has worked and is continuing to work to stop discriminatory changes is like throwing away your umbrella in a rainstorm because you are not getting wet* (emphasis the author's).

But, the Court insists, the coverage formula is no good; it is based on "decades-old data and eradicated practices."

The Court holds §4(b) invalid on the ground that it is "irrational to base coverage on the use of voting tests 40 years ago, when such tests have been illegal since that time." Ante, at 23. But the Court disregards what Congress set about to do in enacting the VRA. That extraordinary legislation scarcely stopped at the particular tests and devices that happened to exist in 1965. The grand aim of the Act is to secure to all in our polity equal citizenship stature, a voice in our democracy undiluted by race. As the record for the 2006 reauthorization makes abundantly clear, second-generation barriers to minority voting rights have emerged in the covered jurisdictions as attempted substitutes for the first-generation barriers that originally triggered preclearance in those jurisdictions.

The sad irony of today's decision lies in its utter failure to grasp why the VRA has proven effective. The Court appears to believe that the VRA's success in eliminating the specific devices extant in 1965 means that preclearance is no longer needed. Ante, at 21–22, 23–24. With that belief, and the argument derived from it, history repeats itself. The same assumption—that the problem could be solved when particular methods of voting discrimination are identified and eliminated—was indulged and proved wrong repeatedly prior to the VRA's enactment. Unlike prior statutes, which singled out particular tests or devices, the VRA is grounded in Congress' recognition of the "variety and persistence" of measures designed to impair minority voting rights. In truth, the evolution of voting discrimination into more subtle second-generation barriers is powerful evidence that a remedy as effective as preclearance remains vital to protect minority voting rights and prevent backsliding.

Beyond question, the VRA is no ordinary legislation. It is extraordinary because Congress embarked on a mission long delayed and of extraordinary importance: to realize the purpose and promise of the Fifteenth Amendment. For a half century, a concerted effort has been made to end racial discrimination in voting. Thanks to the Voting Rights Act, progress once the subject of a dream has been achieved and continues to be made.

The record supporting the 2006 reauthorization of the VRA is also extraordinary. It was described by the Chairman of the House Judiciary Committee as "one of the most extensive considerations of any piece of legislation that the United States Congress has dealt with in the 27½ years" he had served in the House. 152 Cong. Rec. H5143 (July 13, 2006) (statement of Rep. Sensenbrenner). After exhaustive evidence-gathering and deliberative process, Congress reauthorized the VRA, including the coverage provision, with overwhelming bipartisan support. It was the judgment of Congress that "40 years has not been a sufficient amount of time to eliminate the vestiges of discrimination following nearly 100 years of disregard for the dictates of the 15th amendment and to ensure that the right of all citizens to vote is protected as guaranteed by the Constitution." 2006 Reauthorization §2(b)(7), 120 Stat. 577. That determination of the body empowered to enforce the Civil War Amendments "by appropriate legislation" merits this Court's utmost respect.

In my judgment, the Court errs egregiously by overriding Congress' decision....

For the reasons stated, I would affirm the judgment of the Court of Appeals.

Source: *Shelby County v. Holder*, 570 U.S. 529 (2013).

Bibliography

ACLU (American Civil Liberties Union). https://www.aclu.org.
"ACLU History: A Decade of Landmarks for Women," *American Civil Liberties Union*. https://www.aclu.org/other/aclu-history-decade-landmarks-women.
Anderson, Becca. *The Book of Awesome Women: Boundary Breakers, Freedom Fighters, Sheroes and Female Firsts*. Coral Gables, FL: Mango, 2017.
"Announcement of Ginsburg as Supreme Court Justice Nominee," *Clinton Presidential Library*. https://www.youtube.com/watch?v=MHwoosXsybQ.
"The Awakening: Women and Power in the Academy," *Chronicle of Higher Education*. https://www.chronicle.com/interactives/the-awakening.
Buckley, Christopher. "Supreme Court Calendar," in *But Enough about You*. New York: Simon & Schuster Paperbacks, 2014.
Campbell, Amy Leigh. *Raising the Bar: Ruth Bader Ginsburg and the ACLU Women's Rights Project*. Bloomington, IN: Xlibris, 2004.
Canellos, Peter. "Why We Should Worry About the Cult of RBG," *Politico*, December 25, 2018. https://www.politico.com/magazine/story/2018/12/25/on-the-basis-of-sex-review-rbg-223557.
Carmon, Irin, and Shana Knizhnik. *Notorious RBG: The Life and Times of Ruth Bader Ginsburg*. New York: Dey Street Books, 2015.
Collins, Gail. *America's Women: 400 Years of Dolls, Drudges, Helpmates, and Heroines*. New York: William Morrow, 2007.
Collins, Gail. *When Everything Changed: The Amazing Journey of American Women from 1960 to the Present*. Boston: Little Brown, 2009.
Coontz, Stephanie. *Marriage, A History: From Obedience to Intimacy or How Love Conquered Marriage*. New York: Penguin Books, 2006.
Coontz, Stephanie. *The Way We Never Were: American Families and the Nostalgia Trap*. New York: Basic Books, 1992.

Cott, Nancy F. *Public Vows: A History of Marriage and the Nation.* Cambridge, MA: Harvard University Press, 2002.

Dalin, David G. *Jewish Justices of the Supreme Court: From Brandeis to Kagan.* Lebanon, NH: Brandeis University Press, an imprint of the University Press of New England, 2017.

De Hart, Jane Sherron. *Ruth Bader Ginsburg: A Life.* New York: Knopf, 2018.

Douglas, Susan J. *Where the Girls Are: Growing Up Female with the Mass Media.* New York: Three Rivers Press, 1995.

DuBois, Ellen Carol, and Lynn Dumenil. *Through Women's Eyes: An American History with Documents.* Boston, MA: Bedford/St. Martin's, 2019.

Durso, Pamela R. *The Power of Woman: The Life and Writings of Sarah Moore Grimké.* Macon, GA: Mercer University Press, 2004.

Ehrenreich, Barbara. *The Hearts of Men: American Dreams and the Flight from Commitment.* New York: Anchor, 1983.

Fleer, BreAnne. "Ruth Bader Ginsburg Shares #MeToo Experience at Cornell," *The Cornell Daily Sun*, January 23, 2018. https://cornellsun.com/2018/01/23/ruth-bader-ginsburg-shares-metoo-experience-at-cornell/.

Fleming, Mike, Jr. "Oscars Last Call: Lucasfilm's Kathleen Kennedy on Why 'RBG'—The Woman and the Movie—Really Matter," *Deadline*, February 14, 2019. https://deadline.com/2019/02/rbg-ruth-bader-ginsburg-kathleen-kennedy-commentary-oscars-1202556898.

Friedman, Jane M. *America's First Woman Lawyer: The Biography of Myra Bradwell.* Buffalo, NY: Prometheus Books, 1993.

Friedman, Morgan. *The Inflation Calculator.* https://westegg.com/inflation.

Gabler, Neal. *An Empire of Their Own.* New York: Doubleday, 1988.

Gibson, Katie L. *Ruth Bader Ginsburg's Legacy of Dissent: Feminist Rhetoric and the Law.* Tuscaloosa: University of Alabama Press, 2018.

Gilbert, James. *Men in the Middle: Searching for Masculinity in the 1950s.* Chicago: University of Chicago Press, 2005.

Gilbert, Lynn, and Gaylen Moore. "Ruth Bader Ginsburg," in *Particular Passions: Talks with Women Who Have Shaped Our Times.* http://www.particularpassions.com/ruth-bader-ginsburg.

Gilbert, Thom. *Blue Suede Shoes: The Culture of Elvis.* New York: Glitterati Editions, 2016.

Ginsburg, Ruth Bader. "Introduction to Women and the Law: Facing the Millennium," *Indiana Law Review* 32, no. 4 (1999): p. 1161.

Ginsburg, Ruth Bader. "Ruth Bader Ginsburg's Advice for Living," *The New York Times*, October 1, 2016. https://www.nytimes.com/2016/10/02/opinion/sunday/ruth-bader-ginsburgs-advice-for-living.html.

Ginsburg, Ruth Bader with Mary Hartnett. *My Own Words*. New York: Simon & Schuster, 2018.

Githler, Charley. "Jewish Sororities at Cornell: Deep-rooted Groups Born Out of Necessity," *Ithaca*, August 27, 2017. https://www.ithaca.com/news/jewish-sororities-at-cornell-deep-rooted-groups-born-out-of/article_95acd88e-883f-11e7-b9ab-5b668f44ce9b.html.

Grann, David. *Killers of the Flower Moon: The Osage Murders and the Birth of the FBI*. New York: Doubleday, 2017.

Gray, Emma. "Before Ruth Bader Ginsburg Was a Meme, She Was a Feminist with a 'Radical Vision'—*RBG* Tells the Story of Ginsburg's Legacy and Influence Beyond the Internet," *Huffington Post*, May 3, 2018. https://www.huffpost.com/entry/ruth-bader-ginsburg-rbg-movie_n_5ae8b2b5e4b04aa23f279348.

Greene, Meg. *Elena Kagan: A Biography*. Santa Barbara, CA: Greenwood, 2014.

Grimké, Sarah Moore. *Letters on the Equality of the Sexes, and the Condition of Woman*. Charleston, SC: BiblioBazaar, 2008.

Halberstam, David. *The Fifties*. New York: Villard, 1993.

Halberstam, Malvina. "Ruth Bader Ginsburg," *Jewish Women's Archive Encyclopedia*. https://jwa.org/encyclopedia/article/ginsburg-ruth-bader.

Hall, Mitchell. *The Emergence of Rock and Roll: Music and the Rise of American Youth Culture*. New York: Routledge, 2014.

Hardie Grant Books (author). *Pocket RBG Wisdom: Supreme Quotes and Inspired Musings from Ruth Bader Ginsburg*. San Francisco, CA: Hardie Grant Books, distributed by Chronicle Books, 2019.

Hardy, Sheila. *A 1950s Housewife: Marriage and Homemaking in the 1950s*. Charleston, SC: The History Press, 2016.

Harrington, Michael. *The Other America: Poverty in the United States*. New York: Touchstone, 1997.

Harvey, Brett. *The Fifties: A Women's Oral History*. New York: HarperCollins, 1993.

Hendricks, Nancy. *Daily Life in 1950s America*. Santa Barbara, CA: Greenwood, 2019.

Hendricks, Nancy. *Notable Arkansas Women: From Hattie to Hillary, 100 Names to Know*. Little Rock, AR: Butler Center Books, 2016.

Hendricks, Nancy. *Popular Fads and Crazes through American History*. Santa Barbara, CA: ABC-CLIO, 2018.

Hendricks, Nancy. *Senator Hattie Caraway: An Arkansas Legacy*. Charleston, SC: The History Press, 2013.

Herbst, Jurgen. *The Once and Future School: Three Hundred and Fifty Years of American Secondary Education*. New York: Routledge, 1996.

"History of the ACLU Women's Rights Project, The," *American Civil Liberties Union*. https://www.aclu.org/other/history-aclu-womens-rights-project.

"How Far Have We Come on the Arc of Justice?" *CBS News*, September 20, 2016. https://www.cbsnews.com/video/how-far-have-we-come-on-the-arc-of-justice.

"How Ruth Bader Ginsburg Met Her Match," *CNN Films*. https://www.cnn.com/videos/tv/2018/08/27/rbg-film-marty-ginsburg.cnn.

Humes, Edward. *Over Here: How the G.I. Bill Transformed the American Dream*. Orlando, FL: Harcourt, 2006.

Irons, Peter. *A People's History of the Supreme Court: The Men and Women Whose Cases and Decisions Have Shaped Our Constitution*. New York: Penguin Books, 2006.

Johnson, Bryant. *The RBG Workout: How She Stays Strong . . . and You Can Too!* New York: Houghton Mifflin Harcourt, 2017.

"Justice Ruth Bader Ginsburg Eulogy at Justice Scalia Memorial Service," *C-SPAN*. https://www.youtube.com/watch?v=jb_2GgE564A.

"Justice Ruth Bader Ginsburg in Conversation," *WLIW21 Specials*, PBS. https://www.pbs.org/video/justice-ruth-bader-ginsburg-in-conversation-jzwgyq/.

"Justice Ruth Bader Ginsburg Speaks," *CBS Sunday Morning*. https://www.youtube.com/watch?v=HsaHGFQjp0w.

Kanefield, Teri. *Free to Be Ruth Bader Ginsburg: The Story of Women and Law*. San Francisco, CA: Armon Books, 2016.

Kanfer, Stefan. *Ball of Fire: The Tumultuous Life and Comic Art of Lucille Ball*. New York: Knopf, 2003.

Karbo, Karen. *In Praise of Difficult Women: Life Lessons From 29 Heroines Who Dared to Break the Rules*. Washington, DC: National Geographic Books, 2018.

Keyser, Jason. "Justice Ginsburg Weighs Legal Lessons of Opera," *WQXR*, August 5, 2012. https://www.wqxr.org/story/228005-justice-ginsburg-weighs-legal-lessons-opera/.

King, Gilbert. "The Great Dissenter and His Half-Brother," *Smithsonian*, December 20, 2011. https://www.smithsonianmag.com/history/the-great-dissenter-and-his-half-brother-10214325/.

Lamb, Brian, Susan Swain, and Mark Farkas, editors. *The Supreme Court: A C-SPAN Book, Featuring the Justices in their Own Words*. New York: PublicAffairs (sic), 2010.

Lamphier, Peg A. *Kate Chase and William Sprague: Politics and Gender in a Civil War Marriage*. Lincoln: University of Nebraska Press, 2003.

Lancaster, Guy. "Creationists v. Arkansas," *Arkansas Times*, May 31, 2019. https://arktimes.com/history/2019/05/31/creationists-v-arkansas.

Lepore, Jill. *The Secret History of Wonder Woman.* New York: Vintage, 2015.
Levy, Debbie. *I Dissent: Ruth Bader Ginsburg Makes Her Mark.* New York: Simon & Schuster, 2016.
Lopez, Raquel. "Paideia: Education in Ancient Greece," *National Geographic History,* July/August 2019, pp. 30–43.
Manbeck, John B. *Brooklyn: Historically Speaking.* Charleston, SC: The History Press, 2008.
Mansbridge, Jane J. *Why We Lost the ERA (Equal Rights Movement).* Chicago, IL: University of Chicago Press, 1986.
Margulis, Daniel, and John Schroeder, editors. *A Century at Cornell.* Ithaca, NY: Cornell Daily Sun, 1980.
Mauro, Tony. *The Supreme Court: Landmark Decisions: 20 Cases That Changed America.* New York: Fall River Press, 2016.
May, Elaine Tyler. *Homeward Bound: American Families in the Cold War Era.* New York: Basic Books, 2008.
McClay, Michael, and Deanna Gaffner-McClay. *I Love Lucy: The Complete Picture History of the Most Popular TV Show Ever.* New York: Grand Central Publishing, 1995.
McNeil, Liz. "Ruth Bader Ginsburg: Her Great Love Story," *People,* December 31, 2018, pp. 65–67.
Mettler, Suzanne. *Soldiers to Citizens: The G.I. Bill and the Making of the Greatest Generation.* New York: Oxford University Press, 2007.
Miles, Rosalind. *Who Cooked the Last Supper? The Women's History of the World.* New York: Three Rivers Press, 2001.
Murphy, Bill, Jr. "Want to Raise a Trailblazing Daughter? Justice Ruth Bader Ginsburg Says Do These 7 Things," *Inc,* October 4, 2016. https://www.inc.com/bill-murphy-jr/7-things-successful-people-need-to-do-courtesy-of-ruth-bader-ginsburg.html.
Nahas, Aili. "I Designed Barbie's Clothes," *People,* March 18, 2019, pp. 73–75.
Nelson, Michael C. *The Presidency and the Political System.* Washington, DC: CQ Press, 2018.
Neuwirth, Jessica, with Introduction by Gloria Steinem. *Equal Means Equal: Why the Time for an Equal Rights Amendment Is Now.* New York: The New Press, 2015.
Norgren, Jill. *Rebels at the Bar: The Fascinating, Forgotten Stories of America's First Women Lawyers.* New York: New York University Press, 2016.
Norgren, Jill. *Stories from Trailblazing Women Lawyers: Lives in the Law.* New York: New York University Press, 2018.
O'Connor, Sandra Day. *The Majesty of the Law: Reflections of a Supreme Court Justice.* New York: Random House Trade Paperbacks, 2004.

O'Connor, Sandra Day. *Out of Order: Stories from the History of the Supreme Court.* New York: Random House, 2013.

On the Basis of Sex (movie) official website. http://focusfeatures.com/on-the-basis-of-sex.

Ortiz, Victoria. *Dissenter on the Bench: Ruth Bader Ginsburg's Life and Work.* New York: Clarion Books, 2019.

"'Out of Order' at the Court: O'Connor on Being the First Female Justice," *NPR*, March 5, 2013. https://www.npr.org/2013/03/05/172982275/out-of-order-at-the-court-oconnor-on-being-the-first-female-justice.

Oyez.org. https://www.oyez.org/.

Patterson, James T. *Grand Expectations: The United States, 1945–1974.* New York: Oxford University Press, 1997.

Peppers, Todd, and Artemus Ward, editors. *In Chambers: Stories of Supreme Court Law Clerks and Their Justices.* Charlottesville: University of Virginia Press, 2012.

"Pushcarts of the Lower East Side, Circa 1903," https://www.youtube.com/watch?v=yDCo58-XvWY.

RBG (documentary), Magnolia Pictures. www.rbgmovie.com.

Reumann, Miriam. *American Sexual Character: Sex, Gender, and National Identity in the Kinsey Reports.* Berkeley: University of California Press, 2005.

Roberts, Cokie. *Founding Mothers: The Women Who Raised Our Nation.* New York: Harper Perennial, 2005.

Rosen, Jeffrey. "The Book of Ruth," *The New Republic*, August 2, 1993. https://newrepublic.com/article/61837/the-book-ruth.

"Ruth Bader Ginsburg, Justice, Supreme Court of the United States," *Academy of Achievement.* https://www.achievement.org/achiever/ruth-bader-ginsburg/.

Sachar, Howard M. *A History of Jews in America.* New York: Vintage Books, 1993.

Scalia, Antonin. "Ruth Bader Ginsburg," *Time*, April 15, 2015. https://time.com/3823889/ruth-bader-ginsburg-2015-time-100.

Scalia/Ginsburg: American Comic Opera in One Act by Derrick Wang Official Website. http://www.derrickwang.com/scalia-ginsburg.

Schaal, Kristen. "The Future of Gender Wage Equality," *The Daily Show with Jon Stewart*, March 24, 2015. http://www.cc.com/video-clips/poj8lb/the-daily-show-with-jon-stewart-the-future-of-gender-wage-equality.

Sotomayor, Sonia. *My Beloved World.* New York Vintage, 2014.

Stephanopoulos, George. *All Too Human: A Political Education.* New York: Little Brown, 1999.

Stern, Seth. "The Supreme Court's Champion of Women's Rights Who Refused to Hire Women," *Huffington Post*, May 25, 2011. https://www.huffpost.com/entry/a-champion-of-womens-righ_b_780176.

Stoll, Ira. "How One 'Ordinary' Brooklyn High School Produced Six Nobel Laureates, a Supreme Court Justice, and Three Senators," *EducationNext*, March 13, 2019. https://www.educationnext.org/one-ordinary-brooklyn-high-school-produced-six-nobel-laureates-supreme-court-justice-three-senators/.

"Supreme Court, The: Home to America's Highest Court, 2010 Edition," *C-SPAN*, December 20, 2010. https://www.c-span.org/video/?297213-1/the-supreme-court-home-americas-highest-court-2010-edition.

"Supreme Court Interviews," *LawProse.org*. http://www.lawprose.org/bryan-garner/garners-interviews/supreme-court-interviews/justice-ruth-bader-ginsburg-supreme-court-of-the-united-states-part-1/

Supreme Court of the United States. https://www.supremecourt.gov.

"Supreme Interview with Ruth Bader Ginsburg, A," *CNN*. https://www.cnn.com/videos/us/2018/02/12/ruth-bader-ginsburg-interview-entire-poppy-harlow-intv.cnn.

Swers, Michele L. *Women in the Club: Gender and Policy Making in the Senate.* Chicago, IL: University of Chicago Press, 2013.

"Tenement Museum—Lower East Side, NY," YouTube. https://www.youtube.com/watch?v=p4pyX4RwOp4.

Thomas, Evan. "Behind the Scenes of Sandra Day O'Connor's First Days on the Supreme Court," *Smithsonian*, March 2019. https://www.smithsonianmag.com/history/behind-scenes-sandra-day-oconnor-first-days-supreme-court-180971441.

Thomas, Evan. *First: Sandra Day O'Connor.* New York: Random House, 2019.

Thomas, Marlo, editor. "The Honorable Ruth Bader Ginsburg, Associate Justice of the Supreme Court of the United States," in *The Right Words at the Right Time.* New York: Atria Books, 2002.

Toobin, Jeffrey "Heavyweight: How Ruth Bader Ginsburg Has Moved the Supreme Court," *The New Yorker*, March 11, 2013. https://www.newyorker.com/magazine/2013/03/11/heavyweight-ruth-bader-ginsburg.

Turnbaugh, Kristi. "Ruth Bader Ginsburg's Story from Page to Screen," *Columbia College Chicago*, December 4, 2018. https://www.colum.edu/news-and-events/articles/2018/ruth-bader-ginsburgs-story-from-page-to-screen.html#.XOFSROTsbcs.

"United States v. Virginia," *Oyez*. https://www.oyez.org/cases/1995/94-1941.

Urofsky, Melvin. *Louis D. Brandeis: A Life.* New York: Pantheon, 2009.

Vile, John R. *Essential Supreme Court Decisions: Summaries of Leading Cases in U.S. Constitutional Law, Seventeenth Edition.* Lanham, MD: Rowman & Littlefield, 2018.

Wagman-Geller, Marlene. *Great Second Acts: In Praise of Older Women.* Coral Gables, FL: Mango, 2018.

Walker, Nancy A. *Women's Magazines, 1940–1960: Gender Roles and the Popular Press.* Boston, MA: Bedford/St. Martin's, 1998.

Walker, Samuel. *In Defense of American Liberties, Second Edition: A History of the ACLU.* Carbondale: Southern Illinois University Press, 1999.

Wang, Derrick. "Scalia/Ginsburg, an American Comic Opera in One Act Inspired by the Opinions of U.S. Supreme Court Justices Ruth Bader Ginsburg and Antonin Scalia," *DerrickWang.com.* http://www.derrickwang.com/scalia-ginsburg.

Ward, Artemus, and David Weiden. *Sorcerers' Apprentices: 100 Years of Law Clerks at the United States Supreme Court.* New York: New York University Press, 2007.

Waxman, Olivia B. "3 Things We Learned from the New Ruth Bader Ginsburg Documentary," *Time*, August 1, 2018. http://time.com/5247283/ruth-bader-ginsburg-rbg/.

Weiss, Debra Cassens. "Did Alito Roll His Eyes during Ginsburg Dissent?" *ABA Journal*, June 26, 2013. http://www.abajournal.com/news/article/did_alito_roll_his_eyes_during_ginsburg_dissent.

Weiss, Elaine. *The Woman's Hour: The Great Fight to Win the Vote.* New York: Viking, 2018.

Welch, Rosanne, editor. *When Women Wrote Hollywood: Essays on Female Screenwriters in the Early Film Industry.* Jefferson, NC: McFarland, 2018.

Young, William, and Nancy K. Young. *The 1950s.* Westport, CT: Greenwood, 2004.

Index

Alito, Samuel, 141, 142, 150
All Rise (television program), xx
Alpha Epsilon Phi, 20
American Civil Liberties Union (ACLU), 10, 88, 90–91, 94; history of, 60, 62, 80, 81–82; RBG and, 77, 85, 86, 89, 94–95, 98; Women's Rights Project (WRP), xxix, 82, 91, 98–100, 103, 104, 112, 166
Amster, Joseph, 5
Amster, Rose Dick, 6
Amster, Solomon ("Chuck"), 6, 10, 15, 22

Bader, Celia Amster, xxv, xxx, 5–8, 10–11, 22, 32, 34, 52, 91, 117, 124, 126, 131, 138, 142, 145, 194; illness and death of, xxvi, 15–17, 163; influence on RBG, 11–13, 26, 27, 35, 65, 153, 162
Bader, Ida Milstein, 2
Bader, Marilyn, 6, 7, 8, 9, 13, 16, 161
Bader, Nathan, 13, 16, 17, 22, 31, 33–34, 75–76, 163, 166; and Celia, 6–8, 10; death of, 34, 76; early life, 2–5
Bader, Richard, 3, 9, 40
Ball, Lucille, xix
Barbie (doll), 99
Bathrooms (as women's issue), 47, 48, 98, 131, 132, 173
Biden, Joseph, 119, 125, 188, 195
Biggie Smalls. *See* Notorious B.I.G.

Bork, Robert, 119, 120, 124
Bradwell, Myra, 43, 181–182
Brennan, William, xxvii–xxviii
Brenneman, Amy, 48
Breyer, Stephen, 51, 121, 134, 137, 139, 141, 142, 144, 145, 201, 204, 205, 206
Brown v. Board of Education, xxii, 24–25, 44–45, 58, 60, 70, 80, 94, 108, 164
Bruzelius, Anders, 65
Burger, Warren, 107, 121, 127
Burwell v. Hobby Lobby, 140, 145–146, 152, 169
Bush v. Gore, xxiv, 135–136, 143, 145, 168, 200

Califano v. Goldfarb, 102, 167
Camp Che-Na-Wah, 9–10, 16, 31, 91, 163
Caraway, Hattie, 9, 132
Carter, Jimmy, 108–110, 112, 113, 114–116, 117, 167, 184, 192, 193
Chef Supreme (book), 41
Citizens United v. Federal Election Commission, 137, 169
Civil Procedure in Sweden (book), 65, 166
Civil Rights Act of 1964, 85, 142, 165
Clark, Mamie Phipps, 25
Clinton, Bill, 81, 107, 118, 121–123, 125, 127, 134, 168, 171–173, 176, 184, 187, 188, 192

Clinton, Hillary Rodham, 194
Coleman, William Thaddeus, 60, 62
Columbia Law Review (legal journal), 51, 54, 165
Columbia Law School, 25, 31, 43, 51, 53, 62, 63, 64, 72, 89, 122, 132, 159, 165, 179, 181; RBG as professor, 77, 93, 97–98, 103–104, 108, 111–112, 166, 194; RBG as student, 53–54, 55
Columbia Project on International Civil Procedure, 62, 63, 65, 71, 165
Cornell University, 6, 10, 15–16, 19–20, 21–34, 37, 48, 65, 79, 89, 98, 164, 187
Court of Appeals for the District of Columbia Circuit ("D.C. Circuit"), 113–120, 122, 123, 124, 125, 126, 159, 167, 184, 192, 194, 199, 206
Cuomo, Mario, 121, 122
Cushman, Robert, 28, 29

Davison, Kenneth, 103, 167
"D.C. Circuit." *See* Court of Appeals for the District of Columbia Circuit
de Beauvoir, Simone, 74–75
Deuteronomy (scriptures in Bible), 18, 131
Dole, Elizabeth, 118
Douglas, William O., 61, 102, 109
Dred Scott decision, 70
Duren v. Missouri, 102, 167
Dylan, Bob (Robert Zimmerman), xviii

Eisenhower, Dwight, xviii, 23, 46, 55, 57, 67, 164
Ellis Island, 1–2
Ephron, Nora, 100
Equal Pay Day, 154
Equal Rights Amendment (ERA), xxvi, 70, 90, 92, 93, 107, 108
Escoffier, Auguste, 40, 41

Feminine Mystique, The (book), 69, 74, 83, 90, 100, 165
Fifteenth Amendment, 139, 207, 208, 209, 213
Finkbine, Sherri, 67

Ford, Gerald, 108–109, 158
Fort Sill, Oklahoma, 38–39, 40, 41–42, 44, 75, 164
Fourteenth Amendment, 61, 70, 92, 94, 95, 128, 133, 134, 135, 139, 142, 182, 191, 207, 208, 209
Frankfurter, Felix, 51, 58, 60–62
Fried, Frank, Harris, Shriver and Jacobson (law firm), 117, 119
Friedan, Betty, 69, 74, 83, 90, 100, 111, 165
Frontiero v. Richardson, xxvii–xxviii, 100–102, 167

G.I. Bill, 9, 23, 27
Garment District (area of New York City), 6, 126
Georgetown University Law Center, 119, 158
Gilbert and Sullivan (composers), 26, 27, 90, 95
Ginsburg, Evelyn Bayer, xxvi, 31–32, 34–35, 41, 47, 51, 56, 75, 127, 168
Ginsburg, James Steven, 82, 117, 119, 166, 193; birth of, 75; Cedille Records, 112; childhood escapades, 112
Ginsburg, Jane Carol, 7, 52, 64, 75, 76, 111, 164, 193; birth of, 42
Ginsburg, Martin David ("Marty"), xxvi, 31, 37, 75, 76, 110, 116, 122, 127, 155, 164, 165, 167, 168, 193, 194, 197; childhood, 32; cooking skills of, 41, 119, 123; at Cornell, 33, 37; dating RBG, 31–34; death, 35, 138–139, 169; at Fort Sill, 38–40; at Harvard Law School, 42, 47, 51, 53; illness of, 52–53, 138; law practice, 63, 71, 82, 91, 94, 117; marriage to RBG, 34, 35, 36, 112; and Moritz case, 94–96
Ginsburg, Morris, 31–32, 34, 42, 47, 167
Ginsburg, (Joan) Ruth Bader ("RBG") in academia, 55–77; and ACLU, 79–104; birth and childhood, 1–18; college, 19–36; cooking skills of, 40–41; as federal judge, 107–126; at Fort Sill, 38–44; job search by, 54,

55, 56, 59, 62, 64, 72; "Kiki" nickname, 7, 31, 163; law school, 37–54; as meme, xx, 149–162; and opera, 12, 26, 27, 31, 39, 44, 45, 90, 95, 141, 155, 176; at Rutgers, 71–74, 75–77; as Supreme Court justice, 127–146; in Sweden, 62–69; wedding and honeymoon, 34–35; and Women's Rights Project, 82, 91, 98–104, 112, 115, 166

Grimké, Sarah, 101

Griswold, Erwin, 47, 48, 53, 113, 122; dinner party incident, 49–50

Gunther, Gerald, 59

Hand, Learned, 57–58, 59, 197

Hansberry, Lorraine, 56

Harvard Law Review (legal journal), xxx, 51, 58, 97, 111, 164

Harvard Law School, xxx, 33, 37, 42, 53, 58, 60, 72, 110, 111, 113, 122, 130, 132, 139, 164, 165, 172, 174, 179, 184, 185, 187; history of, 43; "Ladies Day" at, 50; library incident, 50–51; movies set at, 43; RBG at, 44, 46–50

Hill, Anita, 125

Holder, Eric, xix

Hughes, Langston, 29, 56

Hughes, Sarah, 70, 71

James Madison High School, 14–16, 163

Johnson, Bryant, 156, 157

Johnson, Lyndon, 62, 70, 71, 96, 121, 184

Jorgenson, Christine, 67

Kagan, Elena, 48, 51, 131, 139, 141, 145, 152, 159, 160, 169, 174, 180, 184–185, 206

Kay, Herma Hill, 103, 167

Kearse, Amalya, 113

Kennedy, Anthony, 128, 141

Kennedy, Edward ("Ted"), 114, 116, 195

Kennedy, John F., xviii, xxv, 47, 55, 63, 68, 69, 70, 71, 79, 94, 96, 121, 165

Kennedy, Robert, xxv, 70, 80

Kenyon, Dorothy, 92–93, 94

Kepley, Ada, 43, 178, 185

King, Martin Luther, Jr., xix, xxv, 69, 80, 165, 166, 211

Knizhnik, Shana, 153–154

Korean War, 21, 37, 38, 163

Lawton, Oklahoma, 39, 41, 164

Ledbetter, Lilly, 136, 144, 168

Ledbetter v. Goodyear Tire and Rubber Company, 136, 144, 152, 168

Lewinsky, Monica, 118

Little Rock, Arkansas, xvii, 23, 164, 171

Lomen, Lucille, 61, 179

Loving v. Virginia, 80

Lower East Side (New York City neighborhood), 2–5, 7, 10–11, 60

Mansfield, Arabella, 43, 177, 181, 186

Marshall, John, 146, 203, 209

Marshall, Thurgood, 44, 45, 80, 94, 113, 117, 121, 122, 159, 166, 175, 184

McCarthy, Joseph, 24, 33, 37, 47, 93

McCarthyism, 28, 29, 30, 58, 177

McKinnon, Kate, 155–156, 169

McLean v. Arkansas Board of Education, 81

"Me Too" (movement), 30

Merchant of Venice, The (play), xxvii

Metropolitan Opera, 31, 39

Miss America Pageant, 80

Moberg, Eva, 66–67, 69

Moore, Annie, 1

Moritz v. Commissioner of Internal Revenue, 95–96, 166

Moynihan, Daniel Patrick, 90, 91, 122, 192, 196

Murray, Pauli, 56, 92–94, 113

Nabokov, Vladimir, 27, 28, 33, 95

National Association of Women Judges, 173, 180

New Deal (government program), 8, 9

New York University (NYU), 86, 87–88, 110, 112

Nineteenth Amendment, 179, 186
Nixon, Richard, 89, 90, 91, 96, 107, 108–109, 118, 121, 124, 127, 155, 157, 166
Notorious B.I.G. (Biggie Smalls, aka Christopher George Latore Wallace), xx, xxxii, 153

Obama, Barack, 136, 142, 144, 158, 168, 169, 185, 188
O'Connor, Sandra Day, xxviii, 120–121, 127, 128, 131, 132, 142, 152, 159, 167, 168, 173–174, 180, 186–187, 193
On the Basis of Sex (movie), xx, 35, 43, 49, 93, 95, 161, 170, 172

Palmieri, Edmund, 59–60, 62, 113, 165
Parks, Rosa McCauley, xviii, xxv, 46, 158, 164, 208
Perkins, Frances, 9
Playboy (magazine), 98–99
Plessy v. Ferguson, 45, 146
Presley, Elvis, xviii, 46
Public School (P.S.) 238, 8, 12, 14

Raisin in the Sun, A (play), 56
RBG (documentary film), xx, 30, 31, 161, 172
Reagan, Ronald, 120, 121, 124, 126, 167, 186, 187
Red Channels (McCarthy-era publication), 29
Redding, Savana, 136–137
Reed v. Reed, xxix, 91–92, 94, 96, 145, 166
Rehnquist, William, 26, 101, 102, 107–108, 127, 129, 171, 193, 200
Richman, Julia, 5, 6
Roberts, John, 51, 138, 141, 142, 150
Roosevelt, Eleanor, 13, 69, 158
Roosevelt, Franklin Delano, 8, 9, 63, 157, 181
"Rosie the Riveter" (imagery), xix, 13–14, 151
Rutgers University Law School, 7, 34, 72, 77, 79, 82, 90, 91, 92, 94, 97, 98, 165, 166; RBG career at, 72–75, 76, 83–84, 85, 88, 89

Safford United School District v. Redding, xxiii, 136–137, 150, 169
Saturday Night Live (*SNL*), xx, 155–156, 169
Scalia, Antonin, xxviii, 26, 51, 119, 120, 126, 128, 135, 138, 141, 142, 155, 159, 176
Scalia/Ginsburg (opera), 26, 141, 155, 169, 176
Scopes "Monkey Trial," 81
Second Sex, The (book), 74–75
Shakespeare, William, xxvii
Shelby County v. Holder, xxi, xxii, xxiii, 135–136, 139, 144–145, 149, 152, 153, 169, 206–214
Simon, Nora, 85–86
Singer, Marcus, 29–30
Smit, Hans, 62, 64, 65, 97
Smith College, 74, 82, 159
Sotomayor, Sonia, 131, 137, 139, 141, 142, 145, 152, 159, 160, 169, 174, 180, 185, 188, 206
Souter, David, 128, 142, 144, 201, 205
Spencer, Jennie, 19–20
Spera, Clara, 125, 130, 194
Spera, Paul, 125
Stanford University, 110, 111, 112, 186, 187
Steinem, Gloria, 100, 111
Stevens, John Paul, 109, 128, 135, 137, 141, 142, 143, 144, 157, 158, 201, 205
Sundance Film Festival, 30, 31, 169
Supreme Court, 1, 24, 25, 44–45, 58, 80, 91–92, 96, 101, 107, 109, 114, 123, 126; building, 128–129; history, 128; law clerks at, 60–61, 119, 130, 132–133, 179; RBG office at, 130–131; RBG sworn in for, 127; rejected nominees for, 108, 124; traditions, 129–130; women on, 120–121, 159
Sweden, 63, 64–69, 72, 73, 84, 97, 165

Text, Cases, and Materials on Sex-Based Discrimination (book), 103
Thalidomide, 67–68
Thomas, Clarence, 124, 125, 128, 135, 137

Thurmond, Strom, 116, 117, 125, 195
Totenberg, Nina, 172, 173, 174, 175
Tryon, Milicent, 103–104
Tydings, Joseph, 113–114, 115

United States v. Virginia, xxviii, 134–135, 168
University of Lund (Sweden), 64

Virginia Military Institute (VMI). *See United States v. Virginia*
Voting Rights Act of 1965, 139, 144, 145, 150, 166, 206, 207, 208, 209, 214

Wang, Derrick, 141, 155
Warren, Earl, 45, 107

Watergate (residential complex), 108, 118, 123, 167
Weil, Gotshal and Manges (law firm), 53, 112, 117, 165
Weinberger v. Wiesenfeld, 102, 167
White, Byron, 121, 200
Women's Liberation movement, 80
Women's Rights Project. *See* American Civil Liberties Union
"Wonder Woman" (cartoon character), xxv
World War II, xviii, 12, 13, 17, 21, 23, 61, 64, 66, 67, 93, 151, 163
Wulf, Melvin L. ("Mel"), xxix, 10, 90–91, 92, 95

Yale Law School, 43, 59, 86, 94, 178, 188

About the Author

Nancy Hendricks, PhD, holds a doctorate in education and is the award-winning author of books such as *Senator Hattie Caraway: An Arkansas Legacy* and *Notable Women of Arkansas: From Hattie to Hillary, 100 Names to Know,* which was represented at the National Book Festival in Washington, D.C. Her recent books for ABC-CLIO include *America's First Ladies: A Historical Encyclopedia and Primary Document Collection of the Remarkable Women of the White House, Daily Life in 1950s America, Haunted Histories in America: True Stories behind the Nation's Most Feared Places, Daily Life of Women in Postwar America,* and the two-volume *Popular Fads and Crazes through American History.*

www.ingramcontent.com/pod-product-compliance
Lightning Source LLC
Chambersburg PA
CBHW070245230426
43664CB00014B/2413